P9-DZY-906

PERSONA
SOCIAL ROLE AND PERSONALITY

PERSONA
Social Role and Personality

HELEN HARRIS PERLMAN

THE UNIVERSITY OF CHICAGO PRESS

CHICAGO AND LONDON

Standard Book Number: 0–226–66030–3

Library of Congress Catalog Card Number: 68–21892

THE UNIVERSITY OF CHICAGO PRESS, Chicago 60637

THE UNIVERSITY OF CHICAGO PRESS, LTD., LONDON

Printed in the United States of America

In Memory of My Mother and Father

Annie and Lazer Harris

Who Understood Love and Work

Since no one is someone without a disguise
And the truths of the parlor in the bedroom are lies
And my everyday self is a shoddy disgrace
I have put on these masks to show you my face

Maurice English, *Midnight of the Century*

And if ever the suspicion
of their manifold being
dawns upon men of unu-
sual powers and unusually
delicate perceptions . . .
they break through the
illusion of the unity of the
personality and perceive
that the self is made up of
a bundle of selves. . . . As
a body everyone is single,
as a soul never.

Hermann Hesse,
Steppenwolf

Translated by
Basil Creighton
© 1957 by
Holt, Rinehart & Winston, Inc.
Reprinted by permission

Division of Labor

The child-wife begets the father-husband,
the babe creates the mother in the womb,
the twisted help to twist their Torquemada,
Abel's cringing guarantees his doom.

Each takes the end of what the other tugs at,
the sister's greed calls out the sister's greed;
fear, love, and dominance are given
to any worthy and to all in need.

We are defined by everyone around us,
each man expands where other men give in;
the sainted must have devils to improve on,
and devils, saints, the more to relish sin.

John R. Platt, *Perspectives in Biology and Medicine*, Spring, 1963

Contents

PART ONE

SOME FOREWORDS AND AFTERTHOUGHTS

Some Forewords and Afterthoughts

A foreword is always written afterwards. When a book's last sentence is written (incredulous relief mixed with separation reluctance) there rise up all those haunting doubts and half-expressed, cast-off, or disregarded ideas and they ask the author, portentously, "Have you really said what you meant to say?" "Is it worth saying?" and, worst of all, "Will anyone care?" So it has become customary for editors to allow the writer one more chance to look backward across what he has set down and to look outward to the persons he hopes will be his readers and to say, in effect, "Look—here's what this book is meant to be about, and let me explain to you why I thought you'd be interested and why I committed this or that sin——and——." Thus this.

The central idea that binds these essays together is an old one. It is simply that human beings are nurtured, developed, shaped, socialized, cut down or built up from birth onwards by their daily intercourse with those other human beings and those circumstances and conditions that they experience as potent and meaningful. It goes on from this to propose that these transactions between the individual person and his dynamic environment (physical, psychic, social) are not haphazard and random. Rather, for the most part, they are contained and aligned by socially defined position and their functions—by roles. Role tasks and role relationships and their interchange of actions and affects, when they are felt as vital by the persons involved in them, are the overt forms in which personality needs find expression, thwarting or nourishment. But our vital roles have been given very little study, either by insightful observation of everyday lives or by careful clinical research. It is as though Freud's maturity criteria—to be able to love and to work—seemed to make such utter common sense that roles in which men work and love and the ways in which roles affect the inputs and outcomes of working and loving have simply been taken for granted. So, to the idea of role as shaper and shaker of personality I have brought the insistent wish to look at what work and love roles are made up of and how they affect personality.

This has seemed to me to be of particular importance in the understanding towards the enhancement of adult life. Most psychodynamic theory leaps adroitly from adolescence to senescence. All those years in between, of young and middle adulthood, have scarcely been scratched for their dynamic contents, even though we carry our most emotionally charged and socially valued roles over their span. This is why I have pondered on what's in a role—especially those that are undertaken and valued in adult life.

What's in a role, in a vital role, is a *person*, with his mind, body, feelings, and, always, at least one other person. "Persona" expresses this merger. Persona is the Latin word for the masks used in the Greek drama. It meant that the actor was heard and his identity recognized by others through the sounds that issued from the open mask mouth. From it the word "person" emerged to express the idea of a human being who *meant* something, who represented something, and who seemed to have some defined connectedness with others by action or affects. (We still use "person" to connote this: we say of an infant who begins to show signs of awareness of self in relation to others, "He's becoming a *person*.") A person makes himself known, felt, taken in by others, through his particular roles and their functions. Some of his personae—his masks—are readily detachable and put aside, but others become fused with his skin and bone.

I first became interested in social roles (as I have written elsewhere) many years ago, in the midst of a dance. It was a square-dance party, large enough so that some of us were strangers to one another. Within one square was a man who was the despair of us all: he went right when the call was "left," he skipped when he was to "stand," he bumbled, collided, stood bewildered—by the round's end he looked like nothing so much as a defeated mouse. One of us went to our host to ask who this poor soul was. "Oh, that one!" he said. "He's X, the famous physicist." What happened? Attitudes and actions in the whole group somersaulted. This was no dancing imbecile—this was a dancing brain; no dolt, but a genius! Warm indulgence toward him took the place of annoyance, eager helpfulness rushed in to fill the vacuum of tolerance. But more than this: in his role as dancing partner Mr. X was inept, apologetic, uneasy; but when he was in his major work role of internationally recognized scientist, he was competent, keen, serenely self-confident. Which, I asked myself, is the *real* Mr. X? How much imprint, I wondered, does a particular role make on a personality? How many adults could know themselves and be able to present themselves as "I am——" without following it by some role designation?

At about this time, along with a number of older and wiser social workers, I had been searching for the particular identity of social casework and role of the social caseworker. I had coined a phrase "put the 'social' back into social casework" that became a popular self-other exhortation among social workers. But had anyone been ungracious enough to press me to say what I meant, I am not sure I could have produced much beyond a belief that we needed to turn from exclusively intrapsychic explorations to exploring person-to-person and person-to-social-situation dynamics. Already this was occurring in a few far-sighted agencies about the country, and in the next fifteen years a flood of social science propositions and findings rolled across social work and into its open stream beds. Among the many notions, ideas, and findings that sociology and social psychology and their sister sciences poured forth, the concept of role, it seemed to me, held most ready usefulness for me and fellow caseworkers—and for other professional helpers too—in our job of understanding the individual person's psychosocial problems to the end of improving the adequacy of his social functioning and of his sense of well-being.

Some transmutations had to take place to bring "role" into practical use. Its usage in the writings of social science not only reflected many variations in its conception and meanings but it was often dealt with at levels of abstraction that made it seem quite remote from the flesh and blood and spirit of real people. I tried, then, to define and describe "role" in terms useful to those who were to use it as a framework for action. I confess that the fact of its multiple and not always consistent definitions among those who fathered it seemed to give me sanction to select its relevant lineaments.

One further personal slant characterizes these essays. I make haste to acknowledge it, with a few explanations that may or may not serve as excuses. It is my persistent belief, not in man's "perfectability," but in his "improvability." This is born, I suppose, of some congenital optimism and hopefulness, but it is maintained by the knowledge that man's improvement does happen and can be made to happen. I hold this belief with what is perhaps a fierce cheerfulness (or cheerful fierceness) in the face of my growing concern about the pervasive defeatism and nihilism that lies like a palpable shadow over our society today.

To view all of living as "absurd" ends in emptiness; to see it all as trivial ends in cheap cynicism; to seek for some tensionless state of harmony or for some continuous state of ecstasy ends only in depression. Among the creators and communicators of our culture there has for too long been an infatuation with what is sick, and now in many places sickness and deviance is being put forth as the only true expressions of "reality." Even among those of us professionally committed to raising the level of human life and enriching human experience there has of late been a fascination, a fastening on, in a literal sense, with death and grieving and mourning. To face and accept death as a fact of life is basic to living in full appreciation of what life holds. To enable people to weather and work up through the inevitable black pit that death and separation gouges into the spirit and viscera of the living is a sober and skill-requiring responsibility for those who would help others. One cannot underestimate such agonies nor such efforts at reparation. My plea only is that this not be all.

Our need, it seems to me, is to come closer to life, to the everyday living experience of the everyday common man and what this may hold of health-giving properties, of opportunities for sensing and savoring and enjoying his work and love relationships in some greater degree than at present seems to be the case. We need some closer, more sensitive examinations of the small details of daily living: What are its unnecessary hurts, its untapped—or actually present—rewards? Its lifting moments that people may learn to be aware of and value and celebrate? We will not achieve "health" or "happiness" or even making things "better" by probing only sickness, problems, decay. Such probes and their consequent actions are necessary. But it is necessary beyond this to do what we have thus far let slip: to find in the daily operations of men and women the means by which they can feel recognized, competent, loved; to blow the obscuring dust of familiarity off them and lift them to the light for keener appreciation of what they hold; and, because they will always be found less than perfect, to work both toward making those means better and toward freeing the push and stretch within the human beings who use them. "We'll make yes" says the poet e. e. cummings.

In a way this book is a self-indulgence. It is freely written. I chose the essay form rather than the tight structure of treatise or textbook because essays are literally and simply "tryouts," "attempts at." This is all I present: ideas, notions, beliefs, hunches. glimpses of aspects of people in the vital roles of their adult life and such implications for professional helpers as seem to evolve from this viewing stance. Such "hard research" as supports some of its hypotheses has been the work of others on which I have drawn.

I have tried to write as simply as I can because I wanted to avoid the self-deceptions that so often accompany professionally ritualized words and because simplicity is the test of whether something makes plain honest sense. I am afraid I have not always been successful— some ready shorthand words like "ego" have sneaked in and have been allowed to stay for want of adequate substitutes. But I have hoped that each reader could translate what he reads into the particular language of his particular professional endeavors.

Despite these disclaimers, this is, I hope, a professionally responsible effort. My professional life has been a rich and varied one. In my years of casework practice my clients were a varied group. They ranged from middle-class European intellectuals newly migrated to this country to lower-class Negro cotton-choppers newly migrated from a southern plantation to a northern slum; from three-year-old twins wrested from their psychotic mother and placed in a foster home to frail old women pushed out of family life and into "homes for the aged"; from the man ravaged by guilt to the man ravaged by rage; from families, black or white, struggling to maintain some secure footing under duress to families tearing themselves apart. In all these experiences, and in work as consultant to other social workers, and as supervisor and teacher too, I have had some small part in trying to release and channel people's innate push and capacities toward less personal pain or more personal gratification, less interpersonal conflict, more interpersonal competence. Along with such efforts I have been a close observer too, if only because action must be guided by what one sees is happening. Among the many clamorous thoughts that my observations called forth is the one that motivates the writing of this book. It is that we—all of us professional helpers, doctors, nurses, teachers, ministers, social workers—have not attended closely enough to the powers for both good and evil that are at work in the immediate present, in the everyday facts of everyday life. Such powers are contained in people's major life roles. So they need study.

Am I making too much of the concept of role? I have asked myself this question in the course of my work on this book. Does it hold real utilitarian value? I am not sure. I remind myself only that all human phenomena seem commonplace or trivial until they are closely examined in their many facets and depths. So childhood seemed to be simply a period of littleness into growth, innocence into knowledge, paradise into purgatory until Freud (father and daughter) and Erikson and Gesell and many others along side them began to explore and explain its depths and forces.

One's thinking is built on the groundwork and insights of others, and one's work is made possible by the cooperation of those others with whom one's living is entwined. So the people to whom I am indebted are more numerous than I know. Beyond my deep-sunk roots in Freud and Dewey I have drawn heavily on the illuminating works of Erik Erikson and in recent years upon the brilliant and buoyant insights of Robert W. White who, it seems to me, "makes yes." My thinking about adult life has had some underpinning by the continuous small-block-by-small-block building of research on adults within the University of Chicago's Committee on Human Development under the leadership of Robert Havighurst; and I am particularly grateful to the recent work of Bernice Neugarten and her associates there. Within my own sector of the University, the School of Social Service Administration, I have experienced among my colleagues that climate of interest and support and those delights of unhostile questioning and probing challenge that are the basic precondition for risking oneself in the hazards of putting notions and propositions into writing. Alton Linford, the School's dean, deserves special mention as a dean whose encouragement to his faculty's creative efforts is underpinned by his concern and arrangements to make such efforts feasible. And especially am I grateful to those students who, in our doctoral seminars, thought and questioned together with me on the subject matter of this book.

To Maurice English and John Platt go my gratitude for their allowing me to use their poems. As poets they understand and can express more sentiently than we who plod in prose the swift interpenetrations of acting-feeling-being.

Mrs. Juanita Brown, my secretary, has, with grace and competence, dealt with all the labors that attend on making a book out of page upon page of script and scratch.

And, always, my gratitude to my husband, Max, on whose life this effort impinged many times and who, throughout, has remained my best friend and gentlest critic.

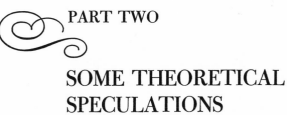

PART TWO

SOME THEORETICAL
SPECULATIONS

1

Adulthood and Personal Change

Do adults change? When a person has stopped growing as a biological organism, has he stopped developing as a personality? Theories of personality development end with the last stages of adolescence. The implication is that if the infant, then child, then that youngster, half-man-half-goat, called "adolescent" has come through his early and crucial life stages and their typical tasks he emerges as a fairly set product of all that he has known. Is it so? Is he so fixed, so cast in the mold that he is destined to live out the long rest of his life acting in the same ways, compulsively repeating his same needs although they may be masked by adult costumes and new role scripts? If he is fortunate enough to come to adulthood as a golden boy, is he fated to be happily occupied and happily married and live happily ever after? Or does he remain a product-in-process throughout his lifetime—a person who is both being and becoming as personality and as social actor—susceptible to changing in ways that are mostly "good" or mostly "bad"?

If we believe he is the latter—a product in process of both being and becoming—what are the forces and conditions that will account for his becoming "better" rather than "worse"? What powers and opportunities will nourish his potentials for self-realization and social contribution rather than quash and constrict his functioning?

These are questions to bedevil anyone who sets out to help people with their problems of making a go of their relationships with others or of coping with the vicissitudes of daily living. Most of the work by social workers, nurses, psychiatrists and other physicians, counselors —indeed, of all people-helpers—is with adults, with people between the ages roughly of twenty to sixty. To be sure, the problems dealt with may often be those of the young children of those people or of their aged parents. But the young or middle-aged adult is almost always part of such problems whether as their victim or creator, their reporter or potential problem-solver. If a child is to be changed, his parent must make some changes. If a child is to have improved developmental opportunities, his parent must shift his ground and his habitual patterns. If conflict festers between adult child and his aged parent, some change of attitudes and actions must ensue between them for that conflict to be resolved. If adults are overwhelmed by personal calamity, some changes must occur not only in their situation but also in their adaptations to it. If chronic psychological strain has come to pervade a marriage or a job situation or a physical condition, some different ways of viewing and feeling about and coping with the situation must come about. These will necessitate changes in the adult in small or large degree, for better or worse. Can they occur? Can they be brought about? If so, how so?

The fact is we know very little about the powers and conditions for development and change in the adult personality. Past adolescence is an all but unexplored plateau (or what is presumed to be a plateau, though to the more discerning eye there are sharp upward peaks and rolling areas and gullies to be seen) on which, having arrived and settled in, the grown-up person is presumed to go about his businesses until he enters his fiftieth or sixtieth year. Then the ground begins to give way beneath him. His time of deterioration—of physical, social, and psychological decrements—has set in and he again becomes the subject of intensive interest and study, now by a veritable army of gerontologists. But between the ages of twenty and fifty, adulthood lies all but unexplored and unexplained.[1]

There are a number of reasons for this knowledge gap. One is the fairly firm persistence of our belief that the person is "made" in his childhood. Another is the fact that adulthood is usually a period of independence and individual freedom even from the avid incursions of interviewers and test givers; no schoolroom or congregate institution holds mature adults ready for study. Yet another explanation lies in the fact that those adults most of us come to know in depth in our roles as professional helpers are people suffering some failure or incapacity to cope with some present problem: We know best those adults whose sickness or whose long entrenched patterns of action and reaction have made them least flexible and adaptable, least able to change their attitudes or behaviors except by help from others. And our own long-entrenched patterns of belief and operation lead us to search for the causes of their personal difficulties within their developmental histories. They will be found there, almost without exception. But they may also exist and ulcerate and be excited by and even created by contacts and conditions in the immediate now of adult life. These dynamic forces that are at work in the daily life of adulthood, and especially those which enhance and enrich that life, have scarcely been identified or searched into.

An interesting paradox attaches to our beliefs about changes in adulthood. We seem to accept rather readily the idea that people can and do change "for the worse." Our faith is not so strong that the opposite may be true; that people can change for "the better." We believe more in the vicious than in the benign circle. We believe in the lurking presence of old wounds waiting to be opened by new trauma, of old hurts waiting to be revived by new threats. Are there no old trusts and hopes that await new proofs of their validity? No old capacities that await release through new opportunities? Are only neurotic potentials, no healthy potentials masked or suppressed, waiting for the signal to emerge? Yet despite this pessimistic view we are incurable optimists, for we cling to the idea of man's capacity to change for the better. If this were not our belief, what would be the possible point of all the person-helper professionals we have developed in our society—psychotherapists, psychoanalysts, counselors, social caseworkers? At the least their efforts are to enable adults to endure the human condition. But at the best, their aim—and indeed, often their accomplishment—is to enable adults to change in the ways they perceive, feel about, think about, and act within their life situations. When such change occurs it must be because potentials for the development or reorganization of elements of personality are yet to be found alive and working in full grown adults. All forms of therapy or personal influence bank on this.[2]

It is in pursuit of notions of how adults may change, of what factors and forces may have some part in their process of becoming that this essay it set down. Some of the ideas to be expressed have already had some preliminary testing in research. Some are heuristic, awaiting tests. The essential base from which my thinking flows, however, is a long-time, continuous observation and inquiry of adults, pushed by curiosity, by discomfort with unfathomed phenomena, and by a professional quest for some further knowledge that would inform efforts to help adults in their development or need for change.

The title of this essay is in line with my effort to be as precise as possible: it speaks of "personal change," not "personality change." Personality is, it seems to me, too global a concept. It refers to the whole structure and functioning of a human being—and thus it is no wonder that even among those who probe it daily and most deeply it eludes agreed-upon definition. When one speaks of "personality development" one implies that all psychic structures are being affected; when "personality change" is spoken of there is some implication that major renovations and reorganizations of the interior life is involved. Whether or not such radical changes can or do take place is as yet more matter of opinion than fact. Recent studies have produced some compelling evidence that temperament and personality bents are genetically determined and that characteristic personality structure is fairly set by adulthood.[3] Yet people repeatedly attest to their feeling "like a new person," "like a changed man," to their seeing things "quite differently," to their expanded (or constricted) capacity to cope and to manage themselves and their situation, and relatives and friends and professional helpers frequently support these subjective reports.

What I believe probable is that certain *aspects* or *dimensions* of personality, singly or in combinations, are susceptible to change under certain conditions. They may have permeation effects upon the total personality in the sense that subjective states of well- or ill-being are often felt whole. Moreover (unless defenses are rigid) there is a continuous two-way intercommunication within the personality between conscious and unconscious experience, between present and past, between behavior and feeling, and shift or change in any of these emotional-cognitive-behavioral processes may be absorbed by connected parts of the personality and certainly into the total sense of self.

Is this attempted differentiation between "personal change" and "personality change" a distinction without a difference? I do not think so, for it points out two directions for further thought. One is the question as to what personality processes and dimensions (or attributes) are most susceptible to development or change. We have yet to identify these. The other is the question of achieveable goals for those whose work is to help people to change their circumstances or their modes of coping. "Personal change" involves modification or alteration in any one or more aspects of a person's feeling-thinking-acting. It is sufficient unto the day. If "personality change" is its accumulated outcome, that is a happy serendipity.

As for the concept of "change," this too requires some definition. It means a modification, alteration, variation, shift in the nature or direction of a structure or process. "Development," unlike "change," implies an on-going change over time. The ideas of "change" and "development" neither define the particular direction that alterations may take nor designate whether that direction or modification is "good" or "bad." They simply name some degree of transformation which occurs in the course of the person's "being" and "becoming" activities. "Change" presents some further pin-down difficulties in that it has both subjective and objective facets. A person may attest to feeling changed, but to those who view him he may appear unmoved and untouched. (This is not an infrequent occurrence in people undergoing psychotherapeutic treatment. They may affirm their inner improvement and sense of well-being as their friends dourly wonder what has been the use of the time and money spent in treatment). Another person may change his overt and visible behavior in some determination to act in ways that will yield better responses from others, but inside him his tensions may be at the same level or even increased. Yet his observers will attest to his being "changed." Often, it is true, since overt behavior brings responses and reactions from others, the actor's social rewards may ameliorate his inner stress. Yet he could not be said to be a "changed personality."

The change one can expect in work with adults needs thus to be both modest and realistic. One asks not whether a major reformation of personality can occur and a new life style be brought into being. One asks, rather, whether within an adult's personality structure such shifts and movements can occur in his actions, feelings, and attitudes as will enable him to say, "I feel better—and as a result I can do better" or the other way round, "I do better—and as a result I feel better." That is all. Yet this "all" may mark the vast difference between a man's feeling trapped and feeling freed, between his acting in self- and other-destructive ways or acting in ways that yield both a personal sense of mastery and the reward of its recognition by others.

Change in a person's views, understanding, actions, feelings, creates some different relationship between him and other persons and the problems in his life network. It is possible that, with change set in motion and with its being felt and experienced as rewarding, a whole benign cycle of interactions may begin to spiral up. Or change may be confined to only one life area. It is also possible that some aspects of personality are more susceptible to modification than others. It is further possible that certain situations call certain personality attributes into active dominance, and subordinate others. So he who tries to promote adult change must add to his modesty and realism an openness, warmed by hope, to all the as yet unexplored possibilities that may reshape, color, push or pull, unfold, develop the personal life of an adult.

It is one thing for any one of us to look at another and think, "He ought to change—or be changed; he ought to take better care of himself; she ought to be a better mother; he ought to look for a better job; she ought to quit undermining herself"—and so on. It is another thing to turn the screw. How does change occur in adulthood? More, how can it be made to happen—what are the powers that drive for change?

People are moved to change by several impelling stimuli. One is their yearning for or wanting something more or better or different than what they have. Another is the feared loss of something they deeply value. A third is their experiencing some situation or circumstance so dangerous or unfamiliar to them as to seem hazardous to their physical or psychological integrity. In each of these conditions will be found the person's deep emotional involvement. His motivation and motions of change are driven by this charged energy.

Past their basic drives to meet physical needs for food, warmth, sex, shelter, what do grown people strive for? What do they want to have and to hold? What do they most fear losing? Two things, I believe, that are not "things" at all but are the very conditions for humanized and socialized life: the security of love and of social connectedness. Given these (and this "given" varies in degree and kind for different people, subject to different expectations and perceptions) there is a base of security from which, then, the adult may look out for those present or potential opportunities by which he may enrich his life or develop his capacities in many kinds of ways. So he may be motivated by the push to stretch out and use himself more satisfyingly or productively, to experience himself to the fullest.

It is in the nature of living that crises occur that may shake the foundations of habit and long-entrenched behavior patterns. Furthermore, since living is in itself a process of adapting to changing age, circumstances, relationships there are phases in adult life that are particularly stressful or that feel crucial because they are decision-times, points of no return when what one does or does not do will determine a whole sequence of consequences. Thus crises and crucial periods of life may upset usual modes of feeling and coping, may threaten love or socially valued relationships or actual physical well-being. At such times the adult may be forced to undertake to change his attitudes, his habitual behavior, his feelings, his conceptions—some or all of these. Otherwise he will be changed, that is he will *be* over-run and subject to the forces that assail him. Change at such crucial times may, of course, be in the direction of "better" or of "worse," adaptive or maladaptive.

Each of these powerful stimuli for change in adults—love, social recognition and connectedness, aspiration towards self-realization, and crucial or turning-point events—calls for some further examination of its dynamic content.

Love is the basic nurture of the human personality, the food on which it grows. Throughout life it remains our never-ending need and our deepest gratification. That children grow and develop on being loved no one doubts. This is no longer an article of faith or sentiment. It has by now been established by numbers of studies that the child's capacity to reach out in affectionate connection to another grows out of his being loved, that his sense of his value and worth grows from consistent and continuous deposits in him of loving feeling from his caretakers, and that his willingness to accommodate to and incorporate social values and behaviors is most quickly and deeply achieved in a climate of love. Actually if an adult is to be open to love, responsive to it, and if he is to be able to give love to another, he must have experienced and have treasured some trustworthy loving relationship in his childhood. He must have felt in himself many times over the leap and play of that warm fountain of feeling towards self-and-other that flowed in him from his core to finger tips, then settled down into a deepening well of security from which he could draw and slake his own love thirsts and, beyond this, give out to others.

Adulthood is a time when sexual love comes to its most full-bodied and many-layered expression and reception. It is a time when love as a caring, tendering, warming, other-attending expression grows and unfolds in the cultivation of friends, of lover or spouse, but mostly of children growing; a time when love of those who have been the love-givers, parents, grows more mellow, more compassionate, both less intense and less fickle. So it is understandable, then, if love is wanted (I was about to say "loved"), cherished, fed upon, if each man in order to feel whole must feel that someone cares for him as himself, that to love and be loved becomes a powerful drive and stimulus to personal change.

What is it? Poets, artists, dramatists, composers, all, have expressed it for us inarticulate ones since the birth of awareness in man and in its every form from mother-love to carnal love to platonic love to tender-faithful love to "love of one's fellow man" and on and on. Yet, like those other common human experiences that both drive into and derive from our visceral core—birth, death, parting, reunion—love defies definition or even adequate description because words, which are the instrument of the mind, cannot contain it. At some risk and folly, I touch on some of its essential attributes.

Perhaps the coolest way to look at love is in its non-sexual manifestation ("sexual" here in its literal sense). Without its glandular and sensory pleasures what goes into love and loving? For one thing to love is to feel and then to give out with concern, warmth, caring, interest in another. Peculiarly, it combines empathy for the other with pleasure in him—as if to say, "I feel with you in your humanness (or littleness or helplessness or strength or suffering or momentary joy) and I find you good, pleasing, worth my caring." At times empathy becomes compassion or pleasure becomes delight. But what is basic is that there be a recognition of the other for his particularness, an affirmation of his selfhood, a concern about his well-being, and then a giving over of one's self in all the ways that will increase it. Now the "miracle" in love occurs. For if the person (or "object") loved responds in kind, if he shows by his reactions that what has been put in to him by the other matters to him, if beyond this he is capable of reciprocating, then that response and reciprocation are experienced by the other as "being loved." Loved and lover, lover and loved, interchangeably are nourished as they nourish, given to as they give. The deposit of feeling from one to the other binds them together so that each feels not only the warming sense of being "lovable" but also the enhancement and expansion of the boundaries of the personality through being part of another.

When, as in heterosexual relationships, sensual pleasures accompany these other aspects of love, it becomes the ecstatic experience of which the poets sing and which young people who "fall in love" can scarcely believe has been matched by anyone else since maybe Romeo and Juliet. When, as in infant-mothering, certain special kinds of body contacts accompany the caring and attending to the child, the sensual and affectional pleasures are heightened too and "blood-bonds" grow more firm. But love can also be a mind and emotion experience only and yet be real as bread, life-giving as the air we breathe, when it is recognized for its essential substance: the investment of oneself—which is to say one's attentive interest, one's caring, and one's responsible actions in the interests of another with the natural expectation that that other (person or sometimes object) will respond to these gifts.

It is no wonder, then, that adults may be changed by love, by loving and being loved—gentled, secured, relaxed, spurred, enhanced, made "real." Love is so hungered for when absent, so potent when present that it is a dynamic change-agent at all levels of the personality. We are both unconsciously and consciously moved and stirred, shaken and shaped by it; and most of us develop and utilize with conscious awareness and aforethought many ways of acting that are calculated to win or hold love.

For the truth is, love and loving must be worked at. One may "fall in love" and lose one's self in the other. But what is fallen into may just as easily be fallen out of. This is the constant disillusionment about love that the romantic, be he adolescent or childish adult, suffers, that love cannot live by passion alone. There must be two whole selves, an "I" and a "thou," and these two selves are different from one another. Their coming together in love involves not just the loss of one self in the other (and then the search to retrieve that self), not simply a merger, but the recognition and acceptance that each is a different, separate self, each yearning for fusion, yes, but needing, also, the sense of own self. With love there must be the reception and pleasure of on-going discovery of the differences and separateness in the two, the I and the thou and the us, together. It is the difference between the I and the thou, as well as the one-ness between them, that love and loving must delight in and celebrate if it is to hold and grow. This is true whether love is between husband and wife, parents' and child, or between good friends.

Difference creates divergences at times, dissimilarities of reaction, of behavior, of attitudes and feelings, of values and aims. So conflicts and struggles may occur between the lover and the loved. The personal differences plus the differences that life roles and conditions involve for every individual make necessary a continuous fine-footwork of accommodation and adaptation, one to another, in the union, self-realization, re-union, other-realization that is involved in loving.

Some of this just happens because we are warmed and made flexible by loving. But often it must be worked at. There are hours and months when, to have and to hold love or to cause it to flourish, a person must act in ways dictated not by his impulse but by his conscious mind. There will be times when he must relinquish temporary pleasure for hoped-for rewards, when reason must be substituted for wilfulness, when the "lecture" must be to himself rather than to the other, when the door must be held open rather than slammed shut, when he must "put himself out" to woo the other with understanding rather than demand that the other "take him in." Loving involves this continuous work upon the spontaneous self and on the transactions between the self and others. It is by such work, such conscious uses of the self in the building of love, not just by its free pleasures, that the deepest recesses of the personality are affected.

People come to adulthood with varying needs and capacities both for being loved and for loving. Some are so hungry for love, having tasted only enough to whet their appetites, that they are voracious and rarely satisfied—always demanding more than others can give, scarcely able to give more than gratitude in return. Some remain unsure of what love is, uncertain that they have ever known it, uneasy about being expected to give it—but even they push inexorably somehow to try to find it or its reasonable facsimile. Some—the fortunate ones—come wanting to be loved, first as a lover or darling, with all the narcissistic delights and mutual surprises that accompany that role; then as a spouse, or love-partner, with all the dependability and security of presence and companionship and responsible reciprocations that are involved in this role; then as a parent—when wanting to be loved normally waits on first wanting to give out with all the love surplus that has been burgeoning in the marital relationship. Voluntary parenthood is undertaken for a variety of reasons, but the dream is always, "I will love—I want to hold, warm, carry, cuddle, nurture." Once the child is born, the loving parent wants to be loved too. She looks into the crib, searching the baby's early impersonal stare for any emerging small signs of recognition and responsiveness that say "I know you and I love you." And the feelings of one-ness, of attachment, of reciprocal and pleasurable connectedness nourish both child and mother. But for those young adults who come to marriage and parenthood and to their work with long-felt love deficiency or whose reaching-out experiences have been responded to by indifference or inconsistency or harshness or even actual perversions of feelings and actions—for those "love" will be experienced differently. It may be pallid, thin, wary, quick to collapse under frustration. Such defects in love capacity may lie at the heart of many marriage failures, of parenting failures, and of the difficulties that patients or clients may show in sustaining a relationship with a helping person. Awareness of these variations in loving capacity among adults needs to accompany a helper's own on-going work to sustain his caring and empathy and concerned efforts to bring about change.

Love is usually spoken of as a relationship of one to another person. But it may also exist and act upon personality, though in lesser degree, as a relationship between a person and some objects or occupation in which he is involved. There may be in adult life not only the work of love with the people who matter but also the love of work. This is not just a turn of phrase. Love, in the sense of its being an emotionally charged investment of one's self in something outside the self, may be deposited in one's endeavors, too. It may be part of any engagement between the self and materials or processes, any involvement of one' self in making something happen that is responsive to one's efforts. So it is that one may "love" one's work when one gives one's self over to it—one's energies, time, interest, but most of all, one's "caring" about it—and when in response it yields up some sought-for outcome or reward. So one may "love" a book or a sonata or a school course. Different as these are, they hold within them certain likenesses if they are "loved": the person puts himself into them, he attends to them in feeling, appreciative, or knowledge-seeking ways. As a result of whatever he puts in—intellect, aesthetic responsiveness, emotion—the book he reads, the sonata he listens to or studies, the course he takes, *responds* to his active investment. By his giving himself to the requirements of the medium while at the same time he makes it his own, the man, his activity, and the object unite and fuse. He works upon the object, it captures him, and he possesses it, all at once. This is how, too, one may say one "loves" certain activities—dancing, hiking, painting, tinkering with car motors. Some push in the person for muscle-pleasure or aesthetic-pleasure or skill-pleasure prompts him to give himself over to an activity which, by its particular responsive yielding to his efforts, gives him in small or great degree the sense of self-enhancement or self-transcendence.

Love of one's work or any leisure-time occupation of the self may ensue when several basic conditions are met: The person must, for whatever reasons, *care* about the objects or material in which he invests himself, valuing it or its outcome. Caring, he must put himself into it (even if only for a brief time) in some responsible or devoted ways. And he must be able to see or feel that what he has put in has made a difference and that the difference is "good." That is to say, he must see and feel himself to have been the "cause," in part at least, of some acts or consequences that are valued. We "love" that which is responsive to our good intents. So the workman or the student or the professional man "loves" those tasks that yield to his investments of skill and knowledge and caring and that, in their outcome, affirm him as competent, a "maker," a creator. So we "love" a square yard of garden that sends up green shoots in response to the labor we've put in and that says, "*You* have been a cause, a force, an influence in my flourishing." When this affirmation is repeated frequently enough the person draws from his efforts the reward of "requited love." More, he is enhanced in his sense of himself as a maker and doer.

The crucial problem of young adulthood has been named by Erikson as "intimacy versus isolation." The young person who is secure in his own identity, he says, is ready and willing to fuse his identity with others, to commit himself to partnership with others. On the other hand, a persisting fear of loss of self leads to persistent self-absorption. It has seemed to me that this period might more truly be called "*investment* versus isolation." Its tasks, whether they be study or paid work or courtship or marriage or parenthood, or all of these, call for the capacity to invest oneself not only in persons but also in tasks and responsibilities. And thus invested and fused, to draw out from persons and tasks both those incitements to new adaptations and different operations, and those rewards of response and reciprocation that make renewed investment possible. He who cannot invest himself in another person or in objects or activities outside himself cannot know love, whether of persons or of work or play. He remains "isolated," a chronic seeker for "meaning" which he will never find because he cannot risk "giving out" in order to take it in. For him who can give himself over to loving and—one must say at once—for whom fortune provides the persons and the occupational or avocational opportunities, the investments, acts, and returns of love—of persons and of occupation, of work or of play—will deeply move and shape the personality brought to them.

Connected with love, sometimes sought as its second-best substitute, increasingly important to the individual as he emerges from the small circle of family life into the ever-widening circles of his society, is the assurance of social recognition, social belonging and connectedness. The drive for "social security" not in the sense of income maintenance but in the sense of recognition, affirmation, and inclusion in the valued social system is a powerful stimulus to spontaneous or consciously undertaken change in adults.

Man is a social animal, the early sociologists announced. But recent experiments with animals show that the need for social relationships, for linkages with one's own kind runs strong and deep in even the lesser animals—more, that the capacity in monkeys, for example, to court, mate, care for their young, to engage in unafraid play activities, is the result not only of mothering but of "socializing" with peers.[4]

The human child is born into a formed society. At first it is a twosome, then the threesome or larger family group. But while he first may be aware only of those with whom he has eye and body contact, these other members of his family are already connected with, impinged upon, and interacting with many other social systems —the several families of their origin, their neighbors and friends, their school, church and work places (past and present), their doctors and other advisors, the newspapers they read and TV programs they watch—and on. The baby comes into a pink or blue world unaware of the surrounding conspiracy to "socialize" him. But he learns it very soon, and when social demands and requirements are made in a benign climate of love he takes them in as his own. More than this, his sense of himself grows on his being measured and judged by the people (social group) to whom he feels he belongs.

For every action he takes—from his first faltering steps to his last— he will look to those who represent his "society" to say, by their smiles and applause, "Good! Well done!" If this occurs he will feel himself affirmed, even empowered. If he finds disapproval or rejection, he will feel shamed or hurt, having fallen short of social expectations. Bit by bit, accretion by accretion, we absorb into our own persons the social recognitions and judgments we have read in the eyes or heard from the lips of those others to whom we feel attached by love or on whom we feel dependent for approval. And after some time the inner-directed man (who is no one other than he who has fully digested social standards) becomes his own best friend and severest critic. Even for him, however, the time never comes when, in addition to this self-judgement and self-approval or self-condemnation, he does not seek—with fear or eager anticipation—a judgement from someone he respects or whose esteem he covets on what he has done or made to happen.

"Social security" consists not only of a sense of being accepted, recognized, affirmed as an "in," a claimed member of society. By adulthod certainly it depends upon the commitment of one's self to entering and taking on some place or status in the social system and to carrying its responsibilities (tasks and relationships). The mark of adulthood, indeed, is this commitment to the carriage of socially sanctioned roles. He who can be called "adult" is one who has taken on a kind of social contract to occupy a marked out and socially sanctioned niche in society, with its socially designated expectations and its ensuing rewards of social acceptance and affirmation if he meets his "contract."

How powerful are these needs for social affiliation and place and recognition has been shown in experiments where adults put into enforced isolation from other people have developed symptoms of psychosis. In punitive institutions "isolation" is considered one of the most severe punishments, feared by the culprit who has experienced it, since he has known, as no one else can know, the terrifying loss of sense of self and orientation when there are no others to affirm one's presence and reality, even if in only negative and hateful ways.

Among the problems of major concern in our society today are several that tie in closely with this human hunger and drive for social place and recognition. Probably as never before are the massed poor aware not simply of the pinch of their poverty but also of their being the "outs," the "cast-offs" in a society in which they want full membership. The burning resentments and hostilities relate not alone, I believe, to the material means that are missing in their lives. Compounding that problem is the sense of being discriminated against, being unaccepted, unvalued as members of the society. Because there is no sense of belonging or social worth, there results either a sense of anomie—rootlessness, aimlessness, nothingness—or a lonely sense of alienation. However, the alienated man seeks his social connections too and it is with other alienated men. They satisfy their social recognition, connection, and acceptance needs thereby. Ofter, however, such a group's sense of identity depends upon its pitting itself *against* the dominant social group; its members know themselves and feel themselves less by what they value and aim for and more by what they denigrate and deny.

This is not confined to the involuntary outcast in our society. In many places in the country today there are young people who have alienated themselves from the dominant mores and values of their society—the "flower children," the beatniks, certain groups of "activists." Like the expatriates of an earlier era who fled to Paris to shake off the shackles of Babbittry only to find themselves huddled together with their fellow Americans but now over sour aperitifs in chilly French cafes, bound together by ties of contempt for America, so these self-alienated young people today seek one another out and huddle together in "pads" and "shacks" for the comforts of mutual affirmation. Most of them (and I hasten to add that these generalizations have their notable exceptions!) are more sure about what they reject than accept, what they deplore than propose. It is interesting that this self-declared social alienation is becoming a formalized role. Its carrier is not just an "off-beat kid," or a "moody adolescent," or a "young man in search of his identity" (although these designations may contain the truth about him). He takes on the group dress and language, he goes to or avoids the places, he obeys the expectations and rules about behavior and attitudes that govern this socially recognized (if not generally approved of) role of alienated youth.

All this simply to point up that even the outcast and the voluntarily alienated person strives for the satisfactions and rewards of social recognition and valuation. For reasons too numerous and complex even to be touched on here there is considerable evidence of a greater need and push for social recognition and approval outside the family than ever before. The press and push for social status and social recognition is bound to be greater in a fluid society than in a rigidly stratified one where conditions of life are taken for granted, good or bad. Not only is present day social status in flux but the ideas of what constitutes prestige and what merits social recognition are in revolution. It is no wonder, then, that among young people who have not yet committed themselves to undertaking adulthood (who have not felt ready or able to do so?) there is the continuous quest for "meaning" and "authenticity." A shifting social scene befogs meaning. What is real? What is to be valued? With what am I—or should I be —connected?

Our domain of privacy is today swiftly narrowing; man's sense of himself as a private person seems rapidly giving way to his public presentations of himself. To some of us, still accustomed to the idea that acts of love are most precious when they are experienced in complete privacy, the open, on the street, even "groupy" exchanges of sexual affection today seem puzzling if not startling. To these same constricted souls among us, the public, group confessionals of various once-held-secret aberrations, the readiness of families to act out their actual family conflicts, to exhibit and speak of their personal problems under the white glare of the public eye, via camera and T.V. screen, is somewhat astonishing. Yet it all bespeaks some accelerated fusion that seems to be occurring between the personal and social self, some sense that "I am only as I am observed and affirmed by others." Whatever the causes and whatever the evaluations of it, the actuality is that people today are acutely aware of needing to be part of a social group and since, for the adult, his family of origin is often remote geographically or psychologically, there is an intensified drive to gain and hold social place and acceptance.

Conformity, anxiety, shame or fear of being shamed, kindness, ruthlessness, sacrifice, courage, exploitation, cowardice—all these and innumerable other human emotions and actions are driven by the wish for the approval or admiration of our fellow men. For some people social recognition is their only proof that they matter; they are in a constant process of reading the cues that they get from others —"other-directed" people, Reisman named them. For others social prestige has become the sought-after substitute for love or self-esteem, and in them the drive for social recognition is insistent, paramount, often psychically consuming. But if one is concerned, as here, only with the commonly powerful stimuli for the commonly encountered person, the need for social connectedness and recognition cannot be underestimated. Just as the need for love holds implications for the professional helper's relationship potency for his client, so does this social-recognition need. A professional helper is a representative of a sanctioned and approved part of the social system. He may be feared or hated because he is within the Establishment, but by this same token his respect for and affirmation of his client may hold more meaning than he suspects.

One further comment on social need and influence. We speak of people's "social environment" and tend to think, then, of the broad, vague neighborhood and cultural surround. Actually we know and feel our environment mostly through the people in it. Our most potent experience of environment is its peopling. Thus family life, the interactions and interplay between its members, is a powerful social environment. We have studied it deeply in relation to children, but studied it little in relation to adults. Work life and its associations may be a powerful social environment. Chiefly it has been studied in terms of its deleterious effects upon the personality of the worker. Indeed, most powerful social environments which have been examined in relation to the changes they wrought in the adult personality have been malignant ones—concentration camps, battle stations, prisoner-of-war camps. The probability is that no benign environment can be as moving for an adult as a malignant one because the latter threatens life itself and the person's total integrity. Benign environments probably act upon adults more in the fashion that Montaigne described in writing of the rearing of children: they "pat them into shape." Meantime one remains acutely aware that studies of adults show that "powerful environments" may produce changes in intelligence, attitudes, and personality characteristics.[5] Those who would help people to change must seek, continuously, to find the "powers" in the common social environments of adult life.

The person who feels a floor of security beneath him, whose physical well-being is secured by adequate means and adequate health, whose psychological well-being rests on a sense of selfhood, product of having been nurtured by love and social affirmation, can look outward and forward. He has free energy, ready for investment in explorations and endeavors beyond the level of stability that is his base, and he is likely to have some confidence that he can achieve something more or better than he now has.

It was once thought that human beings strove only for release of drive tension and a consequent pleasurable state of stability, and that once this was achieved there was effort only to maintain the sense of balance. But observations of how people act, now buttressed by studies of both human and animal infants, show that the push for maximal use of innate powers, for exploration beyond what is customary and routine, a desire for further engagement with things and people, and, more, as several ego psychologists suggest, a drive to be a "cause" or to master new experience is an impelling motivation. It is most likely to be seen in the animals, human or other, who feel that their survival-level needs have been satisfied. Perhaps this explains why those of us who have worked with needful people, whether as clinicians with emotionally hungry or debilitated people, as relief workers with physically hungry people, or as physicians with physically debilitated people, have not seen this push with greater frequency. What we have seen, rather, is the drive to re-achieve a once-held level of stability or to recoup losses, and sometimes, of course, we have seen a hopeless relinquishment of drive in those persons who have known only defeat and frustration for all their efforts. These new views—of the human being's innate drive to exercise his ego muscles, so to speak, to reach beyond the level of present satiation, even at the risk of heightened tensions (which in themselves may be felt as pleasurable)—have considerable import for those whose work it is to enable and enrich people's social functioning. They posit the prior necessity for a base of physical, social, and psychological security. Beyond this they suggest that environmental opportunities for people's growth and stretch must be present and open.

The third source of stimulus for change in adult life lies, then, in the energized motivation of the person to use himself or his opportunities to their fullest. As he feels some restiveness or discontent with what he is or has, and as this is combined with belief and hope that he has the inner powers and can get hold of the outer resources by which to bring about change, he may be said to be driven by aspirations. A man may aspire to advance in his job, a woman to be a better mother or homemaker; people pour their energies into developing skills, know-how, recreational interests, aesthetic pleasures, in expanding their circle of friends, their orbits of influence, their knowledge of the terrestrial or intellectual worlds. All these efforts at new or extended usages of the self are powered by the inner push of confidence and the wish for some greater self-realization and self-development.

When that which is aspired towards is of vital importance to the person, such as achieving an education or work promotion, it is often necessary that there be conscious, laborious efforts to change the self. Habitual patterns of daily operations may have to undergo reformation, ways of relating to other people may have to be modified, all manner of natural, impulsive forms of behavior may come under self-scrutiny and self-control, shaped to the ends and the role model being reached for. In these ways, people work at bringing about personal change at least in terms of what is visible to themselves and others. At the same time some unconscious changes may take place too. If those consciously made efforts yield the sought-for outcomes, if the person finds that he is competent, capable of coping, if what he is putting himself into responds to his doing, and especially if, from the people who matter to him, he receives affirmation of his own self-judgement, then his level of hope and self-confidence is likely to rise and he is likely to "feel his strength," to gain an enhanced self-image. This kind of change frees and makes flexible many aspects of the personality.

The fourth kind of powerful stimulus to change in adult life inheres in those circumstances or happenings that are realistic crises and in those that are felt as turning points, potentially hazardous. The one, the actual crisis, is some unforeseen blow to normal life processes and expectations or the coming-to-a-head of a long-festering problem that is felt as crucial because the persons involved are bereft of the means either within themselves or in their natural resources by which to deal with it. The other, the turning point crisis, is usually a phase or period of change in living that comes about as a natural part of the life process but that may be felt with heightened acuity because what is done about it, how the person involved copes with the read-justments or life style changes that must ensue, will determine whether what follows will take him on an upward or downward course.

No adult's life is free from crises, though some of us are more fortunate in having few rather than many or in having cushions of resource to lessen the shock. But death of parents or of a spouse or of close relatives or friends comes to all adults; death of a child comes to many. Sickness or physical losses occur in all lives, all with their social and psychological undermining. Loss of job, loss of income source, threats to marriage or to the parent's control of his child, failures in work or school, deviance from the "norm" in ways that spell "social disgrace"—these and other misfortunes and hazards are not uncommon to adult life.

Everyone is hurt by such blows, whether they are blows to our cherished stability or to our perilous balance or to our sense of self-esteem and confidence. But each of us defines "crisis" differently. An event or situation may be the same for two people. Yet each will experience it in different degree and will interpret it differently: what one finds overwhelming, the other may find mostly annoying; what one finds anguishing, the other may find only saddening. A crisis, then, has its objective and its subjective aspects. But whatever the reality, the *feeling* that one is in a crisis is the same for all of us.

It is an earthquake beneath us; the ground drops out from under our feet; terror possesses us because the terms of our existence are threatened; and—worst—we can muster no means by which to cope with it.

What will impel a person to change his habitual behaviors, his sentiments, his sense of himself and/or others, his deep feelings is his subjective sense that "I am in danger of being demolished, hurt, losing what I want to hold on to, and I am at a loss as to what and how to do." He must turn dependently, helplessly, to persons or resources outside himself for support and guidance and for restitutive means. It must often happen that the crisis-ridden person will have to cope with himself, with his feelings and perspectives and behaviors as they are involved either in the causes of the crisis or in its amelioration. He may, in short, need to do change-work on himself, not only on his circumstances.

The moments of felt crisis are moments when the iron of personality structure and patterning is white hot. This is because of the pervasive inner sense of shake-up and disorganization; emotion is intense; self-mobilization to fight or to flee, to struggle or to collapse, is high, though it often cannot be sustained for long and may end in capitulation. The feeling is that something radically different must happen at once on the outside or within the self.

That "something" may often be self-engineered, and innumerable stories of people's heroic rise to meet and conquer crises attest to this. But often crisis can only be met by help from outsiders, among whom are professional helpers—doctors, nurses, social workers, clergymen. Their help may require that the person be aided to shift or reorganize or reaccommodate his usual modes of operation. Changes of his feelings, of his perspective, of his grasp of cause-consequence relationships, of his ways of acting and responding, may all take place in a crisis-swept person in the course of his being helped. He may be empowered to cope with his problem with some greater sense of competence and some actual evidence of it. Or he may only be helped to endure with greater equanimity such problems as cannot be resolved or undone. In either case he may learn and change parts of himself in the course of his efforts at dealing with himself or with the problem or, as is usually the case, with both. If this occurs, it will be because in a period of deep needfulness he has felt attached to and supported in a reassuring and strengthening way by his helper; because he has had another, hopefully clearer, pair of eyes lent to him by which to see the situation more plainly and himself in relation to it. Moreover he has been helped to search and find what resources exist outside and within him that he can use for his problem-solving. If he comes out of the crucial period feeling cared for, relieved, affirmed, even to some small extent in better mastery of himself or the situation, then he will value and hold on to what he has learned that may stand him in good stead as he goes forward with his daily problem-solving.

Adolescence to senescence is a long span of years, and in those years many of the most important events of life occur. The commitment to an occupation or even to a series of jobs, the commitment to marriage, the undertaking to bring children into life and to rear them, the relinquishment of those children first to teachers, then to peers, then to new love attachments and new families—all these occurrences in the course of a happy life may yet, for the persons involved, feel crucial. They may have been looked forward to, and *still* feel crucial because what has been anticipated, often, has been the objective event ("Of course Jonnie will go to kindergarten," "Of course Jeannie will get married") and not the particular circumstances that will give it its special character ("Jonnie is afraid of the teacher," "Jeannie's boy friend isn't what her parents would have wanted," etc.). Nor—and this is most important—has pre-cognizance been taken of the subjective involvements that might be roused by those particular circumstance. These normal life events are felt as "crucial" then, when entrenched ways of acting or dependable relationships are unsettled or broken up and also when the entry into some new and unfamiliar role, with its unfamiliar tasks, relationships, and expectations, has been inadequately anticipated or prepared for.[6] This latter, the entry into a new situation that necessitates different and new adjustments, may be compared to a migration into a new culture.

These changes and evolvements in the sequence of living may require changes in habitual expectations, in usual behaviors and ways of operating, and in attitudes towards the self or another. For those persons aware enough of the normal demands of the new situation, prepared well enough by knowledge and by fantasied rehearsals of how they must change, for those flexible enough to carry their fore-planned behavior into action, the necessary changes may not present anxiety or unease. But even they may be fooled. They may find to their surprise that *living* through is rather different from *thinking* through. Certainly for those persons who are quite unprepared for change, either by their internal rigidness or lack of knowledge and know-how, or simply because they have had to "keep running to stay where they are," the shifts of place and persons and tasks may constitute points of crucialness. The person's efforts to cope may be inappropriate, even blind, unsuited to the situation—and thus he will perpetuate his unbalance and even exacerbate his difficulty. Or, on the more fortunate side, the change-point may be for him what Havighurst has aptly called a "teachable moment."[7]

The idea of "teachable moment" is simply that it is a point of felt crucialness; the person is mobilized and open for the cues and aids to the new directions he must take. The early encounter with the unfamiliar alerts all our senses to the new possibilities in it, possibilities for pleasure or for pain. All our antennae poke out to take in new signals and cues. We hold our habitual behaviors and reactions in temporary suspension, waiting to select what the new situation seems to call for. Particularly when the new situation rouses anxiety or discomfort or when it promises great pleasure if it is well utilized, we are eager to learn how to avoid its difficulty or gain its rewards. We may need to change aspects of our usual selves then. We may need to take in new knowledge towards understanding the problems that inhere in the role or new culture to which we are committed, to review ourselves in relation to it, to anticipate and rehearse the attitudes and actions it will require or prohibit, and so on. By such conscious talking over, thinking over, by the imitation of competent models, and by the trial efforts of new actions people adapt themselves to the demands of new roles. If those adaptative efforts "pay off," if the responsive reaction of the people or objects with which he transacts is a rewarding one, then the person's awkward efforts at learning new ways begin to slip into being "second nature."

Studies of the effect of new environments (and it seems plausible to include in this new roles with their new configurations of people and functions) suggest that the most "teachable moments" are those in the beginning experience of crucialness or in the initial phase of a new set of circumstances.[8] Thus the early months of college, the first year in a professional school, the early months of marriage and of parenthood, the first weeks following the migration from rural south to urban north—these are the "moments" when readiness to take in the new situation and to adapt oneself in new ways is at its height. The import and impact of *now* in the lives of troubled or unsettled adults cannot be overlooked. Nor can the motivation for personal change be underestimated when shifts in role or status or habitual behaviors upset a person's equilibrium and send him groping for new ways by which to cope.

So we are driven and spurred and drawn forward by multiple needs and motivations, some unconscious, some half-conscious, some clearly in the forefront of our minds. We drive to relieve ourselves of frustration and tension; we push out to escape stalemate and boredom; we are drawn by hope to reach for satisfactions and pleasures beyond those we have; and we are both pushed and pulled when we encounter life circumstances that threaten our well-being or that throw us off our customary trackage. Our conscious motives may derive from and still be linked to deep and old unconscious drives. But as they are known to us, and as we attend to them, they are clothed in the garments of rationality. These in turn have been fashioned by our whole psycho-social milieu, the culture of which we are both the creators and the creatures. These conscious drives push and pull us to achieve "more" and "better," to fashion and modify our actions, attitudes, mental sets in appropriate ways, insofar as we can, and in small ways to accommodate ourselves, to adapt, to manipulate circumstances. By such efforts and actions we change.

The powers of love, of social recognition, of aspiration towards self-realization, of crucial turning points—these, I have proposed, are the major movers and shakers of the adult personality, the motivators for personal change. Where are they to be found? It has seemed to me that the major, all-consuming life roles of adulthood—work, marriage, and parenthood—are shot through with these change powers. And with one other power which is only now beginning to be recognized for its impact upon emotion and cognition—that of action.

Any vital role is "where the action is," to borrow a plangent term from popular speech. The search for and insistence on action seems to me to be a search for what is experientially real, actual. It is through action that a person knows his actuality. He can know his feelings and his thoughts most truly, most vitally when he plays them out in verbal or muscular expression and becomes aware of the responses they evoke. The scholar who said that he did not know what he thought until he wrote it down was only half-joking. The student of social work or medicine who knows his facts and his principles by heart and by head finds them driving into his viscera only when he must put them into *action* in relation to a client or patient.

The place of action as a moving force in personality development is only now beginning to be explored.[9] For many years after the discovery of unconscious drives and of those emotions of which we have only small or dim awareness, we banked upon changes in feeling as the only way to affect change of behavior. We believed that feeling change must precede behavioral change, that change in actions must wait on modifications or alterations of attitudes and emotions. But recent thinking and experiments suggest that in some instances action precedes or creates feeling, and, moreover, that action does not always follow on mental grasp but may be necessary and instrumental in producing it.

Certainly there can be no question but that any change of behavior must at the least be motored by the *feeling* that one wants or needs to make a change. That is the emotion basic to making any move at all. But given that motivation there may be conscious changes in action undertaken that *precede* changes in understanding or feeling. Such changes, to be sure, are very piecemeal efforts. They take place by some conscious, creaking efforts to act in certain ways in certain selected situations and relationships. It may take a long time (after sleepless nights and hours of therapeutic talk and tears) to come to the point of deciding that one can and will try to change some piece or small complex of behavior in some particular situation. The first step may, then, be taking some action as if one felt as one should rather than as one does. This action or behavior sequence, always taken in relation to some other person or some thing that is invested with feeling, evokes some reciprocal response. If the response is what is wanted, it is felt as rewarding, good. Then there is some release of tension, some sense of confidence for the next try. Change in feeling thus may follow on the action. Feeling alteration—slight and transient though it may be—gives support to the next try at modified behavior. Again, if the modification, made consciously, whether out of wish and hope, or out of anxiety, fear, love, or wish for approval (often love or approval of the guiding helper), it does not matter which—if the modification is experienced as adaptive, there is release of tension and some consequent modification of feeling. It has been postulated that when a mode of action becomes repeated and entrenched because it is releasing, gratifying, and pleasurable, emotional alterations occur which are felt and/or perceived as change in personality.

These propositions have gained additional support in recent

studies of how children learn and develop. There is evidence that only as the child takes action upon another object—be it person or thing—does he "know" it in any real sense. His grasp of the nature of a person or a thing and his responsive reactions to it, feelingful or thoughtful, follow on his active engagement with the object. Moreover, there is evidence that the child's sense of selfhood grows on his sense of capacity to act and do. The triumph of "I did it!" says Murphy writing of the young child, is the base for the sense of "I am."[10]

This mode of experiencing cannot be transferred whole from childhood into adulthood. One mark of maturity, indeed, is the capacity of the adult to substitute symbol for actuality, thought for action, and the capacity to turn action over in the mind ("interiorized action") rather than always to experience it in the doing. But even among those "mature" adults who have long learned to look before they leap, to think before they act, to substitute internal dialogue and mental rehearsals for trial and error behavior, even among these reasonable men, actions often speak louder than words. They "speak louder" in that they seem to test and verify what is "true" and "real"; but also, because their consequences—and all actions have consequences—rouse emotional reactions in the acting person himself which he tastes as gratifying or frustrating, affirming or negating.

In their continuous action-to-a-purpose, adults can hardly be conceived of as simply having things "happen" to them that either leave a new but faint impress upon them or reactivate old patterns. As a person acts in the role of worker or parent, for instance, can one assume that no new organizations of self-to-object are called for, no new demands made, no new experience savored, digested, or reacted to? Do parents just stand there, so to speak, in a state of *being*, "being gratified" by their child, "being hurt," "being proud," "being angered"? Does a worker simply remain open to "being exploited" or "being fulfilled"? Adult experience seems to be far more than a matter of absorption by addition of experiences. The adult is in continuous transaction. His actions, reactions, responses, comprehensions, attitudes, sentiments, drives, are all in active intermingling within the person himself and between him and the others with whom he has vital interrelationships. The concepts of "impress" and "reactivation" or "repetition" are not enough to name the nature of his experiencing. Change, alteration, development, reorganization, modification— these shifts and internal movements keep him in process of *becoming*.

Unless he has retreated from active engagement with the usual life tasks of the adult, he carries that illusion so essential to human dignity that choice and decision to act continue to be his to make. So he makes them, and he acts, and there are consequences for him as personality and for the others with whom he transacts.

Personal change in adulthood, then, in large or small degree, of one or more dimensions, may be given thrust, undergirding, direction, and shaping by the person's experience of action, of making things happen, in the adult roles he undertakes to carry. The tensions generated within transactions between persons bound in role relationships, the emotional involvement of mutuality or conflict, the investment of self—of anxieties, hopes, fears, wishes—in the struggle for gratification and rewarding outcomes, the discharge of tension in the "doing" of a role, the feedback from other persons or from circumstances that give evidence of competence and "payoff"—all these moving forces are involved in active performance of vital roles. The substance of vital roles and their relation to personality is the subject of the essay that follows.

2

Social Role and the
Adult Personality

No bell rings to tell the time for adulthood. Not even age years mark it off. "Twenty-one" once designated arrival, but in this day of ever-lengthening adolescence and extended dependence upon parental or governmental supports to continue one's education or to find oneself, the twenty-first birthday seems increasingly to mark chiefly the coming of age to vote and to order an alcoholic beverage without fear of arrest.

Adulthood—its respect and privileges—is generally set by the person's entry into some recognized and valued social status and his responsible commitment to carry its role tasks. The first rung of adult status occurs either with the establishment of economic self-sufficiency or/and with the decision to invest one's time and interests in some form of work or work preparation. The second rung is the commitment of the self to a mate and contracting for the responsibilities and mutualities of marriage. The third and probably the most crucial step and irrevocable comitment is the production of a child and the unbreakable personal and social contract this involves to nurture and socialize and bring him, in turn, to adulthood.

No matter that the time-sequences are sometimes turned about—that marriages sometimes precede both the capacity and intent to be self-supporting or self-reliant, or even that impending or actual parenthood may precede marriage. Parents, friends, society convey, and the person himself expects, the "rights" of adulthood, and they and he expect reciprocally (and in varying degree) that he will take the concomitant obligations, when one or more of these three statuses have been entered into: worker, spouse, parent. These are life-tasks which, it is assumed, the usual person will, if he can, choose to undertake. They are viewed as the culmination of all previous preparatory stages of rearing and education. With apprehension or pleasure, or both mixed, they are seen as the beginnings of a "new life." What is "new" is that the person, young man or young woman, is held to be able and willing to enter into and shoulder new tasks, to make the decisions and take the actions they require, and to reap the rewards they promise. His society, whether as a whole or in the small groups within it (of the latter he is most conscious), has developed sets of rules of action and attitudes that roughly outline what he is supposed to do and not do within his several roles. Sometimes explicit, sometimes implicit, sometimes inconsistent and even ambiguous, these norms of rights and responsibilities express the requirements and the expectations of the person in his role tasks and relationships.

It was Havighurst[1] who suggested that the mark of adulthood was the exit from an age-graded society and the entry into a status-graded society. Until the person is about twenty-one or so the question he is asked in first encounter with a stranger is, "How old are you?" or "Where are you in school?" Past that point these seem to become impertinent or irrelevant questions. The inquiry becomes, instead, "What do you *do*? What *are* you?" When we encounter a new adult person, we all seek first to place him by ascertaining his status and role, finding where he fits into adult society. This seems to be the essential orientation we need in order to go forward with our relationship.

It is the thesis of this essay that the major vital roles of adulthood contain the dynamic experiences that shake and shape the adult personality. For a number of reasons the concept "role" rouses resistances; certainly manifold meanings have been imputed to it. So perhaps I should begin by clearing away some common problems that accompany the idea of role.

To begin with, definitions of role are almost without end.[2] Each social scientist who writes on it shapes it to his perspectives. One may deplore this solipsism—or one may take it as license to shape a definition oneself, especially since we have only to examine our own daily experience to know role. Not only are its definitions numerous but the term often refers to different phenomena. Sometimes role is used (as it is here—and I will explain later) to denote a social status in action: the role of a husband, of a professional worker, of a student. At other times and places the word is used to denote certain attitudes and affects: the "role of listener"; "a passive role." What is most confusing is the use of both meanings interchangeably. (Thus, in a recent book which sets forth "role theory" as part of its guiding framework, one reads that "role is a goal-directed pattern or sequence of acts tailored by the cultural process for the transactions a person may carry out . . ." and, a few pages later, "The worker's implicit role was an understanding, listening one . . ." and "She accepted his implicit role of hopefulness and sensitivity.")[3] Moreover, role definitions often are so abstract or in such convoluted jargon that they seem to have lost all relation to the plain flesh and blood human beings who live them out. Add to this technical vocabulary problem that of the "acting as if" words that surround the noun "role" and carry it into action. "Role" is spoken of as a configuration of actions that are "carried," "performed," "played." The person is referred to as a role "occupant" or a "role carrier," as "playing" or "performing" a role. In all these designations there lies the implication that person and role are only artificially attached, that role is something entered or left casually, put on or taken off, assumed transiently and at the very outer boundaries of the personality, as one might drape a cape over his shoulders to strut forth upon a stage and, once in the wings, drop it off. There is no getting away from it: "role" by long usage and associations has a stage-actor artifice about it that has made it a suspect concept for those who want to know the "real" man.

Certainly in the ordinary course of a day every one of us does indeed assume transient, time-limited roles that touch nothing beneath our skins. In the role of a bus-passenger one acts in certain prescribed ways vis-à-vis the driver and other passengers. In the role of a hostess one conducts oneself in approved socially-designed ways towards guests, family members, kitchen helpers. One takes on the role of committee member at 9 A.M. and leaves it at 11 A.M.; and what one thinks of, speaks of or holds back, does or desists from doing, who one relates to and how one does so are all determined by norms and expectations that inhere in this role. But none of these transient roles are vital to the personality. All are on the surface of our being, although it is conceivable that with some turn of circumstance any one of them might drive a shaft into deeper layers of the personal self. These casual time-limited roles may indeed be said to be "performed" or "played." But, as will be explained further on, these are not the roles with which we are here concerned; here I am searching only into those roles to which people commit themselves wholly and deeply.

Still another conception often blocks our recognition and acceptance of the experiential significance of social role. It is that "role" is sometimes conceived of as if it were a cut and dried plaster cast, imprisoning the personalty, pressing certain norms and standards in upon the helpless, pliant person, imposing the Establishment's will and shackles on his freedom. Thus many social workers, among others, have turned away from incorporating the concept into their explanatory and therapeutic theory systems, afraid that the individual personality with its few and precious freedoms, its self-determination rights, will be violated by its being pushed and patted into ready-made "role molds."

Actually nothing inheres in the role concept that would make this necessary. As observation will reveal, and as has been shown in several studies of role norms, the societal prescriptions for role "performance" are written large and loosely. A man is "supposed" to support his wife and family; a woman is "supposed" to give physical and affectional care to her husband and children; a child is "supposed" to go to school, is "supposed" to obey and respect adult authority within reasonable limits—and so forth. Within these and other expectations lie wide areas of diversity for individual and group interpretations of how roles should be carried. The "norm" for either a personality or a role is not one certain pinpoint spot on a line running from "excellent" to "terrible," "well" to "sick," "superior" to "deficient." "Norm" and "normal" cuts a wide swath on that line, allows for a wide range of possible behaviors and interpretations. Jessie Bernard states this well when she speaks of role as providing a basic script for behavior which at the same time allows the individual person wide play for "ad libbing."[4]

Role expectations and requirements come to be finely prescribed, specifically demanded, heavily charged with pressure *not* in the interplay between the individual and Society. (I spell it with a capital S to designate it as that "way out there" ambiguous aggregation of Big Brothers.) Rigid interpretation of roles occurs, rather, between the individual and his own tight and small social network—between him and his role partners. In those intimate, closed-network transactions between husband and wife, parents and child, child and siblings, teacher and pupils, employer and employee, supervisor and worker— here are to be found the complicated, feeling-charged expectations of self and other, the sometimes successful, sometimes thwarted efforts to define and redefine ideas, to adapt and readapt behavior, sometimes rigidly, sometimes flexibly, in order to work out "what you and I are supposed to do with and for one another, what you and I are supposed to get out of this." In the happy congruence and mutuality of such adaptations lie the potential personal gratification in carrying a role. In their conflict lie personal conflict and frustrations.

Finally, in this attempt to touch on the common misapprehensions about role it must be reiterated that the ideas incorporated in the concept "role" are in no sense substitutes for those incorporated in the concept "personality." Nor are they merely additive. It is not that there is assumed to be an id, ego, and superego on top of which social roles come to rest. It is rather that personality can only be perceived and assessed within the context of a social situation where the individual is himself, yes, but himself in some role. Even in the deepest revelations of the inner self, such as occur in psychoanalysis, the analyst does not see personality "plain"; he sees and hears behavior (emotions, thoughts, actions acted out or reported on) that expresses the personality within some role—role of patient, transference-induced role of child, or whatever. What is diagnosed as appropriate or bizarre, infantile or mature, is diagnosed in the context of the analyst's reading of a socially defined situation in which certain expectations and requirements are held for individual behavior. Past the blind narcissism of early infancy (and perhaps in the regressions of active psychosis) no one acts simply as personality. We act as personalities within perceived (sometimes misperceived) social situations in which we have assumed or been assigned task and/or relationship roles. Thus roles from infancy onward are not only the forms in which the personality is expressed; they are also the means through which "object relationships" are experienced and internalized, through which ego capacities develop and are exercised, through which superego anxiety and idealism is incorporated.[5]

"Role" suggests simply that human behavior is socially patterned. For operational purposes it has seemed to me that Ralph Linton's definition is most useable: "A role represents the dynamic aspect of a status."[6] Which is to say that a role is some recognized social position carried by a person into action. A status is a recognized and regulated position in a society. Because it is recognized and regulated it offers some firm footing, some ground rules for what and how and with whom the person claiming that status is supposed to act. The moment he acts he may be said to be carrying the role that the status prescribes, that is, he is carrying the duties and expecting the responses that are generally associated with that socially defined transaction.

In the status and active role of a worker a person will have to meet certain requirements of productivity, quality, time investment, conduct. In turn, he will have certain expectations of his employer, of working conditions, hours, wages, relationship behaviors. In the status of a spouse or that of parent there are configurations of rights and obligations, responsibilities and expected rewards; and their acting out, varied and multiform as they may be from one set of role partners to another, will express the individual interpretations of what he and the other are supposed to be and do. Not only do role behaviors and affects differ by class and culture norms, but they also are charged with all those unique, personal, idiosyncratic needs, expectations, demands, and hopes with which each person invests a status.

In short, certain ground rules are prescribed for all major roles. Each person elaborates upon them or modifies them according to the personal needs and drives he brings to the role, according to his knowledge and practice (actual or vicarious) of what the role requires, and according to the agreements between him and his role partner. These agreements are of paramount importance because no roles are carried solo; all are carried in transaction with one or more other persons. Therein lies the greater part of their meaningfulness.

The undertaking and carrying of any one of his major adult-life roles holds far more significance for the person—his personality and his sense of self—than that he now occupies a socially formed and socially approved position. The roles of worker, spouse, parent are time-extended, emotionally intense, adaptationally demanding life experiences. They involve a person's deepest linkage of self and other, his most penetrating sense of "I" and "thou." At any given time of a day, work, marriage, and parenthood may absorb a person whole. They may involve him from the center of his being—viscerally, sexually, emotionally, up and down through the layers of his mental and reasoning powers, out through his muscles and his skin into his social environment whose signals and meanings drive down, in turn, into the deepest recesses of his body, mind, and feeling. So these roles move and shake and mold adult life and the adult personality. They deserve our most careful study to plumb and probe their dynamic impact on personality, to know what their costs and what their rewards are, and, from this, to come to some notions about how to help people carry them with least waste of self and with greatest sense of pleasure and competence.

Work, marriage, and parenthood—what do they do *to* the person who lives them out? What do they do *for* him? In what ways does he find himself affected and affecting, moved and moving, shaped by and shaping them? We actually do not know this in any sizable or reliable way. The reasons for our ignorance are several. One of them is simply the fact that when we human beings feel competent and relatively happy in our life pursuits, we do not ask ourselves or others "Why?" or "How so?" We take our homely gratifications as our just due. We cry out and ponder and analyze only when there are blockings in our pursuit of happiness. We know thus about conflicts in marriage, about parent-child problems, about frustrations and boredoms in work; but we have taken their happier aspects for granted. Here in what follows there will be some effort to discern what vital roles do to and for those who carry them.

By "vital roles" is meant those that become so interlaced with the personality, so deep-driving in their significance to the person's feelings, perceptions, self-concept, interpersonal relationships that they are essential to his total well-being. These roles are different for different life phases. Of concern here are the roles of young and middle adulthood, already named as those of worker, spouse, and parent. They are "entered into" or "taken on" with high activation of mental and emotional processes. They are invested in depth with the person's hopes, wishes, fears, anxieties, fantasies, beliefs, ideas, expectations, with drives and motivations of many sorts. They call into use many aspects of his personality—feeling, thinking, acting, reacting. Thus the person and his value-and-emotion-freighted role may become all but merged. Such merging may be almost total, which is to say that the person may scarcely know or feel himself except as he operates within his all-absorbing role. Or it may be partial, where the person finds happy congruence between certain aspects of his personal needs and capacities and the demands and rewards within one or the several of his vital roles. Thus, too, the person whose needs and drives persistently run counter to the requirements of his vital roles will find himself not free simply to slough it off as one might drop a costume but he will be locked in conflict between needs and musts, between inner drives and outer directions.

When am I only "I"? It is a question that deserves to be pondered in these days when cliches and half understood concepts of "inner-directedness" and "identity crisis" and "authenticity" fog up our views of what living for most every-day people can be. In part, I am suggesting that the anxious quest for identity, like today's sweated, grim pursuit of "happiness," is the product of some illusion. It is an illusion that the self, the "I," can be found and experienced and maintained in some isolated nirvana, "Silent, upon a peak at Darien." To be sure, there are peak moments when one seeks and revels in aloneness, when the felt yearning is to look into oneself, to taste and feel and listen to one's inner experiences, or to muse and play delightedly with the forms and arrangements of one's "own" ideas or fantasies, or to feel through and think through a problem. One may come out from these self-communions refreshed and strengthened. Strengthened for what? For engaging oneself afresh in some interaction with people or tasks, usually combined, in some "role." Or one may come out from communion with "me," "myself," "I" feeling empty and panicky because, unhappily, not enough was there to be found and the sense of being alive and real is to be found only in social intercourse. One may say that this ought not be. It is a sorry state when one knows one's identity only as it is reflected back by others. But for many people this is in fact the case, and if they are to be helped to build into their sense of self this must be recognized.

What is it that makes one person feel whole and secure at the center of himself while another feels hollow? What makes one person able and even glad to enjoy his own company for stretches of time? What makes it possible for some persons in forced isolation or under cruel stress to live internally, to feed on their inner resources while others, thrown back upon themselves, collapse from psychological starvation? "Ego strength," one may answer, "personality integrity," "sense of selfhood." It is all of these gifts of person. And all of them are the product of a like experience: the person has been in continuous interaction and transaction with people and circumstances, in concurrent and sequential life roles, in which he has been more affirmed than cut down, more effective than inept, more gratified than frustrated. He may be said to be "peopled within." He contains within himself that continuity of others, people and his feelingful experience of them, things and his feelingful and knowledgeable experience of them, circumstances (combinations of people-objects-situations) and his digested experiences of them that now make up his inner self. He knows himself, indeed, by his repeated successful experience of fusion with others, followed by his drawing away from them to do the work of digestion, self-reorganization. And this is followed by his engagement with others again.

When am I only "I"? When I am asleep. (But even then my dreams are of other people with whom I commune or against whom I strive.) When I am physically sick, so that I draw back all my "caring" into my own body, licking its wounds, perhaps in the way an infant feels himself as his own world. When I am psychologically sick, so that again, as in physical disease, I must forsake all others and pull into tending myself. (But even then, within myself, are the memories and voices and images of others.) When I choose to retreat or withdraw from others for purposes of self-communion—musing, or problem-solving, or playing with ideas or words or images or memories that in their fresh up-spurts and patternings are the fountainhead for creativity. I am "I alone," then, under two sorts of conditions: when insults upon my body or psychic self call for my turning in to tend myself, or when unmet love-hunger forces me to feed on myself, on "primary narcissism." And I am "I alone" at those times when I withdraw from others not with misanthropic feelings, but rather to be free from the distractions of sociability in order to better savor and digest the social nourishments I have had, or to reorder and reorganize the stirring "input" that I have taken from other people and their productions. If this "input" feels largely hurtful, I may prefer isolation from those who do me harm. But I am likely to continue to struggle to find gratifying connections with social life, either through other people or through activities. If the inputs are experienced as pleasurable, there is a push, after enjoyment of the pleasure of one's own company for a while, to reach out again to other people to share those pleasures. What I have thought or imagined, how I see or fathom this problem, what I have created or produced yields me, myself, a sense of pleasurable mastery But beyond this, one seeks to share it, test it, have it affirmed or appreciated by some one—at least one—else.

The development of the self and the surest knowledge of the self is through the feelingful actions and transactions from infancy onward, between self-and-other, "I-and-thou," or "I-and-it," to use Buber's phrases. And these actions and transactions are all structured and colored by the reciprocal expectations, normative and/or idiosyncratic, within roles.

All those operating functions of the personality that we group together and call "ego" develop out of the continuous interplay between the infant-person, child-person, adolescent-person, adult-person and his social experiences, between his inner organization and the social organization he encounters. Those social experiences are in no sense hit-or-miss unpredictable happenstances. They are for the most part regularized and expectable transactions between "socializing agents" and the driving developing human being. They are patterned role relationships. Ego potential is born in the child. His "ego strength" is an accrual of reliable and appropriate responses that he has developed within his expanding role repertoire. If we are to understand what is absorbed into the personality from its social transactions, how ego strength is built, we will need to study the emotional and mental interpretations the person (at any life stage) derives from his present (and sometimes past) transactions with "objects," human and otherwise. "Ego strength," writes Erikson, "develops from an interplay of personal and social structure." And "we have studied man's inner world with unprecedented devotion; yet we assign acutely decisive encounters, opportunities, and challenges to a nebulous 'outer reality.' "[7] The "interplay of personal and social structure" and the "decisive encounters, opportunities and challenges" occur in our continuous transactions with other people and circumstances, transactions that are socially defined, shaped, and judged in role terms. A person's ego strength, then, consists of his accumulated competence and confidence derived from what for the most part have been satisfying role relationships.

Superego, too, grows out of role transactions. What a child is "supposed" to be, to say, to act like in relation to his parents, his grandparents, the family pet, the neighbor's child, is prescribed, demonstrated, and firmly demarcated in society's regulations for children. These regulations and prescriptions have often been so fully incorporated by the parents that it seems to them that *they* are the arbiters. But scratch the surface of parental authority and you will find a whole system of beliefs about what a child is "supposed" to do in order to be "nice," "good," "normal," and these are translated into expectations of behavior and moral character. Indeed the whole resolution of the oedipal conflict, which is said to entrench the basic superego, turns upon clarification of child-father-mother roles and upon the renunciation by the child of his role fantasies in favor of his role reality—that of boy-child or girl-child whose business is supposed to be in another direction than that of competitor.

Relationships between people—whether between infant and mother, school child and teacher, adolescent and friends, grown man and his employer or wife or children—are attuned to the participants' perception and appraisal of what the particular transaction seems to require of each. As certain behaviors and reactions become entrenched, they may color perceptions, and the role requirements and rewards may be misread. The "formed" person, he who is past the period of high plasticity, brings his personality to any role, and he will view and interpret the role in the light of his personal needs and aims. Yet, except under excess stress or psychic malfunctioning, each person's perpetual effort is to grasp, define, and assess what the outer situation calls for from him and the other. This is the essence of the ego's functions of perception. It is followed by selected behaviors and affects that are the ego's coping and adaptive functions.

What's in a vital role? What does it hold that makes it potentially and actually powerful in the development or changes of the adult personality?[8]

The experience of any one of us shows that in carrying any vital life-role a person makes a substantial investment of himself. We "put ourselves into" such roles as wife, mother, worker, student; we are "libidinally invested" in such roles. These social roles are, for the human being who carries them, charged with emotion and feeling. The greater the deposit of such feeling in the role, the more fully the personality is involved. The more wholly the person is involved, the more he as "self" and he as "role-carrier" merge and become one. Perhaps it is because this merger takes place so often that we have had less than clear vision of what roles include. They have a four-fold dimension which can briefly be set down thus:

1. To carry a role means to act, to do something. So actions and behaviors are one aspect of role performance.

2. To carry a role means to do something in relation to one or more others. So interactions, transactions, and reciprocations between and among several people are a second aspect.

3. Transactions between people are shaped and governed by their ideas, expectations, and judgments of the attitudes and behaviors of self and other. So cognition, conscious ideas, will be a third aspect of role performance.

4. Ideas, expectations, judgments of reciprocal transactions are charged with affect and shaped by drives and emotions. So feelings and sentiments and push-pulls are a fourth aspect of role performance.

Vital roles, then, involve the person in action, in transactions between himself and some human or other "objects," in thinking and in feeling.

As we experience them, the action-feeling-thought-transactional experiences in role performance (one may shuffle this sequence about, for it will be different in different personalities and at different times) seem to occur in simultaneity, in at-once-ness, and one is often hard put to know whether an identified emotion was the cause or the consequence of a certain action. The "personality's" experience of the social situation and the "situation's" response to the personality in and of it is so swiftly and subtly merged that they all but defy separation for analysis. But the powers within role transactions must have close analysis, so I go forward at the risk of bringing the sense of a living process to a jarring stand-still.

An adult's entry to any vital role and its on-going operations is charged with anticipations. They are anticipations of himself as actor, if what he will be expected to do, and they are anticipations of what the "other," the role partner, will do, will "act like." They include expectations of what the "pay-off" will be, what the involvement and deposit of himself will yield him by way of gratification and rewards, and what it will cost him by way of effort and demanding responsibility. Along with his conscious consideration—or as is often the case, his taking certain things for granted—are feelings of himself in relation to what the role requires or promises. He may feel he wants its promised rewards and is willing to pay the costs; or he is afraid of its costs and not sure the rewards are worth it. He feels confident that he is equipped and able to learn the role skills—earning a living and doing well enough to get ahead, raising a family. Or he feels fearful and uncertain about whether he has the capacity to cope. He feels strongly about what he wants and expects from his role partner. Such feelings may range from blind trust to blind suspiciousness, from open receptiveness to plain hostility (the latter, in respect for social expectations, is usually masked by parrying or "kidding" techniques), from the pushing determination to dominate and "run" the whole transaction to the pulling yearning to be carried and supported by the other.

These kinds of anticipations and expectations of self-other, self-action involvements permeate marital, worker, parental roles. They stem from several sources: the person's actual knowledge of what the role usually requires; his actual preparation by education (formal or informal), by prior experience with like tasks, or by mental rehearsals to perform the necessary actions. Accompanying these kinds of preparation there will have been the incorporation, conscious or only partially so, of beliefs, attitudes, sentiments that form halos of emotion about or give heart-felt meaning to the role expectations, actions, and transactions. These feelings derive from the person's whole previous lifetime of role-watching (in his parental home), of role assessment (taken in through his wide open eyes and ears and pores in his impressionable childhood). These usually have been revamped, often to some considerable extent throughout his adolescence when, through his expanding contact with the world—schools, books, TV programs, contacts with friends' families, bull sessions and confidences with friends and admired adults—he may have evolved different ideas of roles and of his desires and aspirations within them.

A person is not always conscious of himself and his feelings and attitudes in relation to the role he shoulders. He may drift into it, as happens when a young man drops out of school and "picks up" a job as a kind of time-killer substitute. He may be catapulted into a role, as when young people enter marriage driven by their sexual passions and some impelling sense that this is their inevitable destiny. He may have a role thrust upon him, as when an unmarried girl becomes pregnant and must take on unwanted motherhood. It may reasonably be expected that in proportion to the person's ignorance of the role, unpreparedness and incapacity for it, or emotional unreadiness for it there will be for him proportionately acute problems in carrying that role with either competence or satisfaction.

The person who has been lucky enough to have had in his most formative years good familial "role models," whose pre-adult experiences have developed and exercised his interpersonal skill and expanded and made conscious his ideas and aspirations of himself in his several adult roles—this person is likely to undertake his roles with forethought and ongoing adaptations. He is, in fact, more likely to be gratified and to find rewards in his roles because his view and expectation of them is realistic and down-to-earth.

On his commitment to undertaking a designated status, or on his being thrust into it, a person links himself with one or more others who stand and operate in relation to him in both socially prescribed and personally interpreted ways. Each of them brings his own baggage of expectations, action modes, attitudes, aspirations, uncertainties with him. Except in very general ways, "the one" cannot know in advance what "the other" will be like in the actual encounter and interplay. Once the interplay occurs, all the factors of knowing, feeling, understanding of role of self and of other are expressed in actions. These actions and reactions, the penetration of one person's feelings and actions into those of the other, evoke emotions of hurt, anger, unease or pleasure, security, gratification—any of which are powerful forces in pushing one or both persons to entrench or to change behavior. Whatever the societal prescriptions for a given role may be and whatever the single individual interpretations of it, it is the dynamic encounter and process of person-to-person interplay, interaction, transaction (call it what you will, there is no adequate word to describe these under-the-skin and into-the-heart-or-viscera impacts and resonances) that are the living reality of self and other and that push and pull the personality towards alterations and modifications, that either undermine or undergird the sense of well-being. When these transactions carry heavy emotional freightage, they feed into the person's capacity to love, to invest himself in others, and they proffer him love-nurture in return. If, unhappily, they are largely frustrating interchanges, they will constrict both his loving and lovableness. Moreover they will leave their impress upon his sense of himself as socially competent and valued or as inept and inferior.

In action within any one of his vital roles, a person may feel himself whole as an acting-feeling-thinking-relating personality. At the same time the nature of role structures and standards will affect his inner self in several different ways.

For one thing a socially recognized status and its role behavior offers anchorage in the social system. It is basic to a person's sense of belonging. More, it affirms that one *is* to a purpose. Identity is firmed up when one's function is explainable and recognizable by those others who matter. This security value of role identity is perhaps best recognized when it is absent. When an adult is neither worker nor student nor spouse nor parent, he is hard put to explain himself to others, or even to himself. He is driven to find some role, some status niche in which he can stand. He may, then, take on and treasure the role of a sick person, a "patient"; he may take on the role of beatnik, of protester against conventional roles. Any one of us rising from his night's sleep, drugged with fatigue, confused by the unreality of his dreams, facing the bleary, ambiguous image that confronts him in the mirror, fumbles for and then finds his footing and his reality as he remembers what he *is*. "I am a shoe clerk—or a lawyer—or—or—." And he pulls himself together, physically and mentally arranged for that role. "I am a mother—or a working woman —and I must get the children breakfasted, or catch the 8:15 bus—." It is as a person steps into his steadying role that he knows how and in what ways he must gather himself together in order to be and to do.

The stabilizing effects of role lie not only in its social support and recognition but also in the fact that in the carrying of roles we find the order and regularities of our lives. It is true that these arrangements and regularities are often the source of boredom and frustration. But they are also a source of steadiness. The roughed out prescriptions for what is to be expected, subject though they are to personal modifications, provide some solid base from which to shape conformity, or make choices of action, or from which to take exception if one will. Moreover, role prescriptions, through their providing some ready-made system and dependability to daily living, free the energies of the ego from involvement in what could otherwise be innumerable decisions and choices. Energies can be poured instead into those aspects of living that may be more freely chosen, "ad-libbed," are subject to play and experimentation. Perhaps it is this "social security," this life stabilization, which role provides that makes young adulthood seem to be a hopeful and integrating time of life. Stability-in-movement is the idea that best describes that equilibrium which frees energy for investment in new ventures. Satisfactory role performance provides that stability. But role tasks and relationships also provide many stimuli for new and expanded uses of the self in relation to other people and things.

Entry into a new role places a person in a new relationship to others. He gains membership into a new group. If he wants this position and its tasks, if he has chosen to undertake it, he feels a connection with other human beings in this group. If he is to feel comfortable in his role, in harmony with its demands and rewards, he will not only need to act in certain ways but will need to take on (or "in") the attitudes and beliefs that are consonant with those acts. Perhaps this should be stated the other way round: only as a person's actions, beliefs, and attitudes are consonant with one another and with what the others in this same status hold to be appropriate will he feel at one with his role and with the others within the role network.

Aware that he partakes of certain common expectations, common problems, and common satisfaction, the person expands his identifications and horizons. He is not only himself but he is a member of the "husbands of the world"; she is identified, in her own eyes and the eyes of others, with the mothers in her society. Jokes about married men, advice columns about child rearing, news of wage or tax increases—these take on new interest and relevance for the person who enters a new "reference group." What occurs is a sense of new attachments which may (though not inevitably) be accompanied by an identification and an empathy with others. It is a commonplace observation, for example, that when grown children become parents, they often for the first time *feel* with parents. They know with some greater appreciation "what it has been like" for their own parents. They come, even, to forgive the parental faults and follies that heretofore called forth in them only intolerance or indulgence.

The shift of attitudes and affects that tends to occur with change in status and roles has been tested in a study of men who were promoted on the job from factory workers to foremen.[9] They became more satisfied with the company, more inclined to defend the incentive system, more positive in their perception of top management: ". . . inside a period of three years those who had remained in their new roles had developed almost diametrically opposed sets of attitudinal position" (opposed, that is, to attitudes they had held as workers). Later, when some of these foremen were demoted to workers and studied again, they reverted to their worker-role attitudes. (This latter finding may give rise to the observation that role-induced attitudes were not deeply incorporated, were experienced at only a superficial level. This is probably true for these particular status changes—they are not "in depth" roles. Moreover the strong possibility exists that the demoted men experienced chagrin, at the least, that their positions were lowered; and therefore their identification with workers against management would be heightened.) The explanations put forward by the researchers for the identified attitude and sentiment changes may have relevance for other role-change situations too. One explanation is that a change in reference groups—that is, a change in the group with which one identifies and which one feels part of—leads to the taking on or actual "taking in" of its attitudes. These, in turn, change the natures of actions which bespeak (louder than words) to outsiders, and to the actor himself, his stance and sentiments. The other explanation is that a change in roles inevitably involves changes in action functions, which then influence both feelings and attitudes about the self in transaction with other persons and/or tasks. These explanations suggest that even an assigned role, if it is valued and is in line with the person's motivations, may finger its way into the under-layers of personality.

Further light has been cast on changes in adulthood, this in terms of the growth of certain aspects of what we call "intelligence." Until not too long ago it was generally assumed that measurable intelligence growth ended by early adolescence. The twelve-year-old cut-off point of intelligence development set in the early army alpha tests has been pulled upwards to a potential seventeen-year-old level by today's most expert psychologists.[10] But more, there is emerging evidence that certain aspects of intelligence may under optimal conditions grow until about age 50.[11] Longitudinal studies of adults support what may be commonly observed—that in such ego capacities and social intelligences as interpersonal competence, judgement, social and technical skills, and staying powers there is apparent growth in early and even middle adulthood. Such development does not "just naturally" happen. It is probably the product of "powerful forces in the environment," of both the demand and the opportunity for the exercise of nascent or latent intellectual capacities. Such demand and opportunity inhere in new, expanding, and rewarding roles. Good judgement, self-control and self-management, purposiveness, accurate reading of reality, capacity for concentration—these measurable and testable attributes of intelligence are both the requisites and the by-products of successful performance of valued roles.

Entry into a new and unfamiliar role, whether forced or freely chosen, may be experienced as a crucial event. As such, the taking on of a new role—a new kind of work or a new position in the work hierarchy, becoming a spouse, becoming a parent, becoming an in-law, may be a "teachable moment" at best, or a treacherous one at worst. The early stages of new and valued roles are charged with heightened sensitivity to self-and others, heightened concerns about hazards or hoped-for gratifications, mobilization for coping. So these are times of behavioral change and sometimes, from this, personal change. Change after childhood, as has been said, is most likely to occur when the individual is dislodged from entrenched, habitual operations and must migrate, so to speak, from a familiar environment (peopled-circumstances) into an unfamiliar one which is experienced as "powerful" either because it promises high fulfilment or danger, high hope or fear.[12] The import of these migrations from a familiar to an unfamiliar role deserves the particular attention of those who work with adults, either toward prevention of breakdown in personal-social functioning or in its restoration.

The sense of self as one who is capable of self-governance, who has competence, who is held to be of worth by others derives from the repeated transactions in valued life roles in which there is repeated experience of oneself as able and adequate *plus* repeated experience that this adequacy and ability yields recognition or admiration or affection from valued others. So it is that the self-image and self-esteem may develop in adulthood subject either to the slings of an outrageous fortune or to the bouquets of a beneficent one. If the regularities, the attachment to others, and the anchorage in a social identity proffer floorboards of security to the personality, it may be said that enhancement of self-esteem and concept of self-as-competent proffer it buoyancy and forward pull. The capacity to strive, the forward-looking hope, the freedom to express one's innate potentials in new-found ways (which we call "creativity") all grow on the person's central confident sense of selfhood. This, in turn, feeds on his self-and-other affirmation of effectiveness. When a person feels or acts "like a changed person," whether in the direction of his well- or ill-being, it is the result of some changed sense of self as actual or potential "effector," as one who has (or has lost) power to influence his environment or to manage himself in relation to it. That this sense and its subsequent affirmation in action will be registered in the under-layers of the personality cannot be proved; it can only be supposed because it is so often felt as actuality.

The more self-aware and insightful a person is, the more conscious and developed his internal communication system, the greater the likelihood that he will perceive and record the connections between what he feels, thinks, and does and what effects his actions and affects have upon others, and theirs, in response, upon him. Such a person affects and is affected by his daily role transactions not only in unconscious ways, in being "acted upon" by others or by his own unknown and therefore un-owned drives. He may also take consciously devised steps, thought-out ways of dealing with either himself and/or the people and circumstances of his environment in order to achieve the maximum reward of gratification he seeks. Such a person may be said to be his own "change agent." He observes himself as actor. He assesses himself in relation to the demands and actual or potential rewards of a valued role. He launches into that dialogue with himself that is a form of self-teaching in which he takes measure of what he wants and talks to himself about how he might change or alter his actions, his views, his aims, or his external conditions—or all of these—in order to achieve some happier adaptation between himself and the situation-complex. If as a result of his internal review of himself and the situation his revised behavior "feels good" or "feels right" (because it has called forth more gratifying responses from the outside), he will have created some conscious change in himself.

In short, while many of the changes we undergo happen to us as a result of our unconscious or only partly-conscious working-over and digestion of experience, many other changes may be the result of our consciously controlled efforts to change the direction or expression-form of our drives. The very determination and decision to change one's ways of acting and responding is in itself a long step towards change. It means self-assessment; it risks disequilibrium; it requires self-discipline. It is a resolution considered almost daily by most adults in one or another of their vital role relationships, but it is a resolution undertaken and carried out by only a few. These few become self-changers.

But there are also many adults who, wanting to change their ways of managing themselves and their life situations, are unable to take themselves on. They turn then to helping persons—sometimes to personal confidants, sometimes to professional helpers. The help they need is essentially that of lifting to their conscious consideration the emotions and attitudes and ideas and behaviors that are affecting their capacity to carry one or more of their life roles with both effectiveness and gratification. Past such new perceptions of themselves-and-others they may gain, past such decisions they may make about their ensuing behaviors, the execution of their interior adaptations will have to be in actual tryouts, tryouts of themselves as actors in relation to those with whom they interact. They will know their greater or lesser gratification, their sense of mastery or defeat only as it is tested in one or more of their daily life roles.

It should not be surprising that the role of client, of user of another's helping services (or of patient, as the case may be), depends for its potency on the same motivators as do other vital roles. When being a client is experienced as a change-process, as "moving," it is because of these several forces: the person is at a crucial point in his life and he is therefore "teachable" or "treatable"; his helper's relationship to him may hold the powers of love, of social affirmation, and of promise for his greater self-realization; moreover, in their

work together on his problem he may be involved as a feeling
thinking-acting person in whatever aspect of his social functioning is
under consideration when he enters it. It may hold much that is new
and therefore disorganizing to him. The client or patient role is
usually time-limited, but for the reasons above it may have emotional
intensity. Those who undertake to give professional help need to
understand these role components as they affect both parties in the
help-taking help-giving transaction.

In sum: It seems to me that in every age phase, from infancy on
ward, the continuous exercise of personality functions occurs within
the relationships and tasks that are governed by role expectations and
their social judgements. These shape and infuse every aspect of the
personality. Vital roles are both time-extensive and emotion-intensive
Because they are the social forms in which living is contained and
expressed, in which the human quest for steadiness and dependability
for anchorage and linkages with other human beings, occur, where the
sense of self-identity and self-connected-with-others is repeatedly ex
perienced, where the powers of mind and muscle and feeling are con
tinuously in play, social roles are the means by which the human
personality is expressed and expanded. Surely the personality's basic
structure and style is laid down in the earliest, most plastic, most bio
logically surgent years of life. Yet, within the adult years there are
tasks in which that personality is engaged, there are impacts upon it
transactions betweeen it and potent outside forces that will stir and
reform its behavioral dispositions, subordinating some, entrenching or
enhancing others. The quest for love and social recognition, the hope
of self-realization, the demands in crucial life events are the stimu
lators and motivators for change in adult life. They are to be found
(or may be sought for but never gained) in the major roles of
adulthood.

Work, marriage, and parenthood are the most vital roles of adult
life. They have not been studied closely except in their failures or in
the bland detachment of research surveys. How are they actually ex
perienced? What are their costs, their rewards, their inroads upon the
personality? How much of the whole man do they engage? We do not
really know. But it would be good to know if we are to understand
what potentials for personal change and development lie in the life
tasks of adults. The essays that follow do not presume to offer that
knowledge; they offer only some observations on the roles of worker
marriage partner, and parent as living experiences.

PART THREE

SOME PERSPECTIVES
ON VITAL ROLES

3

Work

"I don't like work—no man does—but I like what is *in* the work—the chance to find yourself. Your own reality . . . what no other man can ever know"

This is Marlow speaking, in Conrad's *Heart of Darkness*; he utters one major proposition of this essay. It is that work—an adult's occupational role—is a basic force in his stabilization, development, and sense of identity. He may or may not like it. At its worst it may constrict and undermine his sense of self-worth, may damage his motivation, may dull his powers of mind and muscle. At its best it may expand and enhance his sense of identity, of mastery, of social worth and competence as well as his repertoire of social and technical skills. But under either circumstance work provides him an anchorage in the social system, a basic explanation of his identity, an "own reality," a linkage to his fellowmen.

I am aware of how platitudinous and pious this sounds. I set down these flat statements, each of which needs qualification and explication, because from sources as wide apart as Freud and today's automation experts there is a tendency to regard work as a necessary evil or a soon-to-be-unnecessary activity on the part of man. On the part of most of us it is so simply taken for granted that it is scarcely noticed, except when it is absent. Freud noted the importance of work to man's connection with his society: ". . . work has a greater effect than any other technique of living in the direction of binding the individual more closely to reality; in his work he is at least securely attached to a part of reality, the human community." But then, pessimistically, he added, ". . . yet as a path to happiness work is not valued very highly by men. They do not run after it as they do after other opportunities for gratification. The great majority work only when forced by necessity, and this natural human aversion to work gives rise to the most difficult social problems."[1] The question: is there indeed "a natural human aversion to work"? or is there an aversion to certain kinds of work under certain conditions? Of this, more further.

Today's students of work, in another vein, are largely concerned with two of its aspects: the deadening effects of work that reduces men to robots; and the problems of leisure (or do they mean the problems of idleness, which is something else again?) which automation and technology bring in their wake. It is fashionable among many of these writers to point out that the American attitude towards work has been shaped by the "Protestant ethic" (scornful thought!), that working is valued because it is held to be virtuous, idling to be sinful: "Satan finds mischief. . . ." It is not usually clear whether the critics of this ethic would seek virtue in non-work or whether virtue is thought to be a value happily got rid of. Nor is it clear what value or moral imperative would guide men in their daily exercise of their faculties. Most men today seem to want to work. Is the American discomfort with non-work wholly the result of our religious-capitalist inheritance or are the values of work (and therefore the harms in idleness) more numerous and complex than we have taken measure of?

Further pervasive in present day discussions about work is the concern that at every level it is becoming more automated, specialized, fragmented, bureaucratized, pre-organized, and that, therefore, the worker is stripped of initiative, his interest is dulled, his sense of himself as a doer or maker or effector is all but extinguished by the meaninglessness of repetitive part-processes that he switches on, stamps out, checks off; his sense of connection with his work is made tenuous by his distance from its inception, its purpose, its completion. There is scarcely a question of the truth of these conditions and effects. Even a casual visit to a large industrial plant, a city postoffice, a mail-order house will reveal the lackluster eye, the deadpan face, the slack attitude or its counterpart, the robot-like compulsiveness, that characterize large numbers of workers involved in our massive, impersonal, industrial, commercial, or governmental operations. These are matters for deep social concern and immediate and ingenious social planning.

Yet there remain insistent and troubling questions even for these workers. Would no-work be more gratifying or fulfilling than their present some-work? In the event of employment's ending, what would these workers do or be? Can all work be fully satisfying—or even *most* work? Is it possible or realistic to promise, as both glib demagogues and sincere demaphiles do today, that every man's work can be "dignified" and fully rewarding? Are we holding forth some fantasy of work, that for all men it can be "creative" and self-fulfilling, an ideal which can only back-lash with disappointment and feelings of betrayal?

My propositions here are these: that work—the occupational roles that men and women carry—is potentially and often actually a potent force in the sustaining and stabilizing of the young adult's personality; that man, rather than having "a natural aversion to work," is motivated to work, wants to work; and that if social planners and counselors and mental health workers are to train, prepare, persuade, counsel young people to engage themselves in work, we must put ourselves to the examination of motivation for work, the rewards, present and possible, in various kinds of work, the exact nature of what work does—or possibly can do—for people. Only when a man knows what he gets out of work can he know what he's willing to put into it; only when social and industrial planners consider and examine the relation between work and "common human needs" can work (or leisure, or idleness) be assessed as "good" or "bad."

We will not find answers if we continue to cast wistful backward glances to what work used to be in the good old days or to project our dreams of "creativity" and "self-actualization." There are long-held myths about work in the past which rosily mist up the lenses of many of us who turn with despair from our view of work today. There is the myth of the medieval man. If one is to believe these often mentioned myths, most urban men of the middle ages worked on cathedrals; each felt himself to be a contributor to a monument to the glory of God. But, actually, how many artists and artisans could have been involved? How many others—back-bowed, bandy-legged, muscle-locked, hungry-bellied toilers—worked alongside, digging, lugging, hoisting stone, shinnying up precarious scaffolds, falling to their deaths or to lifelong crippling, all but unnoticed? How many of these workers, one wonders, knew themselves to be part of a great vision? Of postmedieval but preindustrial man the image is the happy farmer, sturdy and self-directed, sowing good seed in good soil, reaping good harvest in good weather. Once the machine takes hold the image blurs a bit. Still, the small shop, the small entrepreneur, the open opportunities to land and resources for men of courage and

imagination—all these hold nostalgic lure for all of us. But the fact
is that through all the centuries most men not only led "lives of quiet
desperation" (Thoreau said this more than a century ago) but most
men led lives of desperate body-breaking, sinew-tearing, spirit-dull-
ing, starvation-waged work or, as alternatives, of empty, idling,
catch-penny jobs, enforced beggarly servility. Crawling in mine pits,
collecting slops, shoveling manure, hauling rocks and breaking stone,
plowing stubborn land, and reaping burned out or washed out harvest, creeping up and down chimneys, scraping, pushing, climbing,
lifting, till heart burst and muscles collapsed—these were among the
common occupations of the common man for centuries past.

Did these men feel at one with their work, invested in it, and able
therefrom to draw nurture for themselves? Did it reward and fulfil
them? Nobody knows. No social researcher asked Aesop the slave or
Bottom the weaver or Charles Lamb the bookkeeper whether they
felt "alienated," "fragmented," whether they found dignity, reward,
self-fulfilment in their work. Not only was work considered to be so
natural and necessary to man's condition as to be small subject for
ponder, but the total expectation of what the work role was to yield a
man was completely different even a quarter century ago from what
it is today. This is the second perspective which shapes and colors
our thinking about work and which needs recognition.

Perhaps never before in man's history has so much insistence been
placed as today upon every man's "right" to selfhood, to full actuali-
zation of his powers, full meeting of his needs. In part this is a
countercry against our levelling-off, dehumanizing, computerized
society; in part it is the flowering, even weedy spread, of the seminal
ideas of individual psychology, of some renewed hope and faith in
human potentials, of the heightened pursuit of the elusive "happiness" that had been anticipated when dire economic need was all but
erased. Today there seems to be a growing expectation, not only
among students of work but among workers themselves, that work
should provide not simply the means by which man earns his daily
bread but also the means by which he can express, nurture, and find
himself. How realistic or how wishful this expectation is varies from
person to person and certainly from one sort of work to another. But
perhaps it is not too optimistic to say that there is some turn in the
tide. The use of man for work is turning, perhaps, to considerations
of the use of work for man.

Here our quest is for how work—the everyday kinds of work in which everyday people are employed—may accrue to the personality development of the young adult in beneficial ways.

First is the fact that an occupation provides the security of a place or position in the social system. It names one's function in the networks of functions that constitute society. In adulthood a person must be able to identify himself and define himself in part by what he does. "I work, I carry a certain occupational role" means "I have a known place and connection in society, I carry a socially accepted, economically- or functionally-valued role." A man may feel apologetic, even ashamed, of what he works at; he may dislike it. But without work—what? He is impelled then to explain that he wants, but cannot find, a job; he is "between jobs"; he is "looking," trying to make up his mind, trying to find what will best suit him. That he must have the anchorage of a work role is taken for granted by both him and his society; it is the young adult's base for social recognition.

In our society the question, "What do you do?" (work at) seeks, in part, to ascertain, "Who and what *are* you?" One knows that a man is, or desireably ought to be, more than his job, that only part of his human self is exposed and expressed in his work. But certainly in the superficial touch-and-go of social relationships, what a person works at is the first quick way by which he is identified. And for many people, pathetic though this may be, their work role is the chief means by which they define and know themselves. Everything in our production-oriented society conspires to this end. The question we ask our children from early childhood on is, "What are you going to *be* when you grow up?" We mean, "What are you going to *do*, to occupy yourself with?" (When one child I know answered "What are you going to be?" with a firm "A man!" he was engulfed by laughter from the adults about him.)

True, today's adolescent is being given more time than in the past to "become," to find what he wants "to be." Today we bear at length with the young person who is casting about in his effort to match his drives and talents with available work opportunities, to know himself whole before he invests himself in an occupation which will absorb his time and energies and mind (and by such absorption channel those energies and shape his mind.) Increasingly we allow today an extension of time before the young person must commit himself to a work role. The middle class young adult graduates from college and goes on to graduate school, or he tries to find himself in the spate of new altruistic projects that offer him some chance to know himself before he chooses what he is to *become*. The lower class young adult is encouraged to maintain and extend his schooling, to develop his skills. Held in abeyance but tugging in the minds of patient parents and of the young adults themselves is the insistent question, "When he is finally ready to commit himself, what will he *be* as worker?"[2]

The designation "playboy" may have its envious overtones, but it is still a pejorative term in our society. The boulevardier, the man of leisure who spent his days cultivating people and dabbling in the arts, was never a recognized figure in American society. Indeed one probable reason for the exodus from America of young men of leisure —not necessarily idlers—to Europe in the late nineteenth and early twentieth century was that in this country "not working" was neither understood nor socially tolerated. The social expectation that a man must work has held firm from the beginning of American society. If he does not need work's purchase powers, if he is fortunate enough to have been financially secured through the work (honest or other-wise) of a progenitor, he is still expected to involve himself in some occupation that is socially valued and productive. He may volunteer for philanthropic endeavors; he may work at creating, directing, appreciating, or collecting in the arts—a relatively newly-sanctioned area of work in America. He may put his money to work and occupy himself with its addition or multiplication. But unless he can say, "I am a (certain kind of worker)," he must, to his shaving mirror or to the person he is facing, explain himself as a joke or as being in some temporary state of suspension. If on the other hand he can say, "I *work* at—" or "I *am* a—," he feels socially secured thereby.

Even the chronic beggar, at the other end of the scale from the rich nonworker, begins to consider his daily exercise of begging as "work." In many parts of Asia and in the Western world as well begging may become "professionalized." That is to say it comes to be viewed by its practitioners as a regularized form of work, subject to certain norms of effort, under certain conditions, requiring certain skills, and having certain production expectations. It may, further, be bulwarked by a rationale or "ethic" that gives it respectability at least in the eyes of its workers.[3]

These expectations that one must work were not too long ago confined to men. Within the last generation they have begun to be held for the young woman as well. Time was, not so long ago, when a young woman who had finished school—whether by drop-out or by full completion of requirements—worked only if she needed the money. If she did not, it was quite usual that she waited in her parental home, sharing the work of housekeeping, until marriage opened to her the roles by which she could take her recognized position and place in society—the roles of wife and mother. Her work was within those roles. Today the expectation of the young woman herself and of the society of which she is a part is that she will do some recognized, explainable work in the hiatus between school and marriage, and not just because she needs the money. Why, then? For a complex of reasons, I believe, that have to do with the noneconomic gratifications, the personal and horizon-expansion opportunities that work—even dimestore clerking—promises and often provides. These reasons have taken hold so persuasively today that many women seek to maintain or gain a work role in addition to those involved in marriage and motherhood. Indeed, the controversy over whether being "just a housewife" is a socially respectable role or whether one must be and do something more than this has created new work for numberless lecturers, writers, and editors who work on this never-done subject of woman's work.

Interestingly enough, the arguments for women's working outside the home have focussed upon the personality-building gratifications to be found in work—the exercise of her competence, the use of her talents, the securing sense to her of being part of important or valued endeavors, the broadening experience with people and circumstances that work proffers. These same personality-building values may hold for working men too, though they have scarcely been given a nod of recognition. All of us are creatures of our culture, and even students of work have come to take for granted that males must work chiefly in order to eat.

To earn money is no small part of the personal reward of work. To be paid for what one does is to know that one is judged to have "value" in society's most coolly calculated terms. The pleasure in money reward for one's work is rarely a continuing one. There are, to be sure, the moments when a "raise" gives concrete evidence of the worker's having met or exceeded expectations, and the meaning of recognition and advancement may outweigh by far the increase of purchase power. But by and large, past the pleasure of the first few earned checks, the pay envelope or check comes to be taken for granted. Or it is grumbled over because it is less than the worker feels he is worth, or less than he needs, or less than someone else earns; or it is eaten away by deductions, or spent before it was earned. Nevertheless, to earn money is proof of one's economic utility, and economic utility is a long and firm value in the society of which the worker himself is part.

It is this need to have such value affirmed that one encounters frequently in women who have done volunteer work for many years and who, one day, suddenly decide that they want a "paying job." They often do not need the money. It is, rather, that past the interest and recognition and companionship that volunteer work has offered them over the years, there is some hunger to have their value measured and rewarded by the plainest, hardest means—cold cash. "I am worth money." I know of a sheltered workshop for old people which originally was run as an occupational therapy shop. Attendance was sporadic, production languid. Then someone conceived of paying for completed work (fairly mechanical, simple assembling jobs) even though most of the old men and women did not need the money. Attendance picked up and became regular; production picked up speed and volume. Perhaps these old people were simply back in the old groove: you have to *work* for pay. Or perhaps they were propelled by the feeling that if they were paid they were being valued, and therefore they strove to prove "worth."

At best money earned by work underpins a man's sense of being valued and ranked in the hierarchy of producers. At the least earned money buys necessities and perhaps some small pleasures that may compensate in part for work dissatisfactions.

Moreover, money earned endows the individual with rights to self-determination and choices, to freedom from the psychological dependency on others that economic dependency subtly but surely carries with it. For the late adolescent or the young adult no declaration of independence from parents can ring true or be free of reciprocal acrimony unless it is accompanied by economic self-dependence. For the adult accustomed to the independence that his earned money bestows, the fear of job loss is a compound fear: "How will I pay rent and buy the kids' food" is part of it; the other part, "If I need help—from my family, from 'relief'—what will it cost me? What will I have to pay for it in gratitude, in submission, in excessive obligation?" The price of economic dependence is often a heavy drain upon the personality of the young adult. Conversely the pride of economic self-dependence is essential to a sense of self-respect and self-determination.

Work and earning power are vital in validating the roles of husband and father in his family. Among the few role prescriptions that are universal and firm in our western society is that a husband and father is "supposed" to work and to be the main support of his family. (For practical purposes we need scarcely look at the man who lives on an "independent income." Even he usually finds himself an office in which to study and manipulate the business of money and to which he can, in all decency, retreat during the day's normal working hours). A man's wife must be able to say, to her family, to friends, to neighbors, "My husband works at—" or "—*is* a—." Her household duties are the kinds of work she carries in reciprocal response to the separate work and wage responsibility carried by her husband. His work gives him the right to be tired in the evening, to be irascible or withdrawn. It may cast an aura of interest and respect about him. His earnings may be the source of pride and pleasure or of denigration and dissatisfaction. He may use the purse strings as whips or as bribes. Affectional and even sexual relations will be colored by how work fares for him, by his earnings and their uses. In short, there is no nook or cranny of family life that does not connect in some way with the man's role as worker, earner, and supporter.

A man's children must be able to say to their playmates and peers, "My father works at—" or "My father *is* a—." More, they must be able to say this to themselves when they look at their father with trust and pride (or with unease and dubiousness) because even in early childhood the question is, "What does my father *do* when he goes away?" Before adolescence the child scarcely knows or cares what form of doing is top or bottom in the occupational hierarchy. He is likely to understand only such work as has visible and concrete form. But to be occupied in some work is expected from his father. This is in large part what makes a man a "father," and this fact of his being a worker and money earner weaves a never-ending web of interactions and feelings between a father and his children.

For one thing, it is the working father who sets the model for a man's role. For his boy-child the father's regular, dependable going and coming to and from a world outside the home, his doing something with his hands or head that "makes money," and that connects him with conditions and people to which the family would otherwise have no access—these and all the attendant aspects of working set the child's expectations of himself when grown. The respect and value accorded the father for his work and support does not elude the boy (nor do the opposite attitudes, when they occur); and the father's feelings and attitudes about work, as good (or hard), as stimulating (or exhausting), as gratifying (or frustrating) are absorbed by the big ears of the little pitchers who know their fathers as workers. For the girl-child these same factors that shape work attitudes hold. Her working father is not her adult model as he is for the boy (either a model to emulate or to diverge from), but he is her model for what a husband and father is supposed to do and be, and the transactions between her mother and father about money and needs and spending are food for her feelings today and her fantasies for tomorrow.

Not only does his working give a man his primary role position in the network of his family, but it links his family to the bigger world outside. Depending on his job and his relation to it, the image of that world of work and workers will vary—from a fearful defeating agglomeration of powers and people to an opportunity arena for the investment of one's own powers for various kinds of profit. Each man's work, then, affects his children's ideas of their work expectations and their sentiments about work as something to be feared and avoided or looked forward to. As for the worker himself, part of the authority that he holds as head of the household lies not simply in his being the family's means of support but in his being their linkage to the wider world and its interpreter to them. (When the adolescent child begins to work, he gets "cocky" and "smart," according to his father's view, not simply because he can be money-independent, but because he also gets in on the "know").

For good or ill, then, work binds a man to his family (and his family's fate to his work) in a strong network, and it links him and them to the world outside. When a man finds himself able to carry his role as worker and provider to his and his wife's satisfaction there will grow in him the steadying and gratifying sense that he is "doing all right," that he is adequately meeting the basic expectations of a family man.

It is in the nature of man that he is more aware of his pain than of his pleasure. We tend more to count our misfortunes than our blessings, or if we count the latter it is to reinforce ourselves against a misfortune that has already occurred or is looking over our shoulder. Thus the manifest and ordinary everyday rewards of work are scarcely noted. We take them for granted—they are "coming to us." We know them only, suddenly and acutely, when they are snatched away. The rewards of work that anchor a man in the social system, that secure him in the eyes of his neighbors and wife and children, that furnish his economic independence and the choices that go with it—these are most acutely appreciated and longed for when they are lost, when work is lost and missing. The unemployed man knows what he is missing, if only in a vague, inarticulate way. The employed man rarely knows what he has, rarely asks himself, "How come I feel settled, doing all right, looking forward to my kids' doing even better?" Rather, he dreams the American dream of better jobs, more pay, more interest, more status, more chance for advancement: he owns a small electronics repair shop and customers flock to it; he is promoted over a whole line of senior persons because his ideas and personality are recognized as superior; someone comes along and says, "I've got a cinch proposition—" or "Here's a chance to earn double what you're getting." He dreams of prolonged vacations or leisured months: the fish leap to his bait in a bosky pool; he hits the jackpot everytime in a flashy joint at Las Vegas; his slick little two-seater burns up the road; the museums and cafes of exotic places await his coming. So he grumbles about his work. If he is asked to assess it he will be likely to report on its many dissatisfactions and irritations or on the ways it bores and depreciates him as a person. The man on the job rarely measures his work against non-work. He measures it rather against some image of the work he would like to do under conditions he would like to set—against some ideal of work.

Possibly this is one of the many factors that accounts for the widespread discontent with work when today's worker is studied. Thus when one recent inquiry asked almost five hundred men in an industrial plant whether work or their workplace was a central life interest for them, three out of four men reported it was not.[4] One is left wishing one knew what *was* of central interest to these men. Family? Leisure occupations? Associations with friends, club, or union members? What work would they pose as a desired alternative that would hold such interest?

Another possible explanation of man's disaffection with his work is that he often transfers to it his dissatisfactions in other areas of his life. Changes in many aspects of social living outside of work—the shifting impersonality of neighborhood ties in large cities, the loosening of kinship bonds, the high pitch and press of things to buy and to have—all these fill men with unease and vague distress. Some of these dissatisfactions may be carried to work, displaced onto the work situation. We are sometimes more accustomed to thinking of work as a refuge for many men, as a place and activity that offers eight hours of defense against "home troubles"; but it may also be a place and activity into which home troubles are transferred, disguised and unrecognized. So it is possible that expectations of "happiness" or "fulfilment" brought to work are greater than what can realistically be derived from it.

A different attitude about work was discerned in another large-scale study[5] which asked some four hundred men both in middle-class and working-class jobs what they would do if they inherited a sum of money large enough to make working unnecessary. Four out of five would want to continue working. The unskilled worker expressed the fear of boredom and restlessness if he did not work. He wanted to *do* something. He was more likely than the middle-class worker to want a different job from the one he had, and he usually opted for a business of his own. (This dream of the small business of one's own is fairly ubiquitous among unskilled and blue-collar workers.)[6] The middle-class white collar worker expressed his wish to continue his work because of its interest or its "contribution."

It is a commonplace observation by social workers that the role of husband and father may be severely shaken, sometimes to the point of disintegration, by the loss of his work role and its monetary as well as social status rewards. In blue-collar families the wife's employment outside the home is even today strongly objected to except as it is viewed as temporary or for some special project—buying a new car or getting braces for the kids' teeth. Cliches about woman's "place" in the home rise largely from some fear that role privileges and responsibilities will be lost for the man if the woman becomes a wage-earning worker. In the middle-class family the wife's working is increasingly accepted. It is seen either as an economic necessity for achieving the family's goals or as the woman's right to self-realization. But even with this "enlightenment," if the woman's work turns out to be more prestigious or more economically rewarding than her husband's, he feels some threat to his worker role. He may weather this—by kidding self-deprecation or by blustering self-assertion in other areas of the marriage—but whatever the strategy, the necessity is to right an imbalance created by the man's being elbowed out of his central position as worker and wage earner.

The actual effect of work loss upon men in their relation to their family life has been documented in a number of studies, and social workers' everyday observations attest the validity of their findings today though some of the studies were made more than twenty-five years ago.[7] It was found, for example, that the man's status in his family was lowered by his unemployment, that his inability to carry the role of wage earner threatened his position and rights as family head. There was a breakdown in his previous controls, if these had been coercive. If another family member became chief wage earner, interpersonal relationships were strained. If some inferiority status had previously been cloaked by the habiliments of the worker-wage-earner role, it was now nakedly revealed.

Perhaps more than we ordinarily realize, a man's work may provide a set-up defense system for him. He has a "right" not to be bothered by many problems or relationships that he considers peripheral to his central function. Indeed his work may defend him from himself, from such introspective awareness as may undo a pinned-together personality. The loss of work means not only a loss of income but may mean a loss of work's bulwarks against anxiety or malaise too. For many people these are necessary defenses, essential to their being held together as personalities. The work role validates and underpins their roles as husband and father. Not only is work their most time and energy consuming function, central to their life-organization, but it is also a major source of their self-conception. It provides purchase power not only of commodities but also of position vis-à-vis family members and, in lesser degree, those other persons with whom the worker is in social relationship.

Even in this increasingly mechanized world there remain many kinds of work that proffer more than these essential but perhaps only partial rewards. First among these additional rewards is the opportunity for social contacts, for transactions with other people beyond the confines of family, for peer and workmate relationships. Again, we are aware of this human need far more acutely when it is gone than when it is present. The workers who were asked whether their central companionship or relationship interests were with their co-workers answered to the contrary: they were not.[8] And yet, beyond family and kin, where do most men and women satisfy their hunger for social contact? At beer joints, where fellow workers gather, on bowling teams, at coffee breaks and lunch, at union meetings, at the many contacts of eyes and greeting that, even though they may be touch-and-go, give the worker a sense of human contact. True, anyone who has observed workers coming and going in the mass has seen, perhaps to his sadness, the superficial quality of many of these social contacts, the isolation behind the forced-hearty greeting, the aloneness of five workmen sitting together in the shade of the factory wall munching the contents of their well-filled lunch boxes, silent, empty-eyed toward one another. But are these distances between people work-created? Or are they created by a sum total of present-day life conditions of which work is only a part? There is scarcely any question that people can become drubbed out, flattened psychologically by years of dead-level mechanized work. There is also little doubt that many young people enter the labor market with the capacity to relate to other people—or to tasks— already running thin in them. But everyday observations as well as work studies have shown that workers—perhaps all but the near-psychotic—want and value the proximity to other human beings and the responsiveness of other human beings that work offers. It is wanted even if it is often minimally utilized.[9]

To be recognized by one's work superior as having done a good job, as being conscientious, as making some particular contribution— this augments the sense of self; it is a reward to the personality. Indeed this is the reward most wanted and most found missing by workers in mass production operations. To be part of a working group, recognized and appreciated by one's workmates, united with them whether by bonds of gripes, of interest in sports, or by general camaraderie—this fulfills the ever-present human need to be accepted, supported, even to be authenticated by others.

Certain other aspects of work come even closer than those discussed above to effecting the organization and integration of the personality.

Work regularizes and structures time. It determines our rising up and our lying down; it determines where we should be and with what and whom we will be engaged during certain hours. Sometimes this iron-bound schedule galls us. Frequent absenteeism and impulsive quitting in highly regulated jobs are often break-outs against the clocked lock-step. Yet take this regularity away and most persons are at a loss to use or apportion their time. They "kill time" or find that it has eluded them when they try to account for it. They experience not pleasure at their freedom but a general malaise and "loose-endedness."

"Work buttons me up," said a man of my acquaintance who had

just completed a highly responsible job and had been given a generous year's severance pay. After six weeks' vacation he was becoming edgy. Half laughing, half rueful, he spoke of the burden of his freedom. He woke each day to too many choices of action, of having to decide whom he should seek out, where and with whom he should lunch, where he should go, when to return home. "I miss the constraints," he said. Work "buttons up" daily living for most men, too tightly for some, it is true, but for most of us it serves to mobilize and focus our energies and to give regularity and stabilization to daily living.

To be a "good worker" requires the steady maintenance of certain disciplined modes of self- and task-management. Impulse and irrelevant motivations must be held in leash. It is expected that one will manage oneself in relation to other persons and to other's purposes. One's production is measured and assessed: it must occur within a given time, be of a certain quality and quantity, be done under given conditions. The reliability, dependability, self-control, timing, and cooperation that work requires are exercises of all those ego functions involved in the reality principle. For some persons and in some jobs the requirements inherent in a specific work role remain external impositions, reluctantly accepted, never made part of the self. For others the work role expectations become shackles. But in general it may be said that the undertaking and habitual exercise of regularized and disciplined modes of work strengthens the ego. ". . . man must learn to work," says Erikson, as clinician-philosopher, ". . . so that his ego's power may not atrophy."[10]

How readily work patterns are established and incorporated depends heavily on how congenial they are to the personality brought to the role. They depend also upon the strength of worker's invested motivation for doing and holding the particular job. The stop-gap, make-do, short-term job or the job which the worker feels is beneath him may leave no impress upon him at all. His involvement may be only skin-deep, his submission to requirements grudging and minimal until the clock or whistle frees him to be himself again.

The entry into the work of one's choice, into the work that may become one's life work or career line is probably a crucial point in the development of the young person. He enters a new environment with heightened acuity and sensitivity to its nature and expectations and with heightened self-awareness in regard to his capabilities (or lack of them). He is alert, "tuned in" to the work personnel, especially his work superiors, to the expectations of him and the expected rewards. He is internally mobilized to adapt, shift, protect, cope. He is, in short, at his most malleable point for the establishment and incorporation of work habits and work relationships that will set the pattern for his on-going performance and anticipations.

It is odd how little attention has been given to these crucial beginnings by organized work systems. "Orientation," when it is offered, is often a mechanical rundown of where things are, who people are, and what is to be done. Attention to what and who the new worker is, what he expects, what the congruence or discrepancy is between his expectation and the work reality—these and other means by which the worker could be helped to see his place and purpose in the work system or process and to know the realistic demands and rewards, these aids to his entry to work are more often missing than not. They could shape the new worker's attitudes, interest, and sense of commitment. Instead, the members of the work-place so tend to take it for granted, that they assume the new worker will simply accommodate himself—"he'll learn." He will; he may learn too well and too quickly the example set him of indifference and automatic response.[11]

How much change and self-management must take place in the person's behavior and attitudes varies both with the work and with the person. Some professions—social work is one—require marked changes and reorganizations not only in expressive behavior but also in the attitudes that propel it. Belt-line factory jobs require chiefly suppression of spontaneity and confinement to the use of a set of articulated muscles under clocked conditions. In between lies a whole range of clerical, selling, service jobs with various aspects of personality and behavior, some valued, some not. But even highly "creative" work, even artistic endeavor must, after inspiration, submit to being "worked" in some purposeful, organized, self-disciplined way to bring inspiration into some expressed communicable form. For all that we fancy the artist or the creative man as a "free" soul, the fact seems to be that most creative people are "at work" on their ideas and their problem-solving most of the time. Not only are they inner-directed but they are also *inner-driven* by standards and role-tasks of their own making. They march to the rhythms of their own drums—but march they do.

Of course the young adult comes to his occupational role and its discipline already conditioned in large part by his two decades or so of work required both in schooling and in the self-management that relationships within his family and his play- and school-mates called for. In the period of his early schooling, which Erikson has designated as the stage in which industriousness is learned and exercised or, failing this, where inferiority feelings take over, the child's future as worker is heavily predetermined. School "work" provides the child's first experiences of required self-discipline in line with a planned and regularized program and sequence of tasks, of putting himself into doing things with his eyes and ears and head and hands. If these are well done, they give him a sense of knowing and mastery and accomplishment. If unhappily he cannot "do the work," for whatever reasons, he is left feeling inept, discouraged, and socially shamed. In self-defense he must draw himself out of the defeating and demeaning situation of work, must de-cathect it (to use that awkward but useful psychoanalytic term), or must view it with antipathy. "It's too much like work" becomes the phrase that expresses "it takes too much out of me and gives back too little." This child is father of the school dropout; the school dropout becomes the irregularly employed or underemployed worker. His unsatisfying and unsatisfactory work experience is due not solely to his lack of skill or education for the job. It often derives—and perhaps this has not been closely enough examined—from early or later childhood experiences when he learned that putting himself into work brought him more trouble than pleasure or that the yield or outcome of his efforts did not reward him enough for the input required of him. Or it may have been that his energy and capacity, for whatever reasons of conflict and constriction, fell short of what the work tasks called for and that his efforts yielded only the sense of failure.[12]

There are, however, the exceptions, the "late-bloomers" well-known to anxious parents and dogged teachers. Some young people "find themselves" in relation to school work or occupation in the late afternoon of their adolescence or in the early years of adulthood. To "find oneself" means in effect to find that one is motivated to involve oneself, to manage and put oneself into work towards some constructive purpose. How this happens is often a mystery in the individual instance. Whatever factors of conflict resolution or heightened motivation and hope are operative, the "late bloomer's" capacity to work, like that of his more gradually matured peer, is marked by his willingness and ability to put energy and staying power into learning and carrying out a task and to accept and exercise the disciplined use of self that work requires. What he will "get out of it," in addition to the returns he is consciously seeking, will be an enhanced sense of self-possession, of being master of *himself*, not simply of a job. This subtle but powerful aspect of self-possession and self-mastery as well as object-mastery underpins self-esteem in the personality of the young adult who finds himself able to be both industrious and competent.

One must, realistically, note that not all good workers are happy workers. Some work costs too much in terms of psychological or somatic stress. Competitive pressures that are inherent in the job or that are derivative of early rivalries, driving tension that comes from keeping up with the Joneses or from some compulsion to achieve or to assuage old shames—these and other causes may make a man's work a kind of wracking addiction. Then the work role acts as strait-jacket on the personality. Or it may spill its tensional by-products into psychosomatic symptoms and/or into other life roles.

There remain to be considered those workers who claim to like their work—as much for the work itself as for its secondary gains—and those happy few who unabashedly admit to "loving" it. How many these fortunate ones are in number, how frequent they are in the working population, in what age range and occupation range most are to be found, nobody knows. The happy worker has not been studied partly because of our understandable push to study first what is wrong and what needs change. Yet, if we are to do anything about work and the man beyond pointing the problem and printing the polemic we must try to identify what conditions may make work likeable, more congenial to the person who undertakes it, more conducive to his personal development.

Early psychodynamic theory held that man's drive was to gratify his basic needs and to achieve, continuously and repeatedly, that sense of stability and security that follows on relief of tensional states. Recent theories of ego psychology go beyond this. Proposals, based upon observations of young animals and young human children, suggest that beyond the homeostatic principle is the innate drive for "mastery," "self-actualization," "effectance."[13] What seems to be agreed upon today is that when his basic needs are met man drives to create and encounter new experience, to explore outside himself, to use his senses, muscles, mind upon objects (people, things, conditions), to manipulate, move, push, change, problem-solve—all for the pleasure experienced in working at something that yields to one's powers.

The most persuasive among the current observers and theorists of human motivation, Robert White, puts forward the notion of "effectance" as an innate drive to be an effector, "a cause" of some change or consequence. The well-fed, well-rested monkey, White notes, does not sit in passive pleasure but moves, rather, to exercise himself on his swings, to puzzle over the latch on his cage door; the well-fed, well-rested, loved-up baby explores with his mouth and eyes and hands, makes noise by banging his rattles, makes his crib-side fall down by his discovery that monkeying (apt word!) with the catch releases his prison bars, screams with rage when he finds that all his work on that catch will not bring the side up again. When he is older he is not content that he has jumped down one step—he must raise his achievement level to two; he is not content just to scribble—he must hold his crayon-strokes within the lines (and the intense concentration in his face, his tongue clamped between his teeth show that he is at *work*—not just at play).

The dividing line between work and play may not always be easy to find. So much of the child's play is "work." It takes energy, concentration, problem-solving, discovering and obeying the laws of efficiency, repeated practice towards competence. The use of his various growing powers to effect change in things or in the responses of people, the involvement of himself in actions that make some impress upon others or objects—these, when they yield to his effort, are his proofs of mastery. This is how the child—and later the man—knows his strength. Hard work may be involved, and repetition, and backing and filling and reorganization of his coping strategies. But if it yields a desired outcome or even a pleasurable serendipity, it floods the human being—child or man—with a sense of competence. "I am bigger than the problem or the task," he feels.

So perhaps the human aversion to work of which Freud spoke is less to work and more to the conditions and forms of those kinds of work that keep man feeling that he is so small a cog in the machinery as to be ineffectual and dispensable. Work that uses only a narrow margin of a man's capacity leaves him with a sense of denigration rather than achievement. Conversely, in order for work to be gratifying, to be "liked" or "loved," it must offer the worker the experience of effectance, the opportunity to test and know that what he does, what he puts in of his skills, intelligence, physical powers, or know-how makes some desired or desirable difference. "I *did* it!" is one of the persistent triumphal cries of the human being from childhood on.

One of the most telling and touching examples of this pleasure in being a competent "cause" is set forth in a small book that came out of Russia several years ago.[14] It is the account of one man's day in a Siberian forced labor camp. It is a grueling lock-step day that begins and ends with the bitter harshness of the bosses towards the prisoners and the prisoners towards one another, all brutalized and all brutalizers. Stomachs are empty, clothes are ragged, there is no inner nor outer protection against the knifing winds of the Siberian winter. The men are set to constructing a new building. Ivan is like the rest. Like the others he is cursed and curses, is threatened and threatens, alternately sweats and freezes. But he continues to set his bricks in place, swiftly, not only because of the foreman's pressure but from some inner push and habit of skill. He does not even know what he is building—perhaps another prison house—and he works under gun butt and threats. Yet at the day's end, just before he and his fellow slaves are herded together to be marched back to their barracks, he ventures one more look at his work. A small lick of triumph leaps up within him, for he sees that despite his having had few tools and no leveling string, his bricks lie straight. He "ran back to have a last look. Not bad. . . . The wall was straight as a die. His hands were still good for something!" In every other way Ivan is a slave, but he knows himself to be still master of his materials.

Laboratory experiments with animals at play (work?) reveal another finding that bears on work. Once a problem or task has been mastered, the animal becomes bored and turns from it in search of new stimuli. Every human being knows this boredom with an activity that, once attractive or interesting, has through repetition and sameness become routine. No impress of the individual will make any difference in it, or perhaps no change in it is held to be desirable. So it becomes empty of attention-need. Anticipation of novelty or interest are drawn out of it. It becomes depersonalized. The relation between this state and the loss of effectance is clear; the routine job is empty of the worker and leaves the worker empty in turn. If work is to be "liked," then, it must provide some variety of processes or tasks, some change in a routine grown monotonous. The specter of automation is not that machines will take the place of men. It is that men may be forced to become machines (as men on an assembly-line are today) and that work will diminish the personality rather than enhance it.

Beyond some variety in the work-task, there must be some opportunity for the worker to put his mark on his work, even if it is only a faint one. It is the old principle of reciprocation in human experience: we expect our "take" to be responsive to our "input." Examine the relationship between a worker who "loves" his work and the nature of the work. "Loved" work is that which demands, asks for, or is open to the worker's putting himself—his interest, his energies, his ideas, his powers, his judgements, his self—into it; and then, following as consequence on this investment, the worker finds that there results some identifiable responsive change or difference or modification in the materials of work (things, processes, people, problems); and these effects are held to be good.[15]

"Are held to be good"—by whom? Now, immediately, there enters another vital factor that makes the difference between whether work is only tolerated or is actually found pleasurable. It is the factor of recognition and approval by other persons connected with the endeavor. One hears now and then of persons who are both their own taskmasters and judges, who need no other man to say to them "well done!" If there are such, I have not known them. True, writers and artists close themselves off from friends and relatives for months and years, sweating out their labors, talking to themselves. But are they not, in part, sustained by thoughts of "When this is published—" (that is, when this is read by many other men) or "When the critics see this—" (when those I respect and fear tell me what they think of it)? Scientists burrow into "pure research" in their laboratories and philosophers pursue truth, but does some thought not cross their minds such as "I wonder what old so-and-so would think of this idea—" or do they not dream dreams of acclaim for their ultimate discoveries? Some narcissism is as essential to love of work as it is basic to love of people. Self-love is the start of self-respect and self-investment. And so it is only natural that work, if it is to be gratifying, must proffer some actual or promised social "feed-back" into the enhancement of the self-image.

Most of us know, frankly and openly, that we need the recognition, respect, and, even more, the admiration of other people. We may appraise ourselves, may be our own most fawning flatterers or severest critics, but we also look into the eyes of our fellowmen to see how they reflect us. At work we look first to the assessments of ourselves by those persons why by their positions have judgment power over us and/or to those whom we most admire and respect. Then we look to our peers, whose opinions of us may mean as much or more than the evaluations that come from up the hierarchal line.

If the distance between the worker and those who hold power or whom he admires and respects is too great to give the worker the sense that he is recognized and appreciated, or if the work conditions are such that workmates and bosses alike wear a protective glaze across their eyes, then the worker feels alienated, unrelated to the job because he is unrelated to people. A wage raise may show up in his pay envelope, but he will not be gratified unless some authorized person gives him some personal word and notice. Conversely, recognition of the worker's particular contribution, his specialness, his usefulness, small and occasional though they may be, are bit by bit built into the worker's growing sense that he is valued by his fellowmen, by his superiors, that he is "a man among men." If work is to feel rewarding, in short, it must reward not only by money and the worker's own sense of achievement but also and always by the recognition, appreciation, and affirmation of himself from other people with whom and for whom he works.[16] Work is always judged by others for adequacy of its quality and quantity and for its usefulness. The more invested the worker is in his work, the more he and his work are one, the more he feels judged as *person*. His sense of himself as adequate, competent, worthy of the compensations of respect, admiration, recognition, or money is heavily dependent upon how his accomplishment is assessed. Unless he has some other major occupation which he values and in which he is invested more deeply, unless he has small use for either his work or his judge, a man's sense of himself as person will shrink and suffer or expand and grow full on the social assessments of him as a doer.

Beyond the walls of the work-place lies the community at large which judges work. Work is more likeable when it carries prestige. Such prestige is accorded when work calls for high degrees of education, knowledge, and skill, or when it is held to exert potent influence. (Psychotherapy and advertising-public relations work become bedfellows under this latter rubric!) Work in association with an enterprise that is powerful by virtue of its bigness and richness, even if it is identified more by vagueness than explicitness, may carry prestige. ("I am *with* the Getrichquick Corporation," a man says, rather than, "I am an order clerk, hopefully working my way up.") On the other hand there are many kinds of work that are absolutely basic to the community's welfare, that are clamored for but that have no prestige value whatsoever—indeed, they have only denigration value. Garbage collection and sewer work are two of these. They have no status because they take no knowledge, no skill, and because they are literally "dirty" work. (If jobs such as these are to be wanted and taken by men whose dignity as workers is to be upheld, there must be invented for them some better economic and social rewards than exist at present.) Respect—rather different from prestige—may be accorded many other kinds of work that are held to be "good" for the community and that entail some learning and self-sacrifice on the part of the worker in terms of earning power or drains upon personal comfort. Teachers, ministers, social workers often are accorded this social recognition. Whatever the status accorded the job by public opinion, that status devolves upon the person who carries the job. If prestige, respect, admiration, or general affirmation that it is a "good job" or "important" is the public opinion, the worker has one further form of underpinning and recognition from his fellowmen in the larger community.

Work, at its least, then, offers a man or woman these rewards: a social identity and linkage with other persons of his age, sex, and status; a socially recognized function; an occupation—in the sense of a use of oneself and time towards some end; some purchase power for necessities or compensatory pleasures; the right to self-governance and choices; and an underpinning of other valued life roles. Further, by its regularities, its stipulated requirements of time, behaviors, and production, work provides essential conditions for the stabilization and ordering of daily living. The self-discipline it requires in relation to fellow workers, to work materials, time, and purpose, may come to be incorporated by the worker as part of his self-management. It may pattern his modes of cooperative effort and shared endeavors with others.

At its best, work offers even more. It is a means by which a person comes to know and find pleasure in his own effectiveness, competence, and worth. His successful exercise of his capacities—his prowess, skill, intelligence, ingenuity, inter-personal competences— enhance his sense of self- and object-mastery, and this psychological nurture is both sustenance and thrust for new effort. Self-respect, self-confidence, and that vital life sustainer, hope, expand in the worker who feels his productivity and knows it to be recognized and valued.

At its best, work offers too the rewards of relationships with other persons that are gratifying and ego building in their affirmation of the person or his production; these further underpin his sense of social connectedness and social respect. When the work itself is socially valued and has prestige in the community and when the opportunity for advancement in earnings or recognition is open, the rewards to the worker are obvious ones. Finally, work at its happiest best offers some variety, some opportunity for explorations and the play of mind or skill upon the problems to be solved. It challenges the worker but, it must quickly be added, it must allow him the privilege of failure too, lest challenge be too risky. Work such as this—the dream of all of us, the reality for the fortunate few—asks that a free and informed intelligence be brought to it; and it pays back in kind. The paradox is that because truly rewarding work makes the full man, it is he who is ready and able to use leisure. The man whose work role has only diminished him is left ready and able only to be idle.

It is late in this already over-long essay to come to definitions. My excuse is that some definition seems to have evolved from the foregoing examination of work. It seems desirable to try to clarify the differences between work and labor and drudgery, the differences and likenesses between work and play, and the differences between play, leisure, and idleness. The brief notes that follow are rough beginning attempts to sketch out some outlines of work and play.

Work is the involvement, investment, deposit of the self (or selected parts of the self) in some actions or processes that aim to produce a planned product or outcome. Labor is work that is physically or psychically exhausting not simply because it is consuming of energy but because its feed-back, actual or hoped for, is niggardly. There can be the paradox of "labor of love," work of a mental or physical nature that may deplete the person, but upon which he is nevertheless motivated strongly to spend himself; he engages in it for some special reason. Drudgery is work or labor that is so routinized, repetitive, machine-like that it is de-humanized and so expunges the personality of the worker.

Like work, play is the involvement, investment, deposit of selected aspects of the self in actions or processes that aim to produce an effect or product. But the difference is this: the aim of play, its "product," is simply personal pleasure. The outcome of play is of no consequence to anyone but the player and often not to him. Work, on the other hand, is expected to produce an outcome or product that can be identified, measured, assessed, and valued. The outcome is supposed to be of consequence to the worker himself and, even if in miniscule, to his society.

The actual activities of the worker and the player may be very much the same. They may and often do use the same capacities of the person. The "brain worker" often plays brain-using games for his recreation; the "muscle-worker" often plays in muscle-using sports. Some work may hold much that is playful in it—when it allows for imaginative and exploratory ranging among ideas, or calls for problem-solving strategies. Some play may hold much that is "hard work," demanding concentration, care, skill. The difference, again, is that play may be abandoned, left unfinished and unassessed—it does not matter because it is the action and process that gives the pleasure. Work must be brought to its planned conclusion. Work is clocked, regularized, subject to laws of efficiency. It demands and requires, whereas the demands and requirements of play are subject to player's rules or to agreements between the players. When play becomes strictly regularized or when its outcome becomes a matter of consequence, it becomes work. It becomes "professionalized." The players, whether they are paid or not, work and work hard at perfecting their skills towards gaining some end beyond personal pleasure and gratification.

Play may produce a valued outcome or product—an invention, a poem or picture, a seminal idea—but it was not bargained for; it is a happy by-product. Work on the other hand may produce experiences of personal pleasure, nurture, and gratification, but this too is the by-product, not the aimed-at target of the job. Play may produce a sense of frustration, of personal ineptness, of excess demand; but unlike work, it can be abandoned at will and without cost.

The pleasures and gratifications that may be drawn out of either play or work are several-fold: the pleasure in the use of one's effectance drive and powers in ways that yield evidence of one's competence and mastery; the gains of social or monetary recognition; the nurture in feeding upon and actively "taking in," by the use of the senses, the intelligence, and the imaginative or empathic powers, experiences which are aesthetic or interpersonal. And for those whose work consists of the management and planning of the work of others, the imperious problem becomes how to inject into the work lives of millions of workers such conditions as will yield them the pleasures and rewards men inevitably seek when they invest themselves in the tasks, bonds, and aims of work.

The difference between leisure and idleness is that in leisure the person, again, invests himself, puts himself into some activity in which his use of his powers affirms his competence; or he draws into himself (actively-receptively) such nurture from other persons, objects, or experiences as enrich him. In idleness the person neither gives out of himself nor takes in of others. Except when it is a short-term resting time, idleness is the passive partner of drudgery. It reduces man to an empty shell. The "man of leisure" embarks on doing something, on giving out of himself or taking into himself or both. The man of idleness is passive; he knows only boredom and rolelessness.

All of the foregoing holds implications for the thinking and the action of those whose work consists of helping individual persons gain more gratification and suffer less frustration in the course of their daily lives. It holds implications too for those whose work it is to innovate, bring into being and operate such conditions and programs as will improve the human lot. Work and its meaning in the life of everyday men and women, the problems it harbors, and its potentials for personality shaping and fulfilment deserves our closer attention.

Work by its presence or its absence figures in every situation or "case" known to a social worker, nurse, doctor, teacher—or any other professional helper. Whether the person's problem lies in his physical or mental illness, his interpersonal relationships, his socioeconomic or his psychosocial circumstances, his work or non-work will both affect and be affected by the problem, in good or bad ways. Further, as this essay has repeatedly asserted, the role of worker with its accompanying actions and affects and its consequent rewards (or harms) will subtly but surely influence the person's sense of himself, his sense of social security, his present personal stability, his sense of present "happiness"[17] and future aspiration. The spill-over of the problems or pleasures of work into other life roles, its effect upon marriage and parenthood, its effect upon the growing child's idea of the values and opportunities in the workaday world—these and other considerations are grist for the thought, observation, and helping actions of all those concerned with human fulfilment.

From those men and women already long-involved as workers, already committed to a lifetime occupation, it would be well to draw not only their accounts of the frustrations and hard demands that most work brings but also the gratifications they get—or seek—from it. As I have said, we take our satisfactions as our just due. We rarely savor them, though we are keen to the bitter taste of dissatisfactions. "What does your work do *to* you, and what does your work do *for* you?" The answers to these two simple questions might not only reveal to us the meaning of work to many different people but, more valuable, might reveal to the individual worker himself what he actually has in his work, what he is able to do or make happen, what he needs, what he yet wants. There is much to be said about the value of enhancing a person's experiential awareness. Here it can only be noted that the beginning of a man's sense of being a man and not an instrument, of being free and not automated, is his awareness that he can be an assessor and judge of himself and his life condition.

For young persons about to enter the working world, particularly those youngsters who casually fall into jobs because they have rejected the choice and preparation for a planned occupation or career, there ought to be the opportunity for explorations of what they are undertaking and what they are prepared to do. By "prepared" I mean less their technical or educational equipment and more their psychological attitudes towards work and their expectations about what they will put in and what they will get out of it. The "role rehearsal" that vocational guidance counselors often provide young people consists of necessary advice on what to wear and how to deport oneself. They might well be expanded to include discussion of what the young worker hopes to gain and to give for purposes of clarifying the present actuality and anticipating the future potentials. Along with our having too long overlooked the multiple and telling ways in which a person's work may affect his sense of himself and his world we have too long taken for granted that work is understood, wanted, accepted, anticipated and (paradoxically!) *endured* as a necessary good.

Of the regularly unemployed we know little or nothing. Of the "no-collar worker," in contrast to the white- or blue-collar worker, of him whose work is toil, unaccompanied by skill or social rewards, we know little or nothing. His work is too little or too lowly to make him a captive or accessible interviewee.

Our public programs for continuing education, for job training and retraining, continuously warn against dropout from school and promise that education will lift the level of job and wages. These are sometimes troubling promises: there is danger that an over-sell of education that may result chiefly in disappointment. Graduating from high school or even college does not in itself insure marketable skill or motivation or accurate perception of the transactions that must regularly occur between work and worker. Moreover, are there not many young adults who, for many reasons, remain uneducable? Can they truly all be educated and trained and tooled up? Have the planners of work taken sufficient account of such attitudes as apathy and distrust and feelings of inferiority that permeate the regularly unemployed young? Moreover, are they promising—or seeming to promise—that all jobs will be clean-hand, clean-collar jobs? And if dirty jobs will remain, what rewards and recognitions will need to be devised to give their doers some sense of social approval? Can "made work" be felt by a man as good and valued? Can forced work—in lieu of a relief check? If a guaranteed minimal income were to be established, would incentive to work persist? If so, why or under what conditions? Further problems in social planning are those of shortened work hours in the day and lessened work years in the life-span. How can empty idleness be avoided? How can leisure or play-work be realized?

The problems and questions about work in all its forms proliferate. And the answers, every one, must take into account the psychological-personal meanings of work, not just its socioeconomic meanings. This is because work is the central, on-going life-function of adults in our society. As such it holds deep personal significance for the individual man in some obvious and in many subtle ways. It can undermine and diminish a man; it can steady and fulfill him. The work of the helping professions is to strive toward the latter, and understanding work as an acting-feeling-thinking-transacting role is one step in that direction.

4

Marriage

Perhaps nothing testifies more convincingly to the adaptive-change capacities in adults than the persistence of marriage as a social form and the persistence of most marriages. Despite the high incidence of divorce and separation the fact is that by far the greatest proportion of marriages last, as the original contract provides, until death severs the relationship. Despite the great incidence of "disillusion" among married couples and the disappointments, frustrations, and even hatreds that pepper many and totally flavor some on-going marriages, the fact is that most of them hold together. Despite the remarkable differences between men and women, not simply the biological ones to which the French give their "vive!" but also the frequent differences of sentiment, yearnings, role expectations, ideas of rights and duties—all of which at times are heavily shot through with high antagonisms, all of which in combination have been jocularly called "the war of the sexes"—there exist at the same time remarkable capacities in men and women for changing attitudes and understandings and behaviors that result in mutual gratifications. So, one asks, how is this? How does it come about that two different grown people, each shaped as personality by two different parent personalities, plus all the differences that sex identity and experiential milieus create, how does it happen that they can form and, more, sustain an on-going and for the most part mutually gratifying union? The answer must lie in the common human adult needs that marriage meets combined with the feeling and behavioral changes that the married pair undergo, perforce, or that they willingly and consciously undertake to work at either "to achieve a more perfect union" or in order to hold on to their essential source of nurture and stability.

The common adult needs that marriage meets are those that have been already proposed as the major stimuli or change-producing drives in all adult life. They are both spur and satisfaction, gadflies and goals. To name these needs once again: they are for love, for basic physical and economic security, for social recognition, for self-expansion and greater self-realization. To name them opens, at once the necessity to explain them in the particular context of marriage—and this follows.

But first a few background notes against which to view these factors in marriage.

The combined drives that seek fulfillment in marriage, as they do in any major role we undertake (indeed, it is their presence that makes a role "major"), will vary from individual to individual, within each John and Mary who decide to get married or who have marriage thrust upon them. They will vary in the value invested in one or another of them, by the intensity with which one or another is sought by the priority given one over another. They will vary between the two persons who aim to become "as one." The woman may enter marriage driven by her need for economic security and the social status that is conferred upon a married woman, while the man who wants her may be driven by love needs that in one instance may be simple sexual passion, in another may be a yearning to be attached to a strong, motherly woman, and in yet another (still "love"!) may be a warmly affectionate admiration for a good companion. The fact of these combinations and variations makes obvious how fallacious is the idea of an "ideal" marriage, how futile it is to attempt to understand "what she can possibly see in him" or to generalize that some unresolved oedipal or sado-masochism lies at the bottom of every marriage we cannot understand, or to hold one aspect of this complex and changing relationship as being *the* cause of either its success or failure. The sense of satisfaction of those drives will also vary from person to person depending not only upon the personality needs brought to marriage but also, and heavily I think, upon the person's beliefs about what he has a "right to expect" and what he has an obligation to put in—upon what his perception and actual knowledge of general norms for the husband or wife role are and what he adds or changes by his personally interpreted prescriptions In short, the drives we bring to any social transactions, marriage among them, become translated into or cloaked under role expectations of oneself and one's other. We add or integrate or adapt them to those values and expectations that are transmitted to us by "powerful" others—those we love or admire or feel identified with. (This, of course, is part explanation of the dynamics that operate in marriage to change one or both of the partners.) Thus "what I am supposed to be like and act like" as wife or husband and "what he (or she) is supposed to be and act like in relation to me" are expectations that are amalgams of personal drives, of valued conceptions and norms transmitted by valued sources, of assumptions and beliefs about what is "normal," "nice," "usual" in one's own reference group; and since they "matter" to the persons involved, they will be freighted with feeling.

Actually most people are not aware of their valued role norms or emotionally charged expectations until some violation of them occurs (just as we are not aware of our good health until a headache or a stomach cramp suddenly alerts us to our state of disease). Then, in conflict, role demands and rewards (or frustrations, usually) begin to be expressed, scrutinized, and defended or, often with help, reconsidered and modified. Such awareness of self-and-other expectations and the necessity to consider shifts and modifications of role behavior occurs not only in conflict between person and person. It occurs also in those periods of crucialness that are inevitably part of the married life of even two deeply loving and empathic people.

There is a hoary joke that some of us, as high school sophomores, found hilarious. The straight man says, "Marriage is a very fine institution," and the other responds, "But who wants to live in an institution?" Today's sophomore would probably groan at the obvious word-play, but he probably understands just as little as we did that marriage is not "a state" of being. You *get* married; you hope to *stay* married; but *being* married is a developmental process, not an institution. To take on the role of a marriage partner is to undertake an on-going, changing, and give-and-get transaction that will depend for its stability and satisfaction not only upon the "me and you" or "I and thou" but also upon many factors outside ourselves over which we can have little or no control. It will depend on circumstances and chance, in part: on war, on the society's economic up- or down-turns, on the health of each partner, on the fate of the family one "marries into," on aging and its accompanying decrements, and so on.

Any one of these unlooked for or unprepared for phases or circumstances may cause such tensions or stress as will upset the usual marital stability and may even feel like a crisis—in the sense, again, that usual coping means do not seem to be adequate to handle it. Such periods are crucial also in a second sense: the way husband and wife try to cope with the unfamiliar and stressful situation may either result in a sense of defeat or competence, may bring them closer together or drive a solid wedge between them, may either open them to new learning or close them off from themselves and one another, may either expand and enrich their mutuality or narrow and rigidify their roles. So the to-be-anticipated crucial stages of married life warrant examination for the thrust they give to behavior- and person-changing potentials.

Here I choose to look particularly at the beginning phase of marriage. It is a crucial phase in that two persons undertake new and unfamiliar roles, migrate into a new (to them) culture. It is a legalized, ceremonialized contractual relationship they undertake, high in love power, high in social import, high in potentials for growth and change.

The first months or the first year of marriage is a crucial time because in a very real sense it represents a move into a new culture. Only occasionally has courtship or going steady prepared the couple for this shift of roles, either in terms of the role tasks or of the complexities of role relationships. Dating or going steady has helped them to know one another, to find thrill and delight in affectional and frankly sexual interchanges, to find new wonder in the self as it is reflected back by an adoring other, and wonder in the other that he is so sensitively resonant to thought and mood. Loved and loving, the hunger for connectedness, for belonging together is satisfied over and over. If talk is good between the lovers, there will be shared reactions and experiences and values and future plans. If it is not, if one or both has not been accustomed to express himself in speech or to exchange introspections and emotional reactions and ideas, then this is of small moment in courtship days. There are always the "kicks" or activities of recreation that can be shared (and these may pass as "common interests"); there is always the lightning bond of communion that touch and presence alone provides; there is always the underlying sense of security that "someone is there" at the other end of the telephone wire or at arm's reach. If angers or irritations or hurts occur they are swiftly liquified in the hot sweet fires of sexual approach and response. In brief, the young couple today come to "know" one another, sometimes in the biblical sense only, but often in broader and deeper ways too. But their knowledge is chiefly of one another as lovers and companions.

Everything and everyone joins in keeping it so during the pre-marriage period (provided, of course, that parents give the relationship their approval and blessing). The young couple are encouraged or at least allowed to be alone together much of the time. The relationship to one another's family groups, the beginning of knowing and understanding and coping with "in-laws" is minimal in modern courtship because it is no longer the custom to have intergenerational and family-centered recreation. The careful gathering by the girl of a handsewn or a meticulously shopped-for trousseau, under the guidance and tutoring of an older woman—which served as a kind of preparation for management and planning—has been replaced by a morning's run through the aisles of a Sears Roebuck or its fancier counterpart, by premarital "showers" which literally rain household gadgets and small necessaries upon the bride-to-be, by the secure knowledge that what one does not have one can pick up with money and half an hour to spend. If the girl is a student or a career girl or an office clerk she will generally continue with her usual tasks at least to the point where she must begin to plan her wedding dress and refreshments and to shop for the furniture items that will occupy the new household. But usually she will not take the time nor see the reason to be inducted by her mother into housekeeping and management tasks and concerns (if indeed her mother has these skills). She knows that frozen foods sit waiting at the supermarket and that "anybody who can read can cook." (Or she may already have specialized in a "wonderful spaghetti sauce" which her friends, lulled by the accompanying rough red wine, have assured her makes her an equally "wonderful cook.") Then there is the spiraling excitement of wedding plans and presents and the heady intoxication of taking a socially approved and celebrated, even envied, step; the sense of glamor elevates; the desirability of self and mate is reaffirmed (because everyone approves and is excitedly admiring); the contract is legalized; flowers, laughter, a whirl of kisses and handshakes—and then, depending on one's culture and class, one rides through the streets in a paper-streamer-decorated car, honking to the world that one is just married—or one zips discretely off in a small car to a supposedly secret hideaway.

This description may be somewhat exaggerated. Certainly like all generalizations it has its notable exceptions. Certainly, too, it has its innumerable fine variations that depend not only upon the two unique personalities who join in marriage but also, importantly, upon differences of class, education, and socialization which over the childhood and young adulthood of the couple have shaped and entrenched their expectations and consequent behavior. But the major point here is that today's sweetheart or "steadies" roles offer little preparation or rehearsal for marriage roles. Perhaps this is more true for the young woman than for the young man, since he generally continues his major occupational role as worker or student preparing to work while the woman, even if she continues at hers, must also undertake the tasks of housekeeper and cook and domestic manager. And perhaps it is more true of the middle-class woman than of her lower-class counterpart. The former has been reared, as Margaret Mead pointed out some time ago, by the same educational curriculum as has the boy and man; the latter has been raised in a group where sex role differences have been more sharply demarcated from the first and where, furthermore, the carrying of many domestic responsibilities was a necessary part of large-family-small-resources operations.

What young people—and even not-so-young-ones—in their first year of marriage find is that the new roles they have undertaken are not only heavily freighted with relationship but that that relationship is both more complicated and in some ways different from the love they thought was theirs to have and to hold. Moreover they find that these roles carry certain requirements of behavior not only in transaction with one another but in transaction with jobs that demand to be done and with other people who now, somehow, impinge upon the twosome, because they either intrude themselves or are reached out to by one or both of the married pair. They are on unfamiliar terrain. As was said before, it is testimony to the lively potential in most young adults to learn and to change their attitudes and ideas and behaviors when they are motivated to do so that most marriages not only hold but in many cases grow more gratifying with time.

Few young adults, of course, are strangers to marriage. Most of them have been raised in two-parent families. From the time when, wide-eyed and open-eared, they swivelled their silky heads side-to-side, now to see and hear mother, now father, they have watched and listened to what mothers and fathers do and say to one another. In early adolescence, sometimes before, they have suddenly seen their parents in a new perspective, not only as parents but as a marital pair who have some private life together, separate from the children; this too has been watched and listened to carefully. Unconsciously in the early years and consciously by adolescence, the emotional tone, the kinds of communications between man and wife, spoken and signalled, the actions, open and covert, the verbalized beliefs and assumptions about "ought" and "should" and "supposed to" and "everybody does," and the consistency or discrepancy between verbalized beliefs and actual behavior—all these have soaked in through the open mental and emotional pores of the children. Their aggregate has shaped the growing child's conceptions of (as well as his inclinations toward) marriage and his fantasies of it for himself. All kinds of mutations may occur. One young adult carries a model of flexibility and warmth and tolerance for difference, and consciously he wants to be what he unconsciously is ready to be: as good a husband as his father was. But of course he marries a woman other than his mother (even though he may be drawn to the girl who seems to carry in her his mother's valued qualities). Another, raised by bickering, impulse-ridden parents, may come to marriage determined to do everything in her power to be different from her parents—indeed, her model of expectations is a complex antithesis of what she knew in her parents. Sometimes such conscious determination, warmed and bulwarked by a spouse's love, succeeds. Indeed, this is why no two marriages duplicate one another down the generations and how it is that a child raised in a one-parent home or in a home where marital strife prevailed can consciously work at and become a good husband or wife. (But there will be times when this self-governing newly married person will be shocked at the sudden rise-up in him of angers or cruelties or driving expectations that were absorbed from the parents' marriage, not his own at all.) So each of us comes to marriage prepared for it, badly or well, by attitudes and expectations of self-other behavior incorporated from parental models.

At a more conscious, self-aware level we come with other preparations too. In the course of adolescence and early adulthood our world has widened in varying degrees—in small margin for the person whose education has been cut short and whose lack of money and work skills keeps him close to his family of origin and neighborhood friends, and in great expanse for those whose geographical and social mobility is freed by economic adequacy and whose upper-level education and socialization is enriched by the study of peoples and places and poetry, of times past as well as present, of variations in human beliefs and practices. Moreover, this education is taken in not only from books but also from teachers who often influence their students beyond their fields of expertness, and perhaps most importantly from interminable discussions and confidences with other students, sometimes a diverse group. In the course of this experience, parental norms and perspectives may be radically altered—at least they are modified. Certainly most college educated young people have found themselves "coming to see things differently" than they did at the time of high school graduation, and they have found that seeing and understanding differently has made them *feel* differently, too, about people and issues.

When people marry within their same socioeconomic class and ethnic-religious group they are likely to share and take for granted many of the same norms and expectations of selves and one another. Even so, however, the roles of marriage partners, because they hold new relationships and unfamiliar tasks, require new learning and coping efforts if husband and wife are to experience the satisfactions marriage promises.

Even love—maybe especially love—calls for more than just spontaneity. (Where impulsivity leaves off and spontaneity begins has not quite been delineated by the advocates of the latter.) Love in marriage is a long-time thing. It takes knowledge and know-how; it calls for receptivity to the feelings of the other; it banks on mutualness of expectations that govern even the sensual and emotional transactions of affection and passion. It will have its heedless, headless moments, to be sure. But if it is to hold and grow, it will require some work in the expression and uses of the self on the part of each partner: interest and openness to knowing and understanding the other, some control of self in the interest of the other, some willingness to compromise, renounce, make restitution, forgive, change one's mind and one's behavior. In happy marriages this love-work is on-going, often just naturally a part of the union of two empathic, flexible people; but at other times it must be a learned and practiced art. When it is felt as successful, it becomes "second nature." Love grows on the acts of loving as well as on being loved. So does the personality.

Marriage in these United States is for love. Or so it is said. Yet other than in the works of either poets or cynics, one is hard put to find a definition of what love is. Perhaps that is just as well because a "norm" of love would only add to the already existent anxiousness among young people over whether they are indeed getting what is to be expected in marriage or whether they and their partner are capable of meeting what the norm requires. So, like my betters, I will resist the foolhardy temptation to say what love is. What must be remembered now and again is that love has many faces. "The real thing" will be identified differently by different people. Infatuation passes for love; sexual longing and passion pass for love; feelings of affection and comfortable companionship and connectedness are felt as love; empathy and compassion and self-sacrifice for another feel like love; admiration and worship and loss of self in another may be felt as love. Love is all of these or some of them in combination. At different moments in marriage one of them may be in the ascendancy and another subordinate. For different people one is valued beyond all others. Probably this is what makes many kinds of marriage combinations workable.

It has seemed to me that the resolution of the oedipal complex, that first fierce battle the child fights to stake out his love claims, is in rudimentary form a resolution of the difference between loving and "owning." What the child makes peace with (he who "resolves" the issue) is that it is possible to love and be loved and yet not to possess or be possessed. He compromises with the reality that his parents belong to one another too, not just to him. This is learned again in the resolution of sibling rivalry (in those families, one must add, where there is enough love to go around). In marriage it may have to be learned yet again—or for the first time for some—that love has times of complete at-one-ness with the other, complete fusion, and yet that it must allow for separateness too, for the separate and different person that the partner is—indeed *must* be if he is to be himself.

True, some marriages flourish on a chattel-possessor relationship. It is not simply, as the acerbic comment sometimes goes, that "they deserve one another." They may *need* one another. Or their conception and expectations of the marriage relationship may reinforce their inclinations. Certainly in other cultures today and in our own culture at other times this was the accepted relationship between husband and wife. But our present-day culture holds the flowering and fruition of the individual personality as its topmost value. So the nature of "love" is shaped by this social standard. To love and to be loved, we say, is for the fullest enhancement of the persons involved. Therefore each must feel and know his own full identity, and the enrichment of marital love comes with the fusion and communion of two whole and different personalities.[1] The assumption is that the fulfilled personality is both motivated and competent to reach out from himself to concern for and participation in the larger society.

Yet, one must admit, this concern with individuality, this "personality cult" as some have called it, has had its limitations too—or perhaps it has been too often misinterpreted. Somehow the shining promise of the right to self-realization, to the freeing of energies and generosities has become translated by many today into the "right to happiness." Not the right to the "pursuit of happiness," which implies a questing, a continuous reaching out beyond oneself. Rather it has been taken to mean the right to *be* happy. This problem is several-fold. "Happiness" is as elusive of definition as "love." And to *be* happy suggests that it is possible to maintain a state, a static condition, of elation, pleasure, unruffled contentedness that is manifestly out of line with any knowledge we have of the human personality in any state of life today other than a nirvana, whether thought- or drug-induced. Even Eden grew tiresome and boring after a time, as the biblical sages discerned; else why would Eve have looked for diversion? And they knew too that only the unknowing, those who have not bitten into knowledge (not only knowledge of sin but of the human condition in all its aspects), only those can "*be* happy." Who are they?

The expectation of achieving some dead-level state of happiness has particular bearing upon marriage in its early phase. In the mounting excitement of the prenuptial days, in the rites and celebrations that crowd that period, in the legends that persist despite the everyday evidence all about us that they are wishful fabrications, the naive young couple is promised happiness ever after. Add to this the fact that many marriages are propelled into being by at least one partner's wish for escape from some *un*happiness—from parental domination, from unsatisfying work, from rootlessness—and marriage is seen as a solution to many ills.

One of the common disenchantments of marriage is the discovery that the legalized opportunity for full sexual expression does not bring "happiness." Even among those who find great sexual pleasure in one another there is disappointment in the discovery that the fires of passion that once consumed all hurts and leaped all barriers do not continue to burn as intensely or frequently. This disillusionment, even hurt, at times—often in both husband and wife—is further fed by the plethora of books (and non-books) that glorify sex today. Not only do they persistently sell the myth that if sex is all right everything else in a marriage will fall into line (and, reversed, that if there are sexual problems other problems will inevitably ensue),[2] but they also construct a model of "ideal" sexual relationships that, it is implied, is basic to marital "happiness." The anxieties among young married people grow apace. When the necessity to have ecstasy in equal degree with one's partner, for example, becomes a role norm, tension, malaise, and unhappiness not only interferes with natural spontaneity but the "norm" becomes a continuous measuring rod against which expectations of happiness are assessed.

Disenchantment with sexual love and with other aspects of marriage may harden into indifference, may be compromised into a kind of side-by-side marriage, or may feed the fires of the other frustrations and tensions that are part of all married life. Or, with understanding and motivation, sometimes with outside guidance and sometimes with the assistance only of one another, changes can be worked out. Basic to this understanding is some grappling with the difference between a state of personal happiness and the process of personality growth through the exercise of one's powers, problem-solving powers among them. Beyond this there is the rather touching need for young people especially to understand that familiarity need not breed contempt, but that it must be expected to breed comfortableness. Comfortableness does not occur in peaks. It does make companionship and occasional separateness possible, and from these there results the freshened awareness of the "other" that lights up romantic love again.

No one has said this, I think, better than the novelist Virginia Woolf (she, whose name, used by Albee, has unhappily come to connote violent sado-masochism in marriage).

> Arnold Bennett says that the horror of marriage lies in its dailiness. All acuteness of relationship is rubbed away by this. The truth is more like this: life—say four days out of seven—becomes automatic: but on the fifth day a bead of sensation [between husband and wife] forms which is all the fuller and more sensitive because of the automatic customary unconscious days on either side. That is to say the year is marked by moments of great intensity.[3]

These "moments of great intensity," experienced and afterwards remembered, are moments of self-transcendence. They may melt and temper the structured iron in the personality and condition it for change. But even within "dailiness," the sense of being counted on adds to the person's stature; the sense of attachment and connection adds to his security; the sense that "what I do and say" strikes off a vital response, good or bad, from the other may add both to the sense of one's powers and, desirably, to the sense of responsibility for using them. Of course love power may be used as a whip and destroyer. But it also stirs and moves the loved-lover to act in such ways as will enhance or nurture the relationship and thus, because he is actor-acted-upon, enhance his own personal gratification.

"Love cannot last," goes a stern Gallic proverb, "but marriage must." Thus the Frenchman (or was it a matriarch?) prepares the young and older married couples against the day when romantic love flies out the window and for the day too that occurs desirably even before marriage, when marriage is seen for those other values and rewards that it holds and for which it may be sought, entered, cherished, and worked at.

Even in our country, marriage is entered into and made to last by many forces and considerations other than love. Such forces and considerations are not often spoken of, since love, infatuation, being "crazy about" the mate-prospect, "waiting for Mr. Right" or "my ideal" are all in our most valued romantic lexicon. But to the open eye it is fairly clear that marriages are often made not only for love but also in the search for economic security or prestige based on economic status, for "settling down" into some regularized, dependable, role-clarified way of life, for begetting children and raising a family, for escaping parents, schooling, or other onerous impediments to "freedom," for companionship against actual or anticipated loneliness, and —more frequently than is recognized—because it is the thing to do. It is socially expected of adult men and women for all of the reasons just mentioned. When it does not occur something is felt to be "wrong."

The unmarried man is asked, sometimes with rough and sometimes with gentle "kidding," what his trouble is. Can't he find anyone good enough? (The assumption is that a man can get the girl he goes after.) How long is he going to knock around? (The assumption is that he is just pleasuring himself, or avoiding his responsibility. Sometimes there is a note of envy in the married questioner's voice.) There comes a time, after all—. His more subtle friends scrounge about in their acquaintanceships for likely girls to introduce to him. However it is done, it is clear that his social surround of friends and family expect him to get married.

The unmarried girl is less directly attacked by worried family and friends. The assumption is that she would get married if she had a chance, or the appropriate chance, and that she is not as free to chase and to choose as her male counterpart. She finds herself being anxiously looked at or studied by her close friends and relations as if they were trying to divine, without boldly asking, what the trouble is. She too is paired off by eager would-be matchmakers. She is encouraged to compromise with her allegedly too rigid standards for the good to be found in marriage over and beyond romance. And indeed, when a dwindled supply of available men matched against her increment of years rouses her unease, she may do so.

Despite the sometimes vaunted, often desired, and frequently decried equality of opportunity for the sexes in our society, there remain wide attitudinal differences that show up around the business of marriage and singleness. The young woman who marries is seen by her intimates and acquaintances as having achieved a desirable social status (unless, of course, she marries a man considered undesirable). Even in the most modest bride's mien there is a measure of triumph. "I did it! I made it!" This occurs even with girls who have been sought-after and for whom there has been no question of their marriageability. Economically secure, socially sought after, personally stable though they may be, there is some age-old sense of incompleteness that runs in the bloodstream of women and that makes the step of marriage feel like an achievement. They have stepped into a new and highly approved place in the social system, and a halo of accomplishment shines about them. For men it is different. Bridegrooms are the butts of jokes; they are the victims of female conspiracies. By both their married and unmarried friends they are jocularly held to be entering voluntary imprisonment, giving up their freedoms, "getting tied." And indeed, pleased though he may be at his new status, the groom somehow looks a bit sheepish, as if to say not "I did it!" but "I've gone and done it." (Perhaps, more seriously, this sex difference in social pressure and social approval is among the several reasons for women's generally greater concern with and openness to such changes in habits and behaviors as marriage may call for.) But even though the status of marriage is not so much a social achievement for men as for women, it *is* a form of social security.

Beyond security in an on-going sexual affectional relationship, there comes a time in the lives of most men, apparently, when the regularities and dependability of marriage and the solid social niche it provides are wanted and chosen.

Differences between men and women in regard to their social "place" and approval are open to be seen in the unmarried. The bachelor is viewed as unmarried by free choice; his freedom may be half-envied by his married male friends. Provided he has a decent job and some social grace, he is a plum in the social lists of his female married friends because "an extra man" is somehow never a "fifth wheel." It is interesting how often, in the recent past at least, the word "gay" was associated with bachelorhood. (Unfortunately now that good word has come to mean a homosexual.) Society has assumed that being a lone man can be fun. But only for a while and under certain circumstances. When the "gay bachelor" grows old, or if he is short of money, then he begins to be seen as a "lonely bachelor," and sympathy replaces envy for his grasshopper existence though it is still assumed that if he chose he could find a wife.[4]

There is no acceptable status-setting name for the unmarried woman. "Old maid" is archaic and slightly derisive and so is "spinster." "Bachelor-girl" seems assigned to young women, still nubile, who choose to be "career women" as a prelude to marriage. Somehow, one cannot be a "bachelor girl" after, say, fifty. "Career women" are married as well as unmarried. A widow or a divorcee, by virtue of once having been married, carries the social status of the married woman, though many of her actual problems are like those of her unwed sister. But except for the designation "unmarried," which is a designation by social default, as it were, not of a social status, the woman who remains single is ambiguously placed in the social structure.

Of course, here, as in all aspects of socio-personal problems, there are differences in individual reactions and coping with being "unmarried" and also differences inherent in economic and educational class membership. The unmarried man in the lower and blue-collar class grows isolated, with a widening gap between him and his work-mates, a vague place in his social group. His work-mates are married and raising families, and while many of them are not happily married, nevertheless the married man's marital and family roles give order and purpose to his after-work life. The unmarried woman of low economic and educational status has very little place in her social system, especially in urban settings. She often remains within the parental home, subordinate to her mother. Unless she has unusual work skills or personal talents, her work earnings will not be adequate to support a separate apartment or to buy the social opportunities with which to fill in her after-work hours. She does not fit into her social group's scheme.

So clear, though rarely spoken-out, are these alternative, unsatisfying, and ambiguous roles for the unmarried within the lower class, that marriage is sought early and it is maintained often against great odds of conflict and frustration. It is not simply that divorce is economically all but impossible for a lower class couple, nor that for many of them religious belief forbids it. It is also—and potently—that in the turbulent considerations over the dishpan or behind the truck wheel of "What will I do, then, after I leave? Where will I live? Who will I belong to?" there appear few alternatives or escapes open from the husband-wife roles if they want any sort of security or anchorage. So what may seem to outsiders, especially middle-class ones, to be "impossible" marriages go on by sufferance. In other marriages the meager satisfactions at hand suffice to spur husband or wife, or both, to try to meet the needs or demands of the other, to change what they say or do, to talk to themselves (if not to one another) in order to smooth or steady the both needed and valued marital relationship.[5]

Within the educated middle class there is far more latitude for both men and women who remain unmarried. The man, as has already been said, is often viewed as a social asset, particularly if he seems content and pleased with himself and his free choice. There may be, to be sure, snide speculations among those of his friends brushed by psychiatry about his sexual predilections, but this too, among sophisticates, is coming to be shrugged off as a difference without harm.

For the middle-class and educationally upper-class unmarried woman there are many avenues for her investment and realization of herself. Work opportunities abound that not only hold inherent interest but that may be gratifyingly responsive both to her mental capacities and to the feminine flair or womanly empathies that many jobs need. Moreover, she may find that companionship and stimulation among her colleagues fill after-work hours. Further, her earnings are usually enough so that she can set up a ménage of her own and buy the recreational opportunities that add dimension and color to life and offer connectedness with other people. Yet with some few exceptions there remain even for her those situations where she feels like an outsider, an awkward "extra" in a predominantly married acquaintanceship. The securing sense of belonging—even, indeed, the irritating sense of "being tied," which is in many marriages both a thorn and a security—is not hers. Some of her married sisters may envy her—she is "free," her work is "glamorous," she is "really doing something with herself." But for most middle-class married women, even those who are not bound by considerations of children or religion, the small and occasionally great joys of marriage, the stable niche it offers in a society of "marrieds," the stimulus of human interchange it provides, the socially affirmed correctness of their social position combine to motivate them to work at "making a go" of even such marriages as have faults and frustrations. These same factors motivate the middle-class man as well, since they usually seem to him to be worth the candle, to be preferable to singleness or status shift.

What the foregoing suggests is that marriage is entered into and maintained not by love alone, even in this country, where, by public utterance and reiteration, love is expected to conquer all. Marriage is sought, it is found gratifying, or, if not, it is often worked at by both husband and wife because it is a socially approved arrangement for adult heterosexual life, because it offers social recognitions, social place, and designated roles and thus gives its members a vital form of social security. To gain and maintain these social rewards, men and women will work hard to shape at least their overt behaviors— and if love warms them, their inner ones too—to keep their marriage viable and in relative balance.

"Now you are on your own," young people are told after the wedding is over. It is a somewhat fatuous statement, but the married couple would like to believe it. The anticipation of playing house together, of being free to decorate and plan and do as they will, is an attractive one. But it is not long before the "dailiness" intrudes itself. He goes off to his work by an imperious clock signal and he must be fed beforehand and clean socks and underwear and shirt must be ready, washed if not ironed, returned from the laundry, if not home-done. When he returns from work he must be fed, again by what the implacable face of the clock says; and past the shared eating together, he may fall easily into his long-established after-work patterns of which marriage has not "broken" him—reading the newspaper or watching TV or taking a snooze. Or he must fix this door or drive that nail or hoist this box. If he is a student he must go from helping with dishes to his books and stay with them till bedtime. She must set the house in order if she is to be considered "neat" and mop and dust if she is to be considered "clean" and shop at grocer, butcher, hardware stores and plan and fix what they will eat and be in touch with friends and in-laws now and then. They expect that they are supposed to have good times too, so there are outings to be planned and friends or neighbors to be pleasantly communicated with and arrangements to be made and budget to be consulted for the cost of a movie or a meal out or a new pair of shoes. And so on. In short, the young married couple is on their own in what is for many of them a new environment. This environment is not as open and free as they had expected, somehow; it has its rules and regulations, its musts and oughts, its omnipresent outsiders, on-lookers (neighbors and friends and in-laws) to whether or not the bride and groom are doing what and how they "should." They are on their own—to make their "adequate" or "proper" or "competent" (as the case may be) adaptation to new roles that, with range but with limits too, have governing rules.

The rules are not necessarily rigid or harsh ones. Indeed, like most social rules by which we live, they have become second nature to most of us, unrecognized as socially imposed most of the time because we take them so for granted and also because they have become role-rules for good reason: they oil the wheels of daily living and free us from what would otherwise be innumerable and exhausting small decisions and choices.

But not every person coming to marriage has incorporated them or the skills by which role tasks can be carried out. Moreover, since these role tasks are subject to different interpretations and valuations, there may occur between husband and wife, especially in the early years of marriage, tensions or considerable conflict about what each and both are supposed to carry as responsibility and expect as concommitant rights. "I should" and "he should" is brought to every marriage. It is indeed not simply a love-match but also a contract. In some instances these expectations are driven by personal needs. In others they are the product of ideas and ideals consciously developed from observations and fantasies of married life. Among these are to be found unrealistic ideas of "should" and "ought," or vague notions based upon actual lack of knowledge about what is usual or even feasible. These foggy or skewed notions that guide expectation and consequent behavior are worth the particular notice of those who undertake to help people with marriage conflicts if only because they are often most readily susceptible to change.

Any reading of the "agony columns" of a newspaper reveals the recurrent plaintive voices of the recently married, usually of wives. (Mostly it is the wife who complains or seeks outside counsel. This is because women may have more invested in making a go of the marriage, but also because, more than men, they tend to confide and to draw comfort from talking things out, and also because married women have fewer outlets and escapes from domestic conflict than do their husbands). The problems are most often put in terms of role expectations: What is he or what am I "supposed to do?" "What is right?"

The most frequent complaints and queries center about joint and separate household responsibilities: "My husband says it's a woman's job to do all the housework even if I work eight hours a day on the outside." "My husband has lost his job, but I work. I know he's a good man and is really trying to find employment. But wouldn't it be right for him to do something around the house? He says no." "Who should take out the garbage?" (If the reader thinks this latter query is that of a simple mind, I recall for him that this issue became the moment of truth between two of America's foremost writers: Mary McCarthy slapped Edmund Wilson because he refused to carry out this grubby task, and that was the end of their marriage!)

Second in frequency of complaint are in-law relationships, usually interferences and demands by the husband's mother: "Does she have the right to call her son every day?" "She's always coming over and sticking her nose into my housekeeping." "I say a husband owes his wife more attention than a son owes his mother." A less frequent but recurring plaint has to do with disagreements on the uses and management of money: "What we save for" and "what we spend for" and so on.

In many of these instances, of course, the problem presented may be largely symptomatic of underlying emotional struggles. Yet those underlying disharmonies are usually recognized by their sufferers only in the concrete terms of daily transactions. So the symptom is the point of reference. Moreover, beliefs and assumptions, when put into action, *create* emotions; it is not just the other way around. That is, they call forth pleasant or unpleasant responses on both sides of the transaction. This is how a symptomatic act may become a cause in a whole chain of problematic interchanges both within the person himself and between him and others.

If a young wife does not know that marriage cannot be expected to be a continuation of courtship, if she has no understanding of the naturalness (if unpleasantness) of a mother's continued attachment to her son, if a young husband has not, in his family or acquaintanceship, learned that many men wash tea cups and still are able to retain their masculinity in their own and their wives' eyes, if he has not thought about the fact that his wife's carelessness with money may have some relationship to his inconsistency in doling it out to her and to their joint failure to sit down together and talk over actual income and immutable expenses—then these unrecognized, unconsidered, unshared expectations can be the cause of recurrent angers and hurts even between people who for the most part feel deeply bound to one another.

There is room for breathing space, for nonconformity, even within the routines of marriage roles. Nonconformity that is truly self-expression and individuation rather than only a form of defiance is, in part, expressed in thinking differently and even playfully about the mundane things of everyday life, seeing their fallacies and foibles (and also their purposes and possibilities) and coming thereby to feel free to relate oneself differently to them either in feeling or in act or both. This is based, in turn, on knowing and understanding what it is one is differentiating from or opposing. Within marriage, however, if harmony is to be there, there must be agreement to, or at the least tolerance of, the one partner's not wanting to do or to be the way "he is supposed to be." When, as has been suggested above, the marriage relationship is out of joint because of discrepancies of expectations between partners or because there is no realistic grasp of what the role task calls for and also allows within its range, then the relationship may become edgy and charged with small but accumulating tensions. "Not knowing" or fairy-tale illusions may mar not only the task-carrying aspects of marriage roles; they may penetrate into the most intimate recesses of relationship.

One further example of how all but unconscious yet permeating role expectations may affect people's feelings of self-and-other in marriage is seen in the fact that unrecognized and thus unanalyzed discrepancies within a role itself and within a role network can invade the feeling relationships between people.

It seems to be an increasingly common situation, related probably to both the affluence and the technology of our culture, that young people are marrying while still pursuing their studies. With months or years of college or graduate school ahead of them, students are marrying with the expectancy and usually the assurance from their middle-class parents that they will be supported financially until they are ready to assume this responsibility on their own. This is quite a switch from what was socially expected in their parents' generation: that entry into marriage is predicated upon being able to take economic responsibility.

What becomes problematic—and yet it has scarely been spoken out and examined for solution possibilities—is that a complex of discrepant reciprocal expectations ensues. The parental pair (or both sets of parents) may stand in one of two polar positions: they may be inexorably old-fashioned (yet exorable enough to undertake support!) and maintain the emotionally-charged belief that it is not right to marry without being able to be self-and-wife supporting; or they may be flexibly modern with an emotionally-charged belief in young marriage and romance and even some hopes that "settling down" will enhance their offspring's motivation and capacity. Still, in either instance, there is likely to remain that long-ago incorporated feeling (sense, conviction) that giving carries its reciprocating obligations. It is plainly very hard to give money support without some expectation, not of gratitude (today's parents have learned that they are not to expect that!), but that one might have some voice in the money's uses or (among the more enlightened parents) some evidence that it is being used to the constructive purposes for which it was given. Thus, though there are varying degrees of control in voicing the expectations, they are inevitably present.[6]

On their part the young couple may find themselves grateful, may hope and vow to "pay it back someday," may feel periodic resentments as all of us do when we are in someone's debt because of the tension engendered by being unable to reciprocate. They may have recurrent moments of malaise about their relationship to the one or to both sets of parents: what are they supposed to do to express their obligation—get good grades, telephone every weekend (charges reversed), ask for and take advice? The discomfort will be highest, of course, among those young ones whose adolescent struggles over where their parents leave off and they begin are not yet done, who have not resolved the difference between autonomy as self-governance and autonomy merely as self-assertion. But even in so-called "mature" young people it will be present to some degree because the conflict inheres in the discrepancy of independence within dependency. At times the tension this paradox creates will break out into the marital situation itself with recriminations about "your family" and "my family" and who does what for whom. One of the things that makes this kind of discrepancy tolerable is that it is time-limited.

Numerically, this is a fairly limited group. It is of interest because it illustrates so clearly the pervasive underlay of uncertainty and potential friction that may occur not because of personality problems or interpersonal disharmonies but rather as a result of roles that carry some uneasy combination of internal discrepancies and unclarified expectancies.

The impress of social norms upon personality and its development is nowhere more clearly to be seen than in the differences of expectations—and thus of responsive experience—that socially disadvantaged and socially advantaged couples bring to their marriage roles. That any middle-class helper who undertakes to work with blue-collar (and no-collar) clients must understand such differences goes without saying. They constitute the ground-work from which he tries to identify both the characteristic and idiosyncratic qualities in the individual case. What is of particular interest here is that expectations of self and other in marriage have not only been absorbed so deeply into the growing child's personality as to be all but indistinguishable from self but that there are many above-the-eyebrow expectations, those that are a conscious part of a mental construct, that may operate potently to affect feelings and behaviors. These, because they are in the grasp of the person's consciousness, may be amenable to change with resultant changes of both behavior and feelings.

The differences in marriage expectations by class have been vividly set forth in several recent studies.[7] They confirm the case-by-case experience of those social workers who have worked across class lines.

One major difference lies in the lower class couple's expectation of fairly simple and plainly delineated duties and responsibilities assigned to the roles of husband and wife. The husband is supposed to earn a living, to bring his pay check home, to be faithful, to do the occasional man's work around the house. The wife is supposed to keep the house orderly and clean, to prepare meals (and on time), to be thrifty, to be indubitably faithful and available to her husband's sexual moods and needs. As Komarovsky points out, the proper performance of the *task* aspects of roles is paramount; the *relationship-affect* aspects are subordinate. When they are harmonious and gratifying that is good, and when they are not that is bad; but it is not as upsetting or intolerable as it might be to a middle-class couple.[8]

On their level, the middle-class couple enters marriage with a complex of additional expectations and with different valuations given to the basic ones. One of their high expectancies is that companionship between husband and wife will characterize their relationship, whereas the lower class couple expect that the wife will have her female and the husband his male companions—he, to be free to see them in the evening, she, preferably to see hers during his working hours. While faithfulness is promised and hoped for by the middle-class couple, they are more likely to be concerned (to the point at times of being tied in emotional knots) about whether their sexual relationship matches what the poets or sexologists have promised and whether it is equally gratifying to both of them. The middle-class woman, depending upon whether she is an advocate or an opponent of "the feminine mystique," will undertake her household duties with pleasure or apology, but, in contrast to her lower-class counterpart, she will expect that either through her homemaking or through some additional activities she will find scope for self-development and self-realization.

When dissension arises between working-class husband and wife, it is likely to be suppressed or fought out, often leaving a smoldering residue. Middle-class couples also inhibit anger or exhibit it by open quarrels; but if this becomes frequent, they have some faith that their talking things over between themselves or with friends or professional helpers will enable them to work their problems out. Far more than lower-class couples, they believe in the efficacy of confession, catharsis, and understanding to modify their impulses and behaviors. Far more, too, they are concerned with analyzing and weighing their personal "happiness" and what they are "getting out" of marriage. Communication has become the current key word among middle-class couples and their professional helpers today, almost as if some powers or magic are attached to being able to say out loud to the other what one feels and thinks. (I am reminded of E.B. White's gentle plaint that it isn't silence you can cut with a knife any more, but the exchange of ideas, that intelligent discussions

of practically everything is what is breaking up modern marriages.)
The lower-class marriage is neither plagued nor blessed with this
interchange of confidence or self-other appraisal. Most lower-class
women seem to miss it, though many, schooled by adversity, as are
their husbands, to taciturnity and suppression because "it's no good
talking about it—you've just got to *take* it," push down and deny
even to themselves the recognition of feelings or unfulfillable desires.
But for the middle-class couple there perhaps needs to be some
further thought about *what* is useful and constructive to communi-
cate—certainly not everything, particularly if it is destructive to the
"other" or even to the self. (There is a phenomenon worth more
careful note, and that is that when something is said aloud and is
received by listeners as "true," it begins to *seem* true to the sayer. So
people, whether in individual or group therapy, may often delude
even themselves!)

Back to class differences as they are seen in expectations of marriage transactions: one is struck again with how relativistic are our
conceptions of happiness, of what is good or bad in a marriage, and
of how love itself, deepest of all human needs and emotions, may be
nurtured and shaped, or dwarfed and distorted by socially induced
expectations and gratifications.

The push for self-realization, for achieving the sense of self-
development, of the pleasurable exercise and expansion of our powers
moves us to change. Such change is most likely to be a kind of
unfolding, a discovery and usage of already nascent potentials within
us. It is held, for most people, to be dependent upon the dependable,
relied-upon gratification of the basic drives for physical and economic
adequacy, for love—in at least one of its manifold forms—and for
social recognition and affirmation. When these drives are gratified,
the person feels free; his energy is released for new investments of
himself in new interests. From looking inwards or from keeping his
eyes focussed on the uncertainties or hazards of his daily living, he
can look outwards from himself to experience new relationships and
new expressions of his capacities.

For many people this happens only rarely, sometimes never. Their
lives are lived so chronically in need or on its margins that their
total physical and psychic energies are sucked up by their daily
rounds. And there are many others who, in their anxious effort to win
love or social recognition, push and use their powers relentlessly,

often achieving social position and admiration and acclaim (which for a time may taste like love), but who find no pleasure in their realization. It is as if their aims were realized but not their selves, or as if, in their intense pursuit, they have skipped over some basic nourishments and find themselves at last not fulfilled but, rather, hollow men. For most of us whose wants are relatively modest ones, self-actualization must be found as part of the transactions of ordinary living. "Must be found" suggests that they "may" be found when they are searched for and recognized.

Marriage holds both promise and opportunity for self-realization. Again, repetitiously, it must be said that the *sense* of self-fulfillment (and it is a sense, a feeling, not subject to objective measurement) will vary according to the individual and the pair of personalities, and according to their economic and educational expectations and their personal and environmental resources. Perhaps sex is a differentiating factor too: men typically continue to seek self-nourishment and expression outside of marriage, sometimes in addition to it, sometimes in its stead. So do some women—but the majority of them look to marriage for the place and nurture of their self-investments. Men (by nature? by culture? by combination?) are more task-and-problem-solving oriented, women more nurture-and-relationship oriented; and marriage, of course, is the richest soil for the latter.

For men and women both, it should be said from the first, the production of new life through bringing children into the world, and the rearing and cultivation of infant to child to youth offers the most authentic and most moving sense of creativity, of self-extension and self-realization, of any that life holds. (This will be spoken of later when parenthood as a vital life role is perused.) Probably many more marriages than do so now would fall apart or be broken up if it were not that the spouses were joined not only in the concerns but also in the high sense of purposiveness and self-enhancement that their growing children give them. (This is not to say, I quickly add, that people should have children to hold a fragile marriage together. It is only to note the fact that bad and indifferent marriages are often kept going—sometimes with harm to the children—by parental needs for the sense of purpose and self-extension that children provide.) When one's children seem to be responding to parental love and work, when admiration of them by relatives and friends and neighbors say to the parents "your product is good—you are doing well!"

there rises in them a suffusing, elevated sense of accomplishment—even more, of creativeness.

Before children come, however, and even in childless marriages, a gratifying sense of self-unfolding may occur. Especially for the woman, the tasks of home-maker (if she and her husband and their circle of intimates value this) may express and display her talents and masteries. That she is a good cook, a skillful hostess, a shrewd shopper and manager, a tasteful "decorator" not only may be noted and admired by others but may confirm her own judgement of her competence. As for her husband, if he is recognized by her as a "good provider" or "good lover" or "good company" or "very handy around the house," he will feel himself grown larger by these appreciations of his capacities.

Love itself, of course, is the basic food of self-realization. As anyone who has loved and been loved knows, nothing feels more vital and more sustaining and at moments more exalting than being found vital and sustaining and occasionally exalting by another. Moreover, when strong emphatic bonds are woven between husband and wife, each feels augmented, added to, each experiences some stretch of ego boundaries through living some part of the life of the other.

Self-realization in the sense of fulfilment through marriage is more usual for women than for men. No man would be caught saying, "I'd rather be married than work;" but this is the expected preference on the part of a woman. Men tend to seek the fullest uses of their powers through their work; often they supplement this with such leisure time activities as allows them the *play* of interests and skills that work prohibits. Unhappily many kinds of work cramp a man's style or deaden him by routine and repetition. If he is lucky enough to have a pleasant home and a loving wife, it may be said that marriage offers him both a launching pad and a return haven against his work frustrations. He may project and transfer some of his work dissatisfactions into his home life; his wife may be used as scapegoat for the boss he cannot subdue. But in any event it is safe to suggest that if he were asked he would admit at once that the role of husband was not taken on as his be-all and end-all.

For most women, however, the role of wife *is* so taken (with the often accompanying expectation, of course, that motherhood will come sooner or later). Among such women are those for whom marriage with its acts of home-making and love and social interchanges is experienced as full self-realization. But there is a growing number of women who feel that marriage (even motherhood in its post-infancy stage) does not offer them enough scope for their latent talents or enough range for their multiple interests. It is not that they would choose not to marry; it is rather that they believe their fullest self-development and exercise of powers must have more open opportunity than even the best of marriages can provide.

It is an interesting phenomenon, this recent striving in women to "feel their oats," to experience their powers outside the home, outside the role of wife; and arguments over whether they ought or ought not to want to do this grow strident. There seems to occur an ebb and flow in this push, dependent upon what champion of what position is in the ascendancy at a given time. But that this search to experience oneself in roles other than that of wife will increase seems almost inevitable. The reasons are varied but obvious. The convenience of prepared foods and household gadgets reduces the time and the skills it once took to run a household. With young marriages (quick change from cap and gown to veil and gown) the young woman puts her household in running order, finds contentment with her status and her love life, and is then aware that she has energies and ideas that somehow are not used up in being "just a housewife." She wonders whether this is what she majored in Greek literature for, or whether her good grades in psychology didn't mean that she'd have a lot to offer in some program for needful or disturbed children, or—or—. And fueling this small fire of discontent is, yet again, the middle-class, democratic, personality-treasuring norm that asserts the rightness of each person's seeking to know and use his creative or nurturing powers and talents to their fullest. How is one going to know them until they are tried? So young women who are not yet mothers or those who are mothers of children who need them only part of the time, flock out from their homes to take courses, give courses, work for money, work as volunteers—all seeking to experience themselves as competent over and beyond marriage. Some succeed and bring back into their marital relationship fresh interests and dimensions, or they feel filled-in by the social relationships work provides, or they take pleasure in their happy sense of self-discovery and competence. Some succeed but at some cost—of chronic tension in themselves or stress created in other family members. Some find, a bit shamefacedly, that it wasn't as satisfying as it promised to be, or that they weren't as productive or creative somehow as they had expected to be, and with some mixture of puzzled regret and gratitude they resume marriage and motherhood as their chief source of self-expression and gratification. Yet, the idea that somehow one "should" develop all one's capacities flaps its gadfly wings on every dull or harassing day of married life—and they are, of course, numerous—and women probe and plague themselves with questions of their worth and their proper goals.

Thus the middle-class woman. The wife of the working man complains of marriage too at times (marriage with motherhood, usually) because of its constrictions, its tying her down and hemming her in. But her plaint is not based on a conception of her right to personal fulfillments over and beyond marriage; being a wife and mother is what she believes is her purpose and destiny. Rather, her complaint is an objectively verifiable one. She is tied down and hemmed in because there is rarely the money available to her by which to buy a few leisure hours or, if family or friends will provide these, to pay the bus fares and admission fees of even inexpensive forms of recreation. She seeks not the experience of self-expression so much as that of the nourishment of her senses and contacts with people outside her constricted circle. Churches, neighborhood houses, social agencies, schools, all at one time or another offer such opportunities, but both their programs and their personnel need to come closer to those wives and mothers who, out of resignation or ignorance of resources, have become their own prisoners.

For the greater part of most marriages parenthood becomes the all-consuming complex of tasks and relationships, of high anxieties and deep gratifications. But the on-going marital role brings times and circumstances that, by their upset of customary, ingrained ways of acting and expectation and by their arousal of intense emotion may induce or force change. That such changes will be lesser and more subtle than those in the early years of marriage one can be sure, because the pliability of body and habit and personality will be far less than it was at the pulsing height of adult powers; but changes there will be. These crucial periods deserve scrutiny for their change-powers. Here they can only be touched on.

In the middle years of marriage when the last of the children leaves home, husband and wife find themselves "a couple" again. Parenthood continues, to be sure, but largely in its affectional-relationship aspects, no longer in its tasks of protection and guidance. This is a period often looked forward to, often dreamed of, as a time when responsibilities can be sloughed off with the suffusing sense of a task well done. But when this time comes the parent-couple often find that there is an underside to their pleasure, too, an *un*-pleasure. Mingled with relief and pride are pangs of anticipated loneliness, regrets over all the days and years that were allowed to fly by too swiftly, too little savored. And some sense—more in the woman than in the man—of role loss.

Rarely anticipated are some of the problems inherent in reentry into the exclusivity of the husband-wife relationship. It cannot be what it was before the children came; man and wife must find one another again in their presentness, and in the deafening silence of a childless home. Most couples fumble it out, some successfully, others with growing dissatisfaction. If the marriage has grown in its fullness of affectionate companionship, even if it has lost its high impetuosity, if it has included common interests outside kitchen, children, and office, then this shift to the resumption of a twosome (even celebrated by some as a "second honeymoon") may be felt as a pleasure and a reward. If, however, the couple has lost vital contact with one another except over the bridge their children provided, then some considerable readaptation becomes necessary or a widening gap results.

It is a common complaint among such couples that now that the children are gone there is nothing to talk about. Recent years have seen many divorces take place in this period. Some couples have probably been waiting until the children leave home to carry out a long-planned separation. Others, with children gone, may suddenly become aware of the emptiness of their marriage relationship. How far the depressions of menopause or the indiscretions of the climacterium are the result of actual glandular change or are associated with the necessity to face and manage a new phase in marriage is subject for speculation. That it is a crucial time is evident.

This time is felt most uneasily by the woman. Children or no children, the husband continues in his basic life role, that of worker and doer outside the home. But his wife is freed—or stripped, depending on her view—of her most essential and long-absorbing role. What is she to do now? What is she to be? Where will she invest the time and energies and practiced competences that she has poured into mothering? Where will she find a renewed sense of self-worth and purpose?—for she cannot live vitally only in retrospect or on the edges of her children's lives.

One last period of marital change is fraught with the deepest emotion—the period that follows the death of the spouse. Probably never before has the survivor felt more gutting surge and pain, whether of loss and grief or loss and guilt, or that ever-present admixture of both. Recent researches based on work with bereaved people have brought new understanding to bear upon the workings of grief and mourning. When this most universal, commonplace, and implacable fact of life—its end—is tasted for all its dark bitterness, swallowed, and finally digested, there still remains for the widowed husband or wife the necessity to find a new identity and place. He must discover what he is, alone, and what nurture from the other he still retains in himself and is able to feed upon, and, most of all, how he can once again throw out his own life-line to anchor himself in love and social purpose.

It is not simply the passing of years that makes us grow wiser or mentally withered, more compassionate or cold. It is the penetration and permeation of our innermost selves by the people and the works in which we have most deeply invested and harbored and the sense we have drawn from these transactions of having been diminished or enhanced by them. Marriage holds potent powers for either outcome.

5

Parenthood

Parenthood may just happen or it may be calendar-planned; it may be dreaded or dreamed of; it may, in its long and varied course, be mostly pain or mostly pleasure. But under all and any circumstances its long term commitment, its firm duties and demands, its emotionaly-charged expectations and involvements, its viscerally experienced hurts and gratifications drive deeper into the core of the personality, probably, than any other life role.

Parenthood requires a basic, consistent, continuous willingness and capacity to give or lend oneself to the nurture and protection of another. But it requires more than this. Because that "other" is a growing, changing, developing being in a sequence of evolving life stages under changing circumstances, the parent-person is thrust and pulled, willy-nilly, into moving, changing, and developing himself.[1] He may wish to but he cannot say, "Let me *be* as I am!" for the parental role perforce is a continuous becoming. The mother of the schoolboy cannot be the same as she was when she was the mother of the infant—or ought not to be, if she is to feel and act appropriately. The father of the teen-age girl cannot be the same father as he was when she was a toddler—or had better not be. There are, to be sure, certain constant elements in mothering and fathering, but they must be responsive to developmental changes in the child, to the unique needs of the particular child, and to all the cultural and interpersonal influences that invade and influence parental actions and attitudes. So it is expectable that the role of parent may involve a person in considerable internal unsettling, reorganizing of feelings and habits and, thus, of change as a person. Parenthood is probably a major dynamic in the psychosocial development of the adult.

"The child is father to the man." The beginning of parenthood lies in the person's own childhood, in his observations and experience of his own parents. Unconscious absorptions and incorporations of their feelings and attitudes, nonconscious as well as conscious imitations and identifications, admiring emulation or rejecting reaction formations—all these coalesce (or conflict) to form the potential parent. A formed personality is brought to the parental role. Some parts of it are particularly connected with the loving-socializing tasks of parenthood, particularly congenial to or incongruent with those tasks, particularly vulnerable to or readied for their demands. Mingled with those embedded needs and patterns are a host of consciously held beliefs, expectations, values about what parents and children are "supposed" to act like and be like. These role prescriptions, written large and loosely in the general culture, may, in the individual instance, be tight and complex calligraphies, shaped by misapprehensions, misinterpretations, bad or good advice from authority-persons, lack of knowledge, and remembered models of parenthood devotedly admired or fiercely rejected. All of these preparations, good or poor, past and present, are brought by the married couple to the role of parenthood, and many of them will undergo some changes in the process of parenting. Some changes will be superficial; but others, those that are experienced in depth, will affect the parent-person in depth.

The beginning of parenthood, for our present purposes, is at the point of the woman's first awareness of her pregnancy. A "normal pregnancy" is physiologically the same for every woman—that is to say, the growth and development of the embryo and foetus proceeds according to the laws of ontogeny. But the psychological import for each woman differs, though within certain common kinds of reactions. For the woman who has wanted to be pregnant, the recognition of the signs is a moment of joy followed by a sense of accomplishment and a contented sense of embarkation on a new, growing experience, literally as well as figuratively. For another woman there may be more triumph than joy—"I did it!"—and perhaps some anxiousness along with self-congratulation. Many women are cast into ambivalence at their awareness of pregnancy. They want a baby, but also want "freedom"; they love children, but want more time; their husbands (or mothers or mothers-in-law) want a baby but—; to have a baby, one must be pregnant—"but my figure will be ruined." Some women want pregnancy, consciously as well as unconsciously, but are not so sure they want what follows. Pregnancy and childbirth may bring them status and admiration in the eyes of husband and relatives, may bring them privileges of care and protection; but once the child is there the care and protection and admiration shifts over to the baby, and the mother is expected to become not the "cared for" but the "care-giver."

For the woman to whom pregnancy is an accident, unwanted by anyone, herself included, the awareness of pregnancy may come as a shock, a sickening realization that she is caught in an inexorable development of circumstances that, as she foresees them, can only hurt her, misshape her life as well as her body. The first shock may be followed by defensive maneuvers by which she blots out even the reality of her week-by-week growth, so that it is not unusual for her, as social workers with illegitimately pregnant women will attest, to come almost to the point of childbirth, heavy and bloated, but "not knowing" that she is pregnant. Another woman may make active efforts to rid herself of the embryo; and when they do not work, she carries her growing baby with the constant fear, even certainty, that she has made it abnormal in some way. Or if she wants and loves the man who has impregnated her, she may take some rueful satisfaction in harboring this part of him and holding this link to him.

The variations and combinations are numberless, but the point is that the woman's feelings about her pregnancy and what it presages are a complex of her sense and conception of herself-as-woman and of all the personal-social circumstances that surround her and that say "Good! Well-done! How wonderful!" or that say "Too bad! How could you! What a sorry mess!" Coming from persons whose approval or disapproval is crucial to her (husband, parents, parents-in-law, siblings, and close friends), these judgements shape her self-judgement. When pregnancy is a socially expected and desirable condition, the woman feels affirmed; when, on the contrary, it is considered "disgraceful" at worst or "careless" at best, the woman feels the social censure that comes at her from those about her, carries a sense of "badness" or, in defense against it, a sense of defiance or victimization—"it happened *to* me."

Men, too, have strong and also varied feelings at having impregnated a woman. For the man who, with his wife (and that backlog of relatives and friends always demanding to know when he will undertake fatherhood), wants a child, the knowledge of a successful impregnation holds the double gratification of imminent fatherhood and also the "proof" of his sexual potency. It is an interesting sidelight on the psychology of the male that in every time and class he measures his sexual effectiveness in the last analysis by his capacity to "make something happen," to start a baby. Perhaps the temporary exultation and its outgrowth of satisfaction has less effect upon the personality of the male partner than its reverse state: the gnawing sense of essential unmanliness that besets the man who is held to be infertile. But even men who regard the pregnancy of their wives or sex-partners as a misfortune or an outrage still can scarcely resist savoring the undercurrent pleasure of knowing themselves to be biologically competent.

For the usual pregnancy within marriage, certain common and crucial changes occur in the body and person of the woman. Glandular and metabolic processes combine with deep-running psychological readiness.[2] Social respectfulness and protections added to these give the pregnant woman a permeating sense of herself as fulfilling her most ancient, most valued, most awesome function. In her months of pregnancy she need not be or do much else than be pregnant. Self-concern, tender self-care, expectation that she will have some protections and indulgences from her husband and relatives—all these are allowed, even pressed upon her. When the modern young woman carries her pregnancy with lightness and ease, works at her job or housekeeping almost to the day of childbirth, it is often with an accrual of pride in herself that she can be all this and pregnant too.

"Gravid" is a medical word for "pregnant" and it expresses not only the heaviness of the physical state but the gravely introspective feelings of the pregnancy period. It is a preparation time for motherhood, and fantasies of the future of the child and the self are rich, often quite reality-oriented, sometimes purely wish-fulfilling. These are fantasies of what sex the child will be, what he will act like, look like, become. Husbands fantasy too during this period, together with their wives or alone. For the first child, husbands usually desire—indeed, they are sure that the baby will be—a son. The underlying theme is that "he will fulfill *me.*" He will fulfill me by being just the opposite of what I am, without my faults, or by following in my footsteps and doing me proud or by achieving such love or admiration or fame or happiness as I have longed for but never known. One of the startling aspects of childbirth for the father is that what is delivered is, after all, only a puny, squalling plucked-chicken baby. And one of the major shifts into the role of father (and mother too) is the full taking in of the fact of the child's separate identity, his individuality, and the acceptance of the fact that his destiny is to fulfill *himself*, not his parents.

The gravid woman's fantasies, like her husband's, are shaped by her personal needs, fears and hopes, and also by the expectations and attitudes of the important persons in her current life-space. Fears about whether her baby will be normal (when she feels guilty over past misdemeanors or even bad thoughts) alternate with or are displaced by dreams of what her child will be like, or of what differences will occur in her life situation as a result of becoming a mother. Sometimes these anticipated differences are further fear-producing, for it is quite possible to enjoy the role of pregnant woman and to fear the demanding necessity to "give out" of oneself when the baby comes. Sometimes the anticipations are too roseate—the baby will be a good sleeper, a good eater, a blue-eyed cherub caught and held in the sunny ambience of a women's magazine cover; the baby will "hold our marriage together," and so forth. Then the reality of diapers, bottles, night feedings, crying, regurgitating come as disillusionments. And it is disappointing, too, to find that the baby has purposes of its own that often interfere with marriage intimacies and communications and comfortable habits. But with all of this, most often pregnancy serves as a proper preparation time when the woman begins to feel, with a profound sense of pleasure, the gravity of her new role to come, that of mother.

Pregnancy is a "crucial" period then, even at its most even keel in the sense that it is a period of rapid and deeply felt body change and growth with its accompanying psychological responses. It is a period of heightened emotion and sensitivity both to the self harboring a new life, and to the external world into which this new life will be brought. It is often a period of heightened anxiety and vulnerability too for reasons that have already been noted but also because realistically it is prelude to great changes in family role relationships, duties, plans. In brief, it is a growing time when the woman is highly susceptible to change and open to the preparation of herself in beneficent (or maleficent) ways for entering motherhood. More than being simply a "waiting time," it is a developing time. Were it so conceived by the various persons to whom the pregnant woman may turn for help or counsel—doctors, nurses, social workers, as well as elder family members—its anxious and fearful aspects might be lessened, its securing, personality expansion aspects supported; certainly its readying the woman for motherhood could be enhanced.

Pregnancy ends in the closeted, lonely agony and triumph of childbirth. And now the woman is a mother. Now again there appear all the variations of affect and attitude that are the expression of the differences of personality and social circumstance brought to the moment when the child is laid in his mother's arms.

Mature women and those who have been close to babies are prepared for the wizened face, the skinny legs, the uncoordinated jerky movements of the newborn. Young women, whose short lifetimes confined to schooling have closed them away from birth and babies, are often shocked by the discrepancy between the image they harbored of the child they bore and this homely helpless bundle they've given birth to. Or they may be frightened by the baby's fragility.[3] Add to this the panic frequently felt by new mothers, because maternal love, which they have read and heard about, does not seem to be swelling in them at all as they gingerly try to cuddle the newborn or to get its head to turn to the breast. They will need to learn, alone or with counsel, that love of the newborn baby begins as some mixture of tender pride that this is "a small thing but mine own" and tender pity that he has been given life and must be helped to want it; and that love grows bit by bit on all the small givings and gettings that go between mother and child from the moment she knows herself as "mother."

Nature and society have a happy way of combining to make the entry into motherhood a rewarding experience despite its possible problems. It is one of nature's bounties that for all its being a most commonplace fact, giving birth is nevertheless *experienced* by the woman and by those who love her, as a miracle. "Wonderful!" everyone says, and the general admiration and excitement is such as to make the woman feel she has done something very unusual and laudable indeed. Then there ensues the bustle of helpfulness (sometimes excessive) and gifts and cries of admiration over the baby's potentials, for beauty (if a girl), brawn (if a boy), brains (either sex), plus the all-important pride of the new father in his product, in his wife, in his newly-earned status.

If all goes well then, the obvious and subtle rewards of the entry into motherhood are manifold. Evidence of her competence as a woman is manifest; she has fulfilled the function for which nature and her society prepared her; her production is held to be "good" and desirable—even wonderful; she has, by her production, given added status to her husband, who is now a father, to her parents and parents-in-law, whom she has made into grandparents; and she has begun a new role for herself. Most of all she has opened for herself a whole new prospect of opportunities to live another life vicariously and to widen the boundaries of loving and being loved.[4]

There are those entries or reentries into motherhood that occur under conditions that are likely to be more detrimental than beneficial to personality development. Unmarried women who bear children come to childbirth with foreboding. Some will be biological mothers only—they will give up their babies even before they see or hold them. Some "want" their babies, but often because they conceive of the babies as love-*givers*—"I want someone who will love me"—or because they hope that the baby will serve as bond between them and the reluctant father. Often, because they have had to be highly defended against the whole experience, they have scarcely dared think about what will follow childbirth. (The expectation that the child will be stillborn or that they themselves will die in childbirth must be frequent among this group of women.) For the unmarried mother who keeps her child, unless she has the unusual good fortune to be protected by her paramour or family, a combination of economic stress, social denigration, and emotional needfulness may be paramount. Scar tissue in the form of defenses may come to cover her psychological wounds—but, like real scar tissue, it impedes and mars growth.

There are married women too for whom motherhood is an unwanted accident. Sometimes, it is true, while the accidental pregnancy may be regretted and rejected, the child, once born, finds his way into some as yet warm and open spot in the mother's heart and becomes both wanted and loved. So a rejected pregnancy does not inevitably produce a rejected child any more than a wanted pregnancy results always in a good mother-child relationship.[5] Too many other factors enter in to give tone and meaning to motherhood, factors of personality need, of physical health and stress, of social and economic comfort or discomfort, of psychological distress or well-being—these in all their subtle combinations determine mothering motivations and capacities.

Women who bear children because they do not know how to avoid it may take motherhood as a cross to bear. One may be attached to one's cross, but it is hard to love it. Usually their social and economic circumstances have drained their physical energies and depleted their ego strengths. To hold their meager inner resources together they must wrap themselves in protective armor, and their children find, after a time, that there is little use in trying to pierce it. Neither mother nor child feels gratified; rather, each tries to feed upon the other and each feels love-hunger and thwarting. Mothers such as these have often had such mothers themselves and they themselves feel empty, wanting some fulfilment that they cannot even name. They are only partially grown as personalities, stunted because of emotional-vitamin deficiencies, so to speak, in their growing years. The role of mother is understood by them in its duty-expectations; the love-nurture that warms those duties is missing. Their children come to be known, as they venture outside the family, as "emotionally deprived," "stimulus-deprived," empty-faced, distant, "poor learners."

The implications of the deficits in such mothers for community helpers—social workers, clergymen, public health nurses and doctors in prenatal and postpartum clinics—are manifest. What is needed is open and ready counsel and resources for "planned motherhood" as well as for other problems that erode the family life, and, beyond these "duties" of helpers, the "nurture" supplied by their demonstrated caring and concern—attentions that these women and their families have scarcely known.

In the multiple small interactions and interplay between mother and infant that begin at childbirth, mothering grows, mothering capacities are exercised, developed, and become "second nature" through habituation; and from wanting to enfold, warm, and succor a helpless hungry little thing, maternal feeling opens out into basking in the suffusion of warmth and sensual pleasure and affirmation of one's "goodness" that are produced by the baby's responsiveness.

Love grows on responsiveness to what is given. It grows on the indication that what the "lover" gives out to the loved one, what he or she puts in of caring, nurture, tenderness, concern, recognition is taken in, fed upon, used, reacted to appreciatively in ways that say

"What you give me is good—I love what you put into me of your self."

From the first, the mother-child relationship is a closely reciprocal one. The expectations vested in the role of mother-of-infant are among the most carefully specified ones in our culture, transmitted by peer mothers, own mothers, and by oral and printed prescriptions of doctors, nurses, and other pediatric specialists. The mother must feed the baby certain prescribed food, at certain times (scheduled or "on-demand"), under certain conditions (the battle of the bottle or the breast); must keep the baby clean, must accommodate her sleeping and waking to his, must be tranquil (lest he sense her anxiety and get colic), must hold, cuddle, and play with him (so that he gets the necessary body and sensory stimuli), must, above all, love him—and to this last is often added "unconditionally."

I do not think there is such a thing as "unconditional" love. The "condition" for loving and the growth of love is responsiveness, one to the other. Nurture from one must yield gratification from the other; and this, in turn, nurtures the one so that the two "in love" come to be linked by invisible but powerful skeins of reciprocal givings and gettings. "Reciprocal" does not mean equal either in quality or quantity. Surely it would be impossible to determine who gets or gives more in any gratifying love relationship. Surely the mother of the very young baby seems to be doing all the "putting in," but she alone can assess what she "gets." For one woman the baby's eagerness for breast or bottle fills her with the glowing sense of her nurturing competence; for another the growing baby's facial and vocal recognition of her presence is sufficient delight to reward her for the day's work; for a third, a woman who comes to motherhood with long-felt personal unfulfilments, there is very little the baby's responses will do to compensate her for what she feels is being "taken out" of her. But for every mother there is, and there must be, the commonly felt but rarely expressed expectation that her baby will reciprocate her love by responding to her loving ministrations.

It is, I believe, important that this felt expectation be recognized and spoken of. Many normal young mothers harbor feelings of guilt or fault when they find themselves falling somewhat short of the requirement that they be satisfied to give-give-give unconditionally if they are to be considered truly maternal and truly loving. Professional helpers at times of trouble for mother and child tend more often than not to be child-centered and to view with barely concealed disapproval the mother who sees that her nurture is found noxious by the child, or that her deposit of what energies and efforts she has available yield little in return. Particularly for mothers of infants who are in some way abnormal—blind, deaf, mentally retarded, neurologically damaged, and those babies who seem to be born with defects in out-reaching and relationship capacity—particularly in these instances do helpers need to understand the frustration, defeat, and negation that such babies rouse in their mothers. Nurture, body-closeness, fondling, play—all the modes of loving that the infant's mother gives out with—may in these atypical babies yield small growth, thin response, slow recognition. Such mothers, when they turn, as they must, to others for help, need particularly the feed-in of nurture from those others. In small part, this may assuage their gnawing hunger for reciprocation and response.

In the usual, normal daily interplay between mother and infant there are both subtle and obvious influences upon the mother as person. She is, in the first few months, in body-close, feeling-close relationship with her baby—a symbiotic relationship—and she feels herself reciprocally needed and nurtured. As the baby's individuality begins to come through, as he begins to see with his own eyes and grasp with his own hands and turn over on his own muscle power, not hers, the mother feels proud and rewarded by his growth, even though that growth is actually propelled from within him, only secondarily related to her care. Even for the mother who is able fully to see and accept her child's separate and unique individuality, what he does or does not do will always to some extent seem to be a reflection or an expression of herself. This derives from the deep oneness of pregnancy and early months of infancy. It has had undergirding from psychological theories that place "mother" as central cause in the child's destiny. That a mother feels "to blame" we have come to take for granted; that a mother may also feel approved of, credited, enhanced by her child's achievements we have not so closely attended to. Benedek states, "The mother, through introjection of good-thriving infant [equals] good mother-self . . . achieves a new integration in her personality."[6]

Not only do mothers see themselves affirmed or negated by their children (and assume that others see this too), but their behavior and feelings about themselves are often sensitively responsive to what the child does (unwittingly) to them. In our thinking about mother-child relationship, we have tended to view it as a one-way channel: the mother's potent impress upon the labile plasticity of the child. But the fact is that mother-child relationship is from the first a transactional one, which is to say that each acts upon the other, each affects and feeds back to the other in a continuous spiral of reciprocations, noxious or benign. In this sense "the babe creates the mother in the womb" and continuously shapes and colors her self-image and sense of herself as good or bad, competent or incapable, wise or stupid. More, the baby's and child's reactions trigger their counterparts in the mother. Fed and dried and patted down, the baby who contentedly drops off to sleep leaves a mother suffused with contentment. Fed and dried and patted down, the baby who suddenly flexes his arms and legs and screams with inexplicable rage rouses anxiety in his mother ("What is the trouble?") but also an underlay—or some times an overlay—of anger ("What *is* the matter?" she murmurs, her words revealing her maternal concern, her tone revealing her personal tension at the attack upon her.) One sees the most extreme and shocking evidence of the parental feeling that the infant is acting upon or against them in cases of "battered babies," where mothers or fathers have brutally beaten the child, usually because in their primitive perception it appears that the child is wilfully thwarting or frustrating them. At the other pole is the parent who sensitively understands and accepts the child's own needs and purposes and, because he holds them to be "good," works almost too hard to shape himself to them.

The remolding of the parent-person, particularly of the mother, in the first months of parenthood is due to the many powerful stimuli of this period, including the fact that this is a crucial life phase. Like all crucial periods it is marked by high emotional lability, vulnerability to the impact of significant people and circumstances, unsettledness because of the many shifts and changes that the new family member requires and the new role imposes. It is thus a time when the mother, particularly, is open to all the messages that come at her from the outside and from within her, that push her to shift ground, change habits, take stock of her values and hopes, to gain—or lose— her sense of effectiveness and competence as a mother and wife.

Several studies of parenthood as crisis confirm what most new parents will attest to: that the first few months of parenthood are charged with the strained feelings of unfamiliarity and the high and conflicting emotions that inevitably (and yet unexpectedly, for most couples) accompany shifts of vital roles, shifts of the furniture of the mind along with the furniture of the household. Le Masters suggests that "parenthood (not marriage) marks the final transition to maturity and adult responsibility in our culture . . . the arrival of the first child forces the young married couples to take the last painful step into the adult world."[7]

First the husband-wife twosome is invaded: two has been company for some time, now three becomes a crowd. The pushed-out member is usually the husband because for a time the devoted and sometimes anxious attentions of motherhood absorb the time and energies and interests of his wife. Immediately, moreover, there are personal sacrifices required by this helpless baby—recreation is cut out or limited, sleep is invaded, time schedules are set not by the wishes of the adult twosome but by the baby's imperious needs. Within the privacy of marriage, two child-adults may have had a happy self-indulgent time. But parenthood sternly demands that you "act your age" and act your role. The child-husband, if he is to be a father and not a sibling rival, must give up or suppress his dependent-possessive yearnings; the lover-husband must bide his time, contain his needs, give precedence to another; the companion-husband must shift and adapt his conceptions of "what let's do together" to include now companionship around the pleasures and pains of child-care. He has been husband to a wife; he must now become husband to a wife who is also a mother. The provider-husband becomes acutely aware of doctor bills and diaper service and life insurance and even that far-off college education which is his child's birthright—and so those self-indulgences that cost money must come under scrutiny and control.

All these shifts of perspective, personal drives, and personal habits occur for the woman too, but with greater intensity because the mother role is at this time all-encompassing. More, the woman undergoes, over time, even deeper changes, which are unsettling, frustrating, or gratifying, depending again on the particular interplay of personality and social circumstance.

First among these changes is the woman's subtle but meaningful relocation in relation to her own mother. To the moment of childbirth, she has been her mother's child, a daughter. Whether she has enjoyed this or rebelled against it, it is still a subordinate position. The mother knows more or better, or thinks she does, or the daughter thinks she thinks so. At the point of becoming a mother, a shift in status is achieved. "I too am a mother." It is not only that "I now stand in an equality position to you" with the sense of triumphant arrival, but also—and this is the securing linkage that underlies an individual's sense of at-one-ness with his world—"I am *with* you, I know now (or am about to know) what you have known; we are comrades in the mysteries." Oscar Wilde, commenting wryly on parenthood, once said, "At first our children love us; then they judge us; sometimes they forgive us." The "forgiving" of one's mother is probably never more spontaneous and generous than when the daughter becomes mother in her own right.

Parenthood rouses family feeling. It is not simply that birth brings grandparents and aunts and uncles clustering about the mother and child in admiration and pleasure, nor that grandparents can be called on as convenient sitters or helpers at times of need. It lies deeper in the bloodstream. The family is a bloodline and a lifeline. The new infant brought into the world derives his identity and his fate from it. Beyond this, his connectedness with others, his linkage with a natural source of support and obligation, his coming to know himself as part of a group past and present all will feed his sense of himself and his parents' sense of him. This search for the new human being's connection, sources, and anchorage seems almost instinctive in new parents. Unless friction and dislike have dominated the couple's relationship with their families, there ensues, with childbirth and child-rearing, a kind of reconciliation and reidentification with extended family. Perhaps it is that with the role of parent manifestly achieved, it is safe now to come close to family again—"I have added to the family. I have a new basis of relationship."[8]

The developmental tasks of childhood call forth their counterparts in parenthood. But we know far more about what is happening in and to the child than about what is happening in and to the parents in those first five years of dramatic growth and spectacular yet arcane unfolding in the new human being. If those first five years are fraught with biological and psychological significance for the child, it must be expected that they will carry a heavy freightage of significance for the persons who are in continuous and intense transaction with the child. At the very least the parents are the reactors to the stimuli, pleasurable or painful, that the child's natural growth of motility, of will, of speech, of intelligence provide. But they are more than this. They are expected to be instruments in the promotion, shaping, and direction of that growth, to "socialize" the child, not only nurture him. So they are held responsible, in their respective roles of mother and father, for doing and being what is good for the child and what will make it possible for him to fit into his society. This is so obvious, has so long been taken for granted, that its effect upon the parent has scarcely been closely observed. It has been noticed only in those instances where things have gone wrong. Then the focus has been largely upon how the parents' actions or neglect have harmed the child.

The business of raising a child is taken as a serious one by most parents. It is invested with great emotional intensity, though the emotions may be negative as well as positive. Certainly these emotions may be accompanied and colored by differing conceptions of what a child is like, what can and should be expected of him, what parental responsibilities to him are. Such differences rise up not only out of personality and love capacities in the parents; they are products, too, of knowledge or ignorance or outright misapprehensions; and these, in turn, may be heavily dependent upon such a seemingly peripheral factor as class membership. The education of middle-class parents, formal or casual but pervasive, has trained them to feel that they are the "causes" of their child's development, that the environment with which they surround the child, indeed their every word and act, leaves its mark or makes its thrust within him. They are "to blame" for his faults or unhappiness; in some mysteriously lesser way they may be credited with his successes and contentment. The lower-class parent has not yet taken into himself the doctrine of parental guilt. Despite the recurrent outraged cries of teachers and juvenile court judges when adolescent delinquencies occur, that the *parents* should punish or be punished, the angry and hurt mothers and fathers of these young ones often know themselves as helpless outsiders to their children. They *have* punished, often too liberally and harshly, and they *are* punished by the child's being in trouble. But in his badness the child is not theirs. When he is little the child is viewed by them as having been born "bad" when he pits himself against them, or born "good" when he pleases them. It is blood that tells, though bad influences from outside the home may be held as causative forces too when things go wrong.

Parental perceptions of what a child—their child—is, will differ, and will affect their behaviors toward the child and their reactions to the child's response. The child is a fresh well-spring of potentials —everything must be done to nourish and actualize him. The child is a warming, lovable, delight-giving, needful, and responsive little being—nothing is too much to do or undo, to give or forgive. The child is really a person, unique and particular; I must lend all my senses to experiencing him so that I can pat him into social shape while doing no violence to his special nature. The child is a new edition of me (or a combined edition of *us*), and all the mistakes that were made with me must be avoided, all the opportunities denied us must be his, all our hopes may be fulfilled by him. The child represents me in the appraising eyes of others, so he must measure up, be as advanced, as bright, as trained, as well-behaved as a child can be. The child is a little animal—feed him, shelter him, train him, and he'll be well and good. The child is no part of me; he is an intrusive burden on me, but I will do my duty by him, the best I can.

"The best I can" is what every parent means to do for his child; but, as the above perspectives and feelings suggest, this "best" will be differently defined and implemented according to the parental capacity and by the conceptions and motivations of which he is scarcely conscious. According to these, too, will the parent react to what the child does to him.

Thus, for one parent or parental-pair their child may be a continuous assault upon their sense of competence and value. If he does not meet their standards, conform to their convenience or to their ideas of what is desirable, normal, necessary, if he seems slow or rebellious, if the books all say he is supposed to be dry now and he is still bed-wetting, if his grandmother mourns over his being too thin and pale, he chips away at the parents' sense of adequacy. And as their tension rises over their sense of ineffectiveness or defeat, so does the child's. At the opposite pole are the parents whose child "does them proud." By the happy combination of what he brought into the world and the attitudes that infuse his parents' relation to him, he accommodates and copes with social regularities and regulations; and each step of his mastery (of spoon, staircase, potty, snowsuit, and of himself in relation to his widening circle of people) is felt by his parents empathically. "He did it" or "He is able" feeds back into the parents' sense of gratification and of their own competence.

Certain aspects or stages of child rearing are particularly sensitive areas for particular parents. They stir up small pools of unresolved conflict or unaccepted difficulties that had long lain dormant because they were not in the mainstream of life until the child revived childhood in them. Some mothers most love the infancy time when the child is completely dependent, helpless, receptive, responsive; their difficulties begin when the child stands up on his own two feet, senses his vertical self, trots off in the opposite direction, and says "No!" For some mothers (fathers are usually mercifully spared these problems) the toilet training period is discomfiting and anger-raising. It is not only that the child's dirtiness may rouse unease, but also that it is accompanied by wilful self-assertion; moreover, there are norms that the child is measured against, and thus the mother. The middle-class mother no longer metes out severe reprisals for toilet-failures (she has read too many books that say she must not), but she may need to mobilize other modes by which to cope with her discomfort—if discomfort is there—defenses of compulsive training or of withdrawal into complete permissiveness ("He'll outgrow it"). The little child's explorations of his body orifices at this time and the sometimes frank sexual pleasure that ensues may be particularly disturbing to some mothers—and particularly enticing to others. Here again ethnic and class custom, so long internalized as to have become emotionally charged, become determinants of maternal reactions. Among lower-class Puerto Ricans and in certain American Indian tribes the boy child's sexual pleasure and curiosity is viewed as evidence of his potential manliness, is even playfully stimulated. Among urban lower-class but up-reaching white and black groups it is forbidden, sometimes harshly inhibited, viewed as "bad," even by those mothers who by their own activities make sex open to be seen and heard by the child. Among sophisticated middle-class mothers the period of open sexual exploration is taken as "natural," watched with amusement or barely concealed anxiety, dealt with by lengthy verbal educational explanations or diversion to other interests. Beneath these surface behaviors, however, lie greater or lesser degrees of comfortableness in the mother.[9]

Disobedience is the rage- or anxiety-rouser for some parents. All the small ways by which the small child begins to exercise his own will, to test his autonomy, may rouse in some parents basic fears of their own helplessness, feelings of their dubious authority, echoes of rebellion against their own parents still crying out in them which they have rigorously suppressed; and they may find themselves threatened by this monster in miniature. For other parents, secure in themselves and clear about their rights and limits, the child's self-assertions may hold momentary irritation, to be sure, but also, on second take, amused and/or respectful consideration.

It is possible, with these differing echo-chambers in the parental personality that resound to different calls, plus the everpresent social realities that either undermine or underpin the parental role, that the same parents at one time or phase are less good than at another and that they are better equipped by personality and skills for one phase than for others. In this possibility may lie some of the explanation for the continuous mystery of how this parent—the one we assess at a given moment in time or circumstance—could possibly produce such a fine child or, conversely, such a troubled one.

When the child begins to be highly observant, with open ears and big eyes, asking "How come?" and "Why?" (partly to know, partly to keep a dialogue going), the parent begins to be aware that he is being watched, observed, looked to as authority and as model. Those open, searching eyes can be disconcerting and self-alerting to parents. They must pull themselves together, button up. What they say and act like—whether in the trivial interchange of table-talk and table-manners or in the carriage of daily jobs and interchanges with other people—is observed by the child as a demonstration and is assessed by him with the few criteria he has available—"good," "bad," "nice," "not nice." Benedek suggests that those parents who strive to be good parents may undergo superego modifications to this end.[10] Certainly at the conscious layer of the superego, in the ego-ideal, is the parent's wish to be a good example. Imitation is indeed the highest form of flattery, and the child's imitation or avowed resolve to be like the parent's good self is warmly gratifying. On the other side, the glimpses a parent catches of the child's emulation of his less than admirable traits or behaviors is disconcerting at best, distressing at worst.

All these nurturant and socializing transactions between parents and child go on, it must be emphasized, in a peopled environment. Of these interested and significant "others," the parents are particularly aware. Parenting takes place in the presence (actual or fantasied or remembered) of one's own parents (as they are and as they were), of one's parents-in-law, of siblings, friends, neighbors, even of Dr. Spock who, along with the others, watches from over the covers of his book to judge what and how you are doing in this major life work. The problems of a marriage may be concealed from public view by carefully closed doors and carefully assumed exterior behaviors. But the problems of parenting rarely can be so concealed because there is a live, growing, developing *product* of that process—the child—and he is held by our society to show or, as the case may be, "show up" the parent in public view. It is this social exposure of the parent, along with his primal love bonds to his child, that make parenthood an experience that is potent in personal change.

When the child enters school, he unavoidably becomes a "public" child. According to social expectations, the parents have so trained, nourished, and readied this child that he can enter a formalized setting, cooperate and compete with his peers, conform to adult-made regulations of time, place, and behaviors, and put himself into work. For some hours each day he belongs to the social system called "school" and to another kind of nurturing-socializing person, the teacher, who judges him and, therefore, his parents. When he is judged wanting—no matter whether it is intellectually, in social behavior, in physical appearance—the judgement is received by the parent as a judgement of himself as well. The parent may respond by projecting anger onto the teacher or the school system, or he may ally himself with the judge and attack the child. He may dissociate himself from the whole business, hoping it will blow over, or may agonize in self-recrimination for what he did or did not do that made his child so stupid at arithmetic. Whatever his reactive behavior, it is in defense of *his* feeling of being judged wanting because his child has been.

Reverse this situation. The child judged by teacher and school to be a good student or one who tries his best or one who is likeable, helpful, ingenious—whatever the going values are at a given time— bestows social approval upon his parents. Whether they are responsible for it or not, they bask in his acceptability or achievement.

The child's latency years, when school and play absorb him, but when home and family are still his haven and source of essential security, may hold many kinds of rewards for parents. As the child brings home evidences of his growing skills and learning, he feeds parental hope and aspiration. As he shares with them his expanding experience of garnered (often garbled) facts, jokes, riddles, of game or hobby interests, of discourse between him and his peers, his parents experience again, now vicariously, the small excitements of the opening outside world. More, they may remember and reexperience the warming if silly pleasures of their own childhood when long-forgotten jokes and games and tricks come through afresh in this new generation. As the child ventures further out, knows more teachers, more kids, a club leader here, a den mother there, a camp counsellor yonder, his parents' world expands in unison with his. The home-tied mother feeds on the enrichment of vicarious pleasures, but even the mother endowed with a rich life of her own finds renewed buoyancy in her child's explorations of his world. It is no wonder that parents find it harder to separate from their adolescent children than the children from them! Not only has the parent deposited so much of himself in the child that the pull-away is wrenching, but also the parent's life has for some years before adolescence been fed and enriched by the widening worlds and opening opportunities of the child's living. Paradoxically, in direct proportion to his involvements and opportunities, the child himself has had less and less need for his parent as source of his nurturance.

Of course the above is predicated upon good communication between parent and child, upon the parental freedom to be interested in the small details of the child's out-of-home life, and upon the child's experiencing that his parents' responses are empathic and pleasurable. It has its other side too. If the child fears school and begins to falter and fail, if his shyness or gaucheness or aggressiveness puts him on the periphery of children's groups, his growing sense of inferiority will be transmitted to the parents and absorbed by them in many ways. Then their fears arise, they feel shamed or "defeated again" or anxious about why their child must be "different." They feel themselves judged by outsiders as somehow wanting. More, there is a constriction rather than expansion in their world, for the tendency is to draw themselves and the child back into the security or at least the privacy of the home.

So the parent of the school child may undergo some growth in himself and some reorganization of his sense of himself as he is viewed and judged by the society in which, willy-nilly, his child is his representative.

If ever there is a time when the ordered, patterned personality is subject to the impact and upheaval of a barrage of stimuli and to the necessity for fast-stepping adaptations and accommodations and revisions and reconsolidations, it is during adolescence—during the adolescence of one's children, that is. Everyone knows of the problems and perils of the adolescent period for a child. Scant attention has been given to its significance for parents. Yet it is almost inevitably a long-time crucial period for them when changes in the child's body, status, attitudes, feelings, and behaviors strike off clamorous resonances and haunting echoes in the parental personality and sense of self. Probably not since the child's conception and infancy has the parent as person been so assailed and rocked by changing relationships and tasks.

The "reactivation of the oedipal complex" is held to be a major source of the child's upheaval in adolescence. It has seemed to me that the oedipal problem presents itself in its most dramatic and often disturbing aspects to the parents in this life stage even more than to the child. Even the legend for which Freud named the complex is subject to this interpretation. Before that unlucky child, Oedipus, was born, his father already feared him. What the oracles had told him was simply the articulation of his own unspoken neurotic anxiety: a man-child will grow up, and nutritional advances being what they are today, he'll be bigger than you are and the first thing you know he'll try to displace you—replace you—maybe even murder you. So he put the child out to perish in the mountains. After the rescued babe grew to manhood in another city-state, he killed a stranger at the crossroads. It happened to be his father. There are no details on the courtship of Oedipus and Jocasta, his mother. No question about it, he must have been looking for an older woman. But no question about this either: Jocasta wanted a young man, and this one, Oedipus, was young enough to be her son (as the Thebans must have whispered among themselves). So there Oedipus found himself, a parricide and a husband to his mother, no more victim of his own psychic determinism than of the anxiety neurosis of his father and his mother's maternally-tinged sexuality.

More seriously, the sexual overtones and undertones of adolescence are strong stimuli to the reawakening of sexual concerns and interests in the parents, sometimes pleasurable, often anxiety-producing, and consequent parental behaviors, overt or under-the-surface, may add fuel to already lively fires. These stimulations, plus others to be discussed, make this a period of necessary self-awareness on the parents' part and often of self-change.

For parents, adolescence arrives on the day they suddenly recognize (though the evidence has been accumulating over many months) that their child is sexually nubile. It is not simply that, in the girl, menses have been established and breasts thrust out against tight sweaters or, in the boy, that hair sprouts on his face and underarms and that his bedsheets are stained. It is the combination of these and the sudden (or seemingly sudden) awareness in the child himself that he is, or means to be, sexually attractive. It is the long mirror scrutinies, the tender care of hair, the eye paint, the side-long glances that replace open-eyed stares—these are the further signs that say, "I know myself to be a sexual (hopefully sexy) person."

These combined signs rouse pride and panic, amusement and anger, love and sometimes flickers of lust in the parents. They trigger a whole galaxy of empathic and counter reactions which, depending on all the factors one must continuously take account of, such as the parent-child preadolescent relationships, the current marital situation, the child's actual sexual behavior, may to a considerable extent unsettle the parent and his usual transactions with the child.

By the time of their first child's adolescence, parents who married early may still be relatively young. By the time of the third child's adolescence, they are likely to be well into middle age. The age-stage of the parent may be one factor in his reaction to the sexual ripening of his child, but more subtle factors underlie this. Sketched in the rough only: the child's body changes may trigger off new sexual self-awareness in the parents. The daughter is suddenly seen by her father as being sexually desirable. He may be pleased or disturbed by this, often both, confusedly. He may be further upset (and then angrily projective or punitive) that he feels some quickenings of sexual feeling in himself. Or he may, alternating between guilt and pleasure, make an open bid for a flirtatious relationship. He sees his son with a mixture of pride and resentment, as outgrowing, overpowering him (all those new vitamins! all the chances kids have today to build their muscles!). Comparison between himself, the father, and his son on a physiological basis is all but inevitable; it has been going on for years: ("You're going to be as big as your daddy." "You're almost as tall as your dad!" And now, "You *tower* over your father!") But now if the father's own body has begun to wear down with middle age and if time and work and familiarity have lessened his sexual prowess, his son's accession to physical powers may be a source of pleasure, through identification, or a source of disturbance, through competition, and often both.

For the mother of the adolescent boy or girl, the same kinds of conflicting feelings may arise with subsequent behaviors that call forth pleasurable-guilty or unpleasurable-angry transactions. The marital relationship itself may reverberate to these open and unconscious provocations. The parent-child relationship certainly does. It is not affected simply by what the parent projects into it of his unconscious or merely nonconscious feelings, but also and always by the child's response.

One of the perceptions that suddenly comes clear to the adolescent child is that his parents are simply people. In that awful moment of illumination the adolescent sees—sometimes to his amazement, and sometimes to his amusement—that this omniscient and powerful man and woman are really rather little people, after all. Moreover, they've had sex, as his presence proves—so they're not so pure. Moreover, they're fairly old, so they ought to act their age. Nothing so embarrasses the adolescent as a parent who behaves as a peer. And concomitantly, nothing sets parents back on their heels so hard, forcing them to take stock of their changed bodies and status, as the adolescent's scornful or gentle relegation of them to middle age.

Most adults remember only fragments of their early and even later childhood. But adolescence is a vividly remembered period. This is an additional reason for parents' swift identifications and empathies with their adolescent children. They "know" the sexual temptations and dangers; they attribute to their children the feelings that were theirs; they feel impelled to help their children avoid the mistakes they made or to use the opportunities they muffed. In brief, the parent of the adolescent tends to relive his adolescence with a vividness that has not been possible for earlier stages. The process of this combined reliving and vicarious experiencing of the child's growth and problems calls to the surface many feelings, attitudes, self-other assessments that require stock-taking, rethinking, new perceptions of self, spouse, own parents, and child. The sense of self as sexual object and as parent of a half-adult, rapidly-changing child undergoes considerable jostling and reorganization.

But the sexual ambience of adolescence is not all. The six to ten years that constitute adolescence (a briefer phase, generally, for lower-class youths, whose education ends and adult tasks begin earlier; an often prolonged phase in middle-class youths, who are encouraged economically and educationally to take a longer maturing time) are years fraught with many vital choices and changes for both child and parent. The child must move from dependence, economic and emotional, upon the parents to self-dependence. So the parent must move, reciprocally. The child must decide and take a series of crucial steps in the direction of his future occupation or vocation. So the parent must help make—or, as is sometimes the case, struggle to be allowed some part in—such future-determining choices. Moreover, such forced or planned changes occur not in a relatively stable social setting, where parents can get their footing now and then, but rather in a social surround that is as swiftly shifting, as multiform, multicolored, violent, and cacophonous as the psychedelic night-spot "happenings" the young seek out.

The thoughtful parent knows adolescence—or thinks he knows it—in its intrapsychic aspects, but he is troubled and unsure because his child is experiencing it in a world he, the parent, never made—or at least he will not admit to being its creator. So if he is to be "with it" he must open himself to new learnings, to new perceptions of what seems to be happening, to increased tolerance for differences in values, interests, opinions. He *must*. Otherwise he will find himself out of touch with his adolescent. This is not to say he must take all that is newly believed, valued, voguish to be better than what he has believed, valued, or held either useful, beautiful, or just in good taste. He may remain of his same opinions still. But if he is to have any exchange of opinion with his adolescent, he must have lent himself—*bent* himself, perhaps—to taking in the nature and process of this changed and changing world of the young. Probably no previous generation of parents have had to recognize their own past experience as students, workers, friends, sweethearts, recreation-seekers as being so obsolete in so many ways as to make their precepts and prognoses questionable at least, quaint at worst.

The emergence and entrenchment of a "teen-age culture," empowered by the spending-money and mobility of today's adolescent, makes "foreigners" of even American born and reared parents. In some aspects their position is not too unlike that of European parents of several generations back whose American offspring moved away from their standards and controls because of the culture gap between them. Parent-child reciprocations were shaken, roles crumbled at their edges into ambiguity. The firm expectations of rights and responsibilities on both sides were shaken by conflict between home and the outside culture. Some of these same kinds of conflict, dubiousness, and uncertainty assail parents and their adolescents today. What *is* one supposed to do or say or stand for in relation, say, to chastity before marriage? Is it true that "all the other kids" do this or that, have this privilege, are free of that duty? "In *my* day," say the parents, and the words are no sooner out of their mouths than they know it is no longer the same. So what are they to believe or even measure by? Ambiguity of behavior norms and uncertainty about what will eventuate in the child's best development pull apart the fabric of even well-knit parent personalities. Within this cloudy climate the adolescent struggles for his separate identity and self-dependence.

As part of this struggle, and in order to feel his own powers, the adolescent must often reject his parents. He does this, in part, through his awareness that they are "only people"; if he is mostly angry, by denigrating and demeaning them; if he is mostly loving, by indulgent charity towards their childishness or naiveté. "Anything you can do I can do better" is the theme song of some, while others sing, "Anything you can do I wouldn't be caught dead doing." This is a shaking experience for parents. Those with younger children who still look to them for competence and wisdom or older children who accredit their accomplishments can better bear the shafts of adolescent criticism or disdain. But vulnerable parents, those who themselves feel unworthy or ineffectual, may truly suffer from the child's discovery and undermining of them.

Perhaps most troubling is the attack, verbal or behavioral, upon values and standards that are held to be important, even dear, by the parent. The gulf between parent and child is never so wide as when cherished or long-accepted values are found unacceptable by one or the other. There is no basis, then, for influence. If the parent feels that premarital sex is "wrong" and the child feels that "it all depends," there is nothing between but separation and argument. When the child bolsters his argument with evidence that in the world outside there is no certainty that the parent is "right" or "wise," the parent is left helpless. He may, depending on his characteristic defense system, brace himself and make a rock of Gibraltar of his principles and belief, or he may yield to the aggressor, hating himself for his weakness. Or he may remain oscillating and torn between his need to hold close to his cherished child and his need to hold close to his cherished beliefs. Whichever way he takes, he is pulled apart and forced to defend against, adapt to, or compromise with attitudes and actions that get under his skin and into his psychic life.

The drive for self-assertion at the cost of parental authority is only part of the overall dependence-independence struggle of adolescence. Its symptoms and typical aspects in the adolescent have been recounted and analyzed too many times to need repetition here. Viewed from the position of parent and towards understanding how it is that parenting an adolescent can shape and color the parental personality, one can appreciate the alternate threat and promise to the parent that inheres in this struggle. It is not only the adolescent who is inconsistent in relation to the balance between rights and responsibilities. The parent is too. He finds himself in the slightly dizzying state of shifting vision: he sees his child now looking like a man, reasoning like a savant, now watching a childish TV show, now guzzling milk like an infant. And since the parent is in live, present-moment transaction with this chameleon child-man, his reciprocal responses are likely to be equally labile, shifting from rational discussion to emotional authoritarianism or abject capitulation. The struggle in parents to hold authority yet relinquish it, to be firm yet flexible, to advise yet consent, to find their own new identities (giant or pigmy?), even to find the secure knowledge by which to govern their behavior is a struggle that amounts, at times, to upheaval.[11]

There are some common parental worries about the adolescent that are less interpersonal, more concerned with the young person's making his way into the outside world and with his future. A generation ago it was assumed that if a mentally adequate young person attended to his studies conscientiously he would "get ahead" and eventually "make good." Today's middle-class adolescent is in a brutally competitive drive for high grades and high test scores so that he can be in some "top percentile" in order to be accepted into some "top college" so that he will be "happy" (presumably) and also —though this is rarely admitted—in order that his parents' prestige will be enhanced and that they too will be "happy." His lower-class counterpart may also be driven, when he is intellectually competent, by his own aspirations and the need to compete for scholarships and place if he is to realize them. Or he may be prodded on simply by a school system that holds up college as an inexorable necessity. (Witness the recurrent newspaper accounts of the difference in salaries between those who do and those who do not finish high school, and the implicit promises abroad in the land that anyone who "finishes" his schooling will get a good job.)

So, for reasons that are endemic to our culture, parents push, nag, and hover over their children, seek counseling and tutoring for them, dangle opportunities and choices before them, and worry. These and further preparations for the child's future become heavy traffic between parents and child, especially in middle-class homes. That many adolescents grow tense and "over-trained" in this educational competition, nervous as race-horses at the starting line, is commonly observed today. Their parents are both perpetrators and victims of the system. They are victims in that their own personal sense of success or failure begins to hinge not upon whether what their child is doing and being best fulfils his needs, but upon whether what he does and is offers them social status and promises them "success." Parents naturally "want the best" for their children. What that "best" is seems to be in need of some considerable reconsideration today, parent by parent, child by child.

Sometimes complicating and sometimes easing the stress is the fact that the parent is carrying other roles, working within other relationships and other tasks along wih those of his one child's deci-sions-towards-adulthood. He is occupied in some work, he is a spouse, he is parent to children at other life stages, and he is connected with his extended family, church, or friendship and recreational groups. His energies and his tempers are affected thereby. But more: because late adolescence is held by our society as being crucial to competent adulthood, its choices and accomplishments held decisive, the par-ents' social circle is particularly alert to the child at this stage, particularly interested, curious, concerned, as the case may be, about what and where and with whom the adolescent is "doing" and "going." Small wonder, then, that parents in this stage sometimes feel themselves socially spotlighted and that the wish for social approvals and fear of their loss are intensified.

Now, in the child's late adolescence, the future tense becomes present imperative. The apparent insouciance in many adolescents, the denial of the importance of the conventional workaday world, the open rejection and revolt against its pressures are more often than not defenses against undercurrent anxiety about where to cast one's lot. Parents are anxious too, overly intense at times about the "right" choices, whether of job or study course or mate. They begin to scrut-inize anew this person that their child has turned into, looking for signs of what he is to be and become and whether his choices seem to be wise, to presage success or failure. Their child's indecisions, moodi-ness, his drop-out from school (even when avowedly temporary), his taking up with undesirable companions, or even his taking on some outlandish personal adornment—these serious or mild deviations from parental norms strike cold terror in their hearts. Depending upon the child's course (and, of course, upon the parental sense of selves as cause or as innocent, if outraged, bystanders), parents anguish, they castigate themselves for that which they did and that which they should have done, that which he did and that which they should not have let him do. They examine their past and current behavior and resolve to do differently with the next child coming up. Or they pretend to withdraw into the more comfortable security of their marital roles and of parenting the younger ones, and they congratulate themselves on giving their adolescent child the freedom to find himself, while keeping half an anguished eye on him. Or they involve themselves in a push-pull, coax-resist transaction of ambivalences, *à deux* or *à trois,* the outcome of which may reward them gratifyingly or leave them feeling played out and defeated. Whichever it is, the parents' final thrust to shape life in beneficent ways for their child is an effort that involves their whole being—their deepest feelings about themselves as persons who nurtured well or badly and their deepest feelings about the child who is himself, yes, but whose happiness or unhappiness, competence or incompetence, is theirs too.

Like the physician, the average parent must heal himself. Over and over again, alone and in partnership with his mate, the parent must take measure of the interaction between him and his offspring, of what he does and feels that triggers certain responses in the child, and of what the child does that he finds difficult to digest. Not only must he be aware—as innumerable books and counseling-advice articles and columns reveal to him—of what is usual, natural, normal, expectable in the life-view and behavior of the adolescent, he must also become and remain more self-aware than he has ever needed to be before, conscious of the inner emotions that shape his view of his child and his reactive behavior to him. This is essential if he is to be able to control his own rush-up of feelings and to reason through a strategy of behavior and consistent position that will enable him to be firm and reasonable in the face of flux and impulse.

For those parents who are particularly troubled, either because of their personal involvements or because their adolescent child is realistically particularly troubling, professional help may be needed to find and reinforce some new basis of equilibrium. That helper will be most helpful who understands, compassionately, that parents *also* suffer, that even he who is obviously "to blame," he who is the creator of a frankenstein suffers because he is destroyed by it. That helper will deepen his understanding if he recognizes that the parental role —in transaction with the adolescent as well as with the child at any other period—involves the parents' *feelings* about themselves and the child, their *expectations, beliefs,* and *ideas* about themselves as well as about the nature of the world which surrounds them, and their *actions*, which are both expressive and responsive. Each or all of these aspects of role transaction may need examination and working over.

Coursing through the parent's every effort to cope with himself and his child in different and better ways is that major motivator— love. It cannot be denied. Even when anger and bitterness or studied, self-disciplined neutrality permeates the parental feeling, beneath it lies that organic, visceral tug or passionate (in its basic meaning of "suffering") bond to the child. It is not that the child is "flesh of my flesh," for this kind of love is known to adoptive parents as well. It is, rather, that over so many days and years the parent has deposited in the child whatever he had to give of nurture, hope, caring, tending, instructing. Whatever he had to give, varying from person to person, even if it was in small measure, has yielded up growth, development, responsiveness—evidences, small and subtle or clearly seen, that the child has taken these in and found them good. When, as is sometimes the case, the parent sees rather that "you have taken me into you and found it noxious" or "you have cast out what I gave," there remains the sense of bond, though it aches with guilt or anger; for, insofar as he was able, the parent *tried* to put in what would fulfil his child.

It is not readily explainable, parent-child love, for it runs too deep and primordially to be accessible to words. Its mysteries are perhaps greatest when one views it in the sordid contexts of parental neglect and actual abuse of children. Even there one sees the child's agonized pull back to the parent who has hurt him, but to whom he "belongs," and the parent's incredulous sense, when the law wrests the child away from his harm, that he has been "cut off" (from his possessions? his rights? his extension of himself?) We have not yet probed these warped parental feelings to understand their contents, but some life-long sense of bond is there.

For most parents that bond carries the warming, sustaining, and motivating powers of love. Their children are their product; they are proof of their investment of themselves; they are their representatives now and into the future. So love and social recognition, love and social authenticity, merge to affirm the parental role and the parent person.

Buoying up the parent in his tasks even in times of trouble is hope. Hope comes with a child. Simply in his being, he contains a promise of future. In his growing and unfolding, in his being a continuous "happening," there inheres always the hope—whether wish or expectation—that he will "happen" in desired ways. Hope invested by a parent in his child (or perhaps more accurately, drawn from the child into the parent-self) may be largely a kind of wishing, a dream with scant base in reality. Or it may consist of anticipations and expectancies based on evidence of the child's hale and sound development. The latter is most real and therefore most sustaining, of course. But in either instance one of the child's greatest gifts to his parents is this possibility of renewal, of an expansion of living not only extending further into the future but in the broadening and deepening of daily life experience, and that persistent, recurrent, up-springing, buoyant hope that this next time around will be better. Even if there were little else, hope makes it possible to bear and even digest parental frustrations and to do the necessary work and rework of the personal self towards being a good parent. For most parents in their middle adulthood, aspiration and the promise of self-realization is invested in the outcomes of their children's lives. Sometimes children —particularly adolescents—resent this and protest their rights to fulfil *themselves,* not their parents. And good parents will support those rights. Yet they cannot help feeling cut down and diminished if their child fails or is hurt in some way, cannot help feeling enhanced and expanded when their child masters some task and shows himself to be both competent and content. When the parent begins to find his world closing in, his growing child, pushing at its horizons, keeps it open; when he begins to know his time is running out, his child buoys up his sense of future and hope.

When the last of the children goes off to college or to make a home of his own, the parent sighs with contented relief that he has successfully passed a long anticipated milestone. Then he looks around and suddenly finds himself (*herself,* more likely, because the father continues at his same occupational role) bereft of what has for years been both a consuming and nurturing role. Becoming a parent is a crucial time; relinquishing parenthood—or more exactly, changing the conceptions and expectations of the nature of that role—is another time of crucialness. Particularly for the mother there is a loss of the sense of function and usefulness. Her often mixed emotions— release and empty-handedness, freedom and ambiguity, achievement-pleasure and nostalgic-regret—are carried into behaviors that may result in new ways of self-fulfilment or in a deepening sense of loss.[12] The marriage relationship will inevitably be affected by the now childless state. Husband and wife will draw more closely together to find one another again, and sometimes afresh, or if it was chiefly the parent role that kept their union going, the marriage may rock at the pull-out of parenting tasks. Housing arrangements may change—the uprooting from long-familiar quarters to settle in new and smaller ones, or some radical, even frantic "redecorating" as if to symbolize that a new and different life is to begin.[13] But the major change that occurs—and must be recognized so that its occurrence will be a turning point towards a new equilibrium—is the change in the parent's definition and expectations of self-and-other in his changed role.

Most of the task aspects ("instrumental") of the parent role are finished. The affectional aspects ("expressive") remain, but their quality must be different. Dependency needs (for advice, guidance, protection, tangible evidences of affection)will be considerably lessened even though economic dependency may continue for some time. (As has been pointed out in an earlier essay, this is often a difficult differentiation for parents to stomach!) The intensity of relatedness will be diluted. It is fitting and proper, as most parents will affirm, that the child's most intense love feelings should be poured in elsewhere, to friendship, to sex partners, to own newly formed families, or into "causes" that involve bonds of altruism. Yet, even knowing this, most parents feel the dilution of such intensity and gratifying dependency as a loss; they miss it even if they would now be concerned if they had it. By self-examination and self-awareness, by understanding of the complete congruity between what the grown child's role calls for and the changes that must be expected and accepted in parental reciprocations, "good" parents, or they who are to successfully weather this changed status, will manage their behavior appropriately. Others will find themselves now at odds with their children, now with one another, and now with themselves.

One further note: When a vital role sags because some of its most satisfying behaviors and rewards are withdrawn from it, some sort of substitute behaviors or rewards must be found. This is why so many women turn to altruistic and philanthropic activities when their mothering tasks are diminished. It is not simply that they have "time on their hands." It is their hunger and need, again and always, for either love (that is to say, seeing that what they put in of themselves yields growth or gratefulness or greater well-being in others) or for social affirmation (that is to say, seeing that what they do is valued or is held to be useful).

Class differences elbow their way into these foregoing generalizations, as they do to most. In lower class families the grown children do not move out so far from the parental home or sphere of influence. Married daughters, particularly, cling closely to their mothers or siblings for guidance and advice, for many small services and aids, and for the sense of belongingness. Aging parents live within walking distance of their married children. Recreation (usually get-togethers over meals) tends to be intergenerational and interfamilial. The reasons for these differences are quick to be seen. Again, the high value placed on the child's achieving psychological separation from his parents in order that he come to his fullest self-actualization is an educated middle-class value. Again, money and many job opportunities make geographical mobility easy for middle-class young adults; neither is available to the lower class. Lacking purchase power, one lives close to parents who may serve as resources in times of money-pinch or sickness. So the dilemma of the diluted mother-role may be largely one of the middle class.

Finally, there is the inevitable change in parents that is perhaps hardest of all to cope with in good grace. It is the time of old age when, with the deterioration or loss of physical capacities, of social relationships, of major roles, the parent undergoes that reversal of status in relation to his child (children) in which it is he who must be protected, nurtured, taken care of, comforted. Authority of decisions becomes his child's; advice is the child's to give; the child is his parent's conveyor, interpretor, arbiter. As at any other period of life, the reaction to this role reversal and the capacity to cope with oneself in relation to it will differ from personality to personality, according to differing self-concepts, differing self-other expectations, and certainly according to the lifetime relationship between parent and child. For some it is a bitter or bewildering time, on both sides of the transaction. For others it is tolerable, acceptable if not enjoyable. For a few—(are they those whose children have incorporated good parental models? those who have mentally and psychologically schooled and prepared themselves for this eventuality? those in whom the well-springs of love and the capacity for vicarious pleasures have not yet dried up? it is hard to say)—it may be a time of quiet gratefulness for having "good children."

Yet unless senile psychosis or complete debility sanctions the aged parent's becoming a dependent, he cannot truly take the role of child. The idea of "role reversal" is only partly valid. Having for so long carried the parental role, even in its shifting and varied aspects, one becomes a parent-*person*, and this cannot be dropped off lightly. So there may be hours and days of struggle for old authority, for former self-direction, for small powers, for self-assertion partly in the fight to retain one's old status and role in the eyes of one's adult children, partly to hold onto the personal necessity to have a recognized status and role. For—as will be discussed in a later essay—this is the most saddening and undermining aspect of old age, that one is roleless, that in our society "aged parent" is a rueful and often ambiguous role. Yet I believe this: that he who has known himself throughout his lifetime as a parent, who has expanded his self-awareness and awareness of others in transaction with him, he will carry these practiced capacities, though in diminished degree, even into the tremulous uncertainty of old age. He will still be able to struggle within himself to accommodate and compromise and renounce or to make the many other adaptations that will hold firm his treasury of love, of social place and recognition, and of feeling that he has had his small portion of life fulfillment.

Parenthood is a long story—and so has this essay become! Our view of it here has been for its powers in modifying and molding aspects of the adult personality. I have proposed that if powerful stimuli may change the feelings, beliefs, and behaviors of adults, they are to be found in abundance throughout the course of parenting. Love, passionate involvement in the child's destiny, hope and the rewarding extensions of the self, social approbation (or disapproval), and the crucial turning points in the child's developmental process— all these continuously charge the parental tasks with intensity and sense of moment.

Every phase of the child's life is also lived by the parent, though from his side of the see-saw. Every phase demands constancy of nurturance and guidance. Each phase requires the malleability and flexible modifications of parental behavior that tap and exercise all available ego capacities. That these demands and the reinforcement of rewarding behaviors must resonate back into the deepest recesses of the parent personality seems all but inevitable. That the hurts and pleasures, frustrations and rewards of parenting, when repeatedly experienced, must deeply influence the parent's sense of himself seems self-evident.

Many of the tasks of parenthood are "second-nature": they require capacities that "come just naturally," are ready and free for use. But others are experienced by the parent as unsettling to his personality organization and aims because they call for as yet unlearned or unavailable ways of acting, or they drive shafts into the underground of his emotional balance. With any crisis or crucial point in life, the resolution may be for good or ill. At such points some outside guidance or counsel or thinking-over and feeling-through experience may be needed to gain emotional release or perspective or guiding knowledge. This is where "parent-helpers" come in. Social workers, psychiatrists, teachers, clergymen, doctors, pediatric nurses, all these professional helpers encounter parents at points of high tension or crucialness. Sometimes such helpers tend to be so child-focussed that the parental turmoil is all but over-looked. One thing is certain. The parent cannot work for his child unless something from within him or from the outside is working for *him* too. The turn of the screw at a crucial time, whether towards retreat or towards taking new hold on the problem, depends upon what supports—nurture, understanding, compassion, guidance, and concrete aids—the parent can draw upon. It may come from the other parent or from his natural sources of help. Failing these, he will need some or all of this help from those who understand that parenthood not only derives from the personality but that the personality is affected in depth by parenthood's powerful experiences.

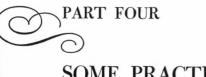

PART FOUR

SOME PRACTICAL
CONSIDERATIONS

6

Role Ambiguity—
Some Common Problems

Some people have no "vital roles." Or, if they are engaged in daily regularities of "being" and "doing" something, of consistently carrying present chores or routines, they are uncertain and dubious about what the norms or expectations of those tasks are, or what their own connection with them is supposed to be, or how they are viewed and defined by the others who encounter them. It is not simply that some faulting of personality integration has detached them from the social roles they carry or drag along behind them. Their "anomie" is, rather, socially induced. They stand in some social no-man's land because, for reasons temporary or long-time, the status or place they occupy has not been given full social recognition. Thus the status, and they with it, remain vague and undefined. They feel themselves floundering about in a fog of uncertainty about what their "called for" behavior is to be. They are haunted by the fact that in the eyes of their surrounding "others" they see only dubiousness reflected.

The relation between personal security and the expression of personality within a viable role network is never better seen than in these instances of role ambiguity. Those who would help people whose sense of identity is adrift need to take note and measure of this continual interlacing between social and personal definition and definiteness. Not only may one individual person need to be helped to find and define himself in terms of his wishes and present powers and self-other expectations. It may be necessary too for the helper to consider what social sanctions and provisions can be called up either to legitimize or to phase out an ambiguous status and role.

Ambiguous roles are those for which no place has been made in the social system, no formal recognition given that the particular status exists, that it is judged "good" or "bad," or that it lacks regularized expectations for what and how its occupants are to operate. They may include, too, those roles that contain inner contradictions and inconsistencies due, usually, to their being in a nascent or transitional stage. Nascent and transitional role definitions occur when a society is in upheaval or rapid change. Hence it is to be expected that ambiguities and inconsistencies would be frequent in the present day and that a sense of rootlessness and a relentless "quest for identity" would be widespread. In what follows I shall only touch upon some common instances of role ambiguity for the consideration they merit.[1]

Foremost among those who suffer role ambiguity are the aged. It has seemed to me that just as entry into adulthood is marked not by a set age but by the conscious choosing and shouldering of one or more vital life roles, so entry into old age is marked not by an arbitrary date but rather by the felt loss of those roles that have been central to adult life. This loss of vital roles comes at different ages for different men and women. But given a long enough lifetime it comes to us all. After his first weeks or even months of freedom from work, relished as his just desert, the old man without a regular job begins to feel lost, somehow, missing the affiliation and regularization of his daily life that was present in his work role. He may find these in part in some forms of leisure activity or in various kinds of volunteer good works. He may attach himself to other old men for shared opinions and fragmentary chit-chat and for the comfortableness of being in the company of his peers, the "retired." But with a few exceptions, the sense of being-to-a-purpose has gone out of his life, and it is hard to know whether his unconscious need for withdrawal and for husbanding his energies makes his investment in relationships and activity superficial or whether some increasing emotional withdrawal and lack of social purposefulness and value results from his loss of role. The old woman holds on to her householding duties long after her role as mother and spouse has ended. But when she has tidied up the house and washed her cup and saucer and talked to her grandchild on the telephone—what, then, is she to be or do? And when she is no longer able—sight dim, hearing dulled, legs a-totter— to manage for herself and is taken into her child's home or put to live in a "home for senior citizens," when all tasks are dispatched by the swifter, stronger, more efficient others, what is she? What is her role? Typically, she will outlive her husband by ten years, so she will be a widow. But widowhood is only half a role. She may be a mother. Yet her children more and more take over her long-held functions:

They protect her; they decide for her; they may love and respect her, but as she grows less competent, she becomes more subject to their authority, more aware that she fulfils no purpose for them. She may be a grandmother and draw from her young grandchildren that spontaneous, uncalculated, carelessly spilled out loving and attention that refuels her sense of worth and source. But as the grandchildren grow older, and as she does too, the pleasure of her company grows less and her use narrows; for they compete with the hundred other things and people that fill up young people's lives today. So her grandmother role grows thin as the blood in her fine blue veins. "What am I?" she muses. "For what or whom?"

Sixty-five is not the age at which this occurs—though it may be. Nor is seventy-five—though it may be. It occurs when, for whatever combination of physical, mental, and psychosocial breakdowns, the aging person finds he has no satisfactorily designated place in his social network (except his chair, his room, his customary *spaces*) and that no expectations are held of him except that he take care of himself. There is some tendency among us all to want to see only the sunny side of aging. We put euphemistic names to the period and the group—"the golden years" and "senior citizens." We acclaim the late-in-life work of a Leonardo or a Churchill or a Schweitzer as though these were ordinary men whose works could be copied if only one were willing enough. We devise recreational schemes by which to give the aged a "good time." In part this affirmation of the pleasures of "being old" is the self-protection of those of us not yet old, the defense against our own discomforts.

No one can be held "to blame" for these well-meant efforts nor for the role ambiguity which imperceptibly engulfs the aged man and woman. Perhaps that is the inevitable pathway to death. But perhaps too, our viewing old age full-face may, in individual instances and in overall social provision, enable us to postpone the too-early encroachment of rolelessness or to better ameliorate its effects. Actually, workers in the field of geriatrics have been moving in this direction. The schemes by which old people are enabled to remain in their own homes, carrying their functions as housekeepers and grocery shoppers and next-door-neighbors, the use of old people as foster grand-parents for relationship-starved children, the groups formed in community centers for learning and discussion of problems, even discussing these very problems of role-loss—all these move in the direction of maintaining the sense of purpose and competence and eliciting some investment-of-self from the aged. The questions for the families of the old and for social planners are: What kinds of meaningful *doing* can be devised by which they can know themselves to be something more than "old man" or "old lady"? And, added to this assurance, what kinds of social and affectional rewards can be provided to warm and nurture them?

A far smaller but equally poignant group of the ambiguously defined persons in our society are the ex-patients of mental hospitals. Indeed, "ex-patient" names the ambiguity: formerly "sick," now discharged, not as "well" but as "well enough to take a chance" and "provided he stays on drugs" and "on the assumption that his family will take him back" and "with the proviso that he may return to the hospital if necessary"—. So he walks out of the hospital, where his role as "patient" was explicitly prescribed and implicitly demonstrated, into—what?[2]

If he is fortunate enough to have a concerned family who have kept his "place" for him (and this latter tends to be more rare than usual) he is taken back as husband or father or son. But even here there is vagueness and uneasiness on his part and on the part of all others in his role network about what he is expected to do and be and what the reciprocal behaviors are to be. Is he a convalescent, the others wonder, subject to relapse at a slight or a pressure? Must we walk on egg-shells, guard our actions, think twice before we speak? If he is still on medication, is he still a patient with the "right" to be sick and self-centered and the responsibility only to take care of himself? If he has been discharged, is he to be expected to resume work and husbanding and affectional relations with the children? And he is caught in his counterparts of these questions.

If the discharged patient is one of the many whose family has neither house-room nor heart-room left for him, who is consigned to a boarding home or, worse, a crib in a dilapidated hotel, his sense of exile and isolation joins with his role ambiguity. Because he often has few skills or capacities to offer (or what he has had is impaired by his sickness or its medicated aftermath), his ability to get and carry work that is regular and rewarding is minimal. So he drifts from job to job. Because his capacity to extend himself to others is likewise impaired, his relationship roles are thin and often one-sided. It is no wonder that readmissions to hospitals occur in massive numbers. Unpleasant and ugly though it may be, the hospital offers security of shelter and dependability of food, regularity of "program." More, the ambiguity of status is cleared up. To be a patient is a clearly recognized role with delineated reciprocal expectations.[3] As such it may hold temptations to the person who finds himself in limbo.

Again, the ambiguity of the ex-patient's role is no one's "fault." It inheres in the situation of the migrant who goes from one "place" to another "place" that is obscure. But again, it calls for the attention and pondering of all those persons whose own designated role includes motivating the sick man to want to get and stay well. Perhaps the role of ex-patient or dischargee can, indeed, be more explicitly defined in terms of valid expectations of the person himself and of those persons and circumstances with whom he will engage immediately on his exit from the hospital gate, and of the hospital's present and future relations with him. Certainly on a case-by-case basis there can be more careful delineation of the realistic expectations "on the outside," the feasible aims, the desirable actions that would mark out this transition from role of patient to ex-patient aiming to carry some more rewarding role, even though he may have to be sick now and again. These expectations of self and others, together with aims for the self and the problems of role transition, ought to be the grist for the mills of discussion between the patient and his designated professional helpers before he leaves the hospital.[4]

True, in many hospitals today there are groups of patients organized for discussion and rehearsal of their out-of-hospital roles. What has scarcely been touched, however, are the persons and circumstances on the other end, the reciprocal side of the role relationship. Wives, parents, children, whether willing or unwilling to take the patient home, are themselves fearful and uncertain about what they are supposed to do or be, with and for the patient. The ambiguity of their position and actions vis-à-vis the discharged patient raises the family level of anxiety, makes for faltering and inconsistent actions, intensifies their already existent ambivalences with all their consequent double-message behavior. So the already blurred perceptions of the ex-patient are put further out of focus. So, too, one of the basic conditions for "crazy" behavior is set: The person cannot perceive or take in his social situation clearly; thus he does not know what is called for from him; thus he may act in ways that are read by the others as inappropriate or seemingly without meaning.

Among those people fallen or thrust into ambiguous roles are the hosts of women who are unmarried mothers. It cannot be said that they are not recognized by their society. They are, with social eyes either averted from viewing their disgrace in full or accusatory, as the case may be. They are socially recognized as a category of role "violators" since the role of mother prescribes the counter-role of father, and both within wedlock. Their children are recognized and accepted as needing economic support when the mothers have no private resources or are unable to both go to work and provide mothering care, so public funds are available in lieu of earnings. Until fairly recently these funds were called "aid to dependent children," but "aid to *families* of dependent children" has within the past few years included the mother as a rightful "needer" too.

Now a relief receiver, a mother who has never been legally married, who has no role partner, who is often an adolescent whose schooling, recreational activities, and associations were cut off by an accidental pregnancy—who and what is she? How does she view herself? What does she hold herself responsible for? And what does she believe is expected of her by her family, her peers, and those more remote and also more powerful representatives of society she encounters—her doctor and visiting nurse, her social worker, her child's teachers? Indeed, it is not always clear how she is defined and thus what is expected of her by them.

She is expected to take care of the children, to love them, train them, cook and clean for them, and so to make healthy good citizens of them. But she is "on relief" which, in most states at most times, means that she is on a below-the-poverty-line budget. Money and resource deficits lower the possibility of being a good housekeeper as they heighten the possibility of stress and frustration. People on relief are supposed to try to get off relief. This means that while on the one hand she is adjured to give good mothering care to her children she is also often encouraged, even urged, to get work to supplement her inadequate finances. In this blurring of clarity as to whether she is, indeed, entitled to money assistance or is given it on sufferance, her relief investigator often is expressing not just his own but the community's ambiguous definition of this woman.

She, the unmarried mother, is expected not to repeat her sin of the flesh. So she must keep free of danger. Is she then not to look at men, to seek them out, to flirt, play, date in some hope that she may achieve marriage? When she acts in such ways as to attract men, she is viewed with censure or apprehension, not only by her relief worker or the doctor and nurse at the well-baby clinic, but by gossiping neighbors as well and even her friendly peers. ("When I frug at the Settlement," said an eighteen year old unmarried mother, "the kids all think it's not right.") As an unmarried woman (but a mother), what are her "rights" to seek associations with men, and what are her balancing responsibilities? Considerable confusion exists here in the minds of all of us about what is right and wrong, good or bad for this mother and her children. That confusion leads to censorious attitudes and prohibitions (when we are not sure about what is proper, it is safest to condemn it!) against the mother from the community that financially supports her. On her part, dishonesty may become the best policy. That it does not do so more often is a tribute to an essential integrity in many of these beleaguered women plus the understanding relationship they have been proffered by their helpers. But there remains this undeniable inconsistency— perhaps an insoluble one—between being an unmarried young woman and an unmarried mother. Particularly when this young woman is little more than a child, psychologically and socially, although physically a woman, her becoming and being a mother must often be a vague, split, confusing role.

For the "first offender," the young woman who becomes illegitimately pregnant for the first time and who, perforce or by choice, keeps her baby, the transition from the role of single woman (with its sub-roles of school girl or worker or daughter in a family) to that of mother is one of those migrations that are held to be crucial in their demands for readaptation. Such adaptation involves the total person—her feelings and emotions about her changed status and all its personal and social implications, her ideas and anticipations of what the new role will require of her and she of it, what it will hold of good and bad, of hurt and pleasure, her impulsive or planned behaviors that attempt to cope with all the new circumstances and attitudes she encounters, and so on. It is no wonder that this "migration" is often run from, that the pregnant girl denies and cannot even perceive the blatant growing evidence of her own body changes. It is not only that she is not motivated to take on motherhood. It is not only that she is shrunk in the esteem of her kin and peers (and often in her self-esteem, too, less with guilt, perhaps, and more with shame at having been exploited). It is also that she is in no way ready, prepared, knowledgeable about what she can and will do as a mother, how she will act, what the baby will expect of her and what she can expect in turn. Is she to stay in her parental home, or is she to leave? If the former, will the baby be hers or her mother's? If the latter, will she be "a girl" again? Once the baby arrives and some of these decisions have been made with or for her, there loom ahead all the complex transactions that go into being a mother. The fact is that even the married young woman, economically advantaged, supported by a loving husband and family, often experiences panic in the transition between the role of gravid woman and that of mother-of-infant. And she is supported by love, social admiration and affirmation, physical care, and the achievement of a hoped-for goal. The unmarried mother has her travail alone; no one paces the floor during her agony; no one says "Well done!" (though a kind doctor and nurse may tell her she has delivered "a fine baby"); no one, in most instances, helps her to anticipate, to know, feel through, to rehearse what her new role will ask of her and will give her. So she enters it blind, vaguely frightened because it holds both social and personal ambiguities.

When only these few facets of the unmarried mother's role are recognized, those persons who are involved in helping her in the medical, financial, or child-rearing aspects of her life may be challenged to think through for themselves and with their client (or patient) how some of the personally experienced vagueness and consequent ineptness may be modified.

As has been said, role ambiguity is inherent in certain transitional statuses or in statuses that are socially undefined either because they are held to be impermanent or are "wished off" as impermanent. Parts of the conflict between adolescents and their parents derives from ambiguity on both sides about what rights and responsibility norms are and about where peer standards leave off and parental standards take precedence. "Is everybody really doing it?" the parent wonders. "Am I out of line?" And on his part the adolescent pushes to find the limits and rules that will offer him security.

Part of the long-known but little plumbed difficulties in foster home placements of children lies in the ambiguous role of the foster parent. They are sought out for their capacity to love and nurture and care for children. Yet they are not supposed to care too much nor love too much lest they be unable or unwilling to detach themselves from the child when, for whatever reasons, he must be removed. They are expected not have financial gain as their motive in taking a child, yet they are expected to bear the stress of tasks and problems with few other kinds of rewards. Are they to be Mr. and Mrs. Doe to the child or "Dad" and "Mom" or "Uncle and Auntie"? Are they to be the agency's staff member, client, supervisee? Are they to be antagonist or aide to the child's true parents? The shifting nature of this role must often lead to inconsistencies and ambivalences towards child, agency, and the role-tasks.

One of the most interesting examples of shift from clouded ambiguity to clear and open definition has occurred within recent years in the status and role of parent of the mentally retarded child. Until a decade or so ago this status and its accompanying actions was hidden from public view, pushed out of sight into the hushed, dark closet of ambiguity. Stigmatized, disgraced, associated in the public and private mind with all sorts of superstitions of guilt, sinfulness, and "bad blood," mental deficiency and the mentally defective child were out-cast from society, hidden away, or ignored except when mental deficiency was held to be, as in the first decades of this century, the cause of social delinquencies.

What was the role of parent of this deviant child? What was he expected to do or be? What was he to expect from the child? From the sisters and brothers of this child? From friends and relatives in relation to the child? From the school system?

Perhaps the idea of "role-of-parent-of-a-mentally-retarded-child" is an awkwardly expressed idea. Indeed it has been an awkward role. At that moment when the parent faced and stared, unbelieving, at the bitter fact that his child was "retarded" or "mentally defective," he was at a point of crisis. Past his personal anguish and self-castigations and nameless angers, he faced the questions of what he was going to be expected to be and to do. What was to be involved for him? Was he to act as if nothing in this child was different from his others? Was he to give himself over, body and soul, to making every sacrifice for this child to make up for his sin against it? Was family life to be molded around this child, or were they to act as if no deviance existed? Then, was he "right" to feel hurt or angry when relatives averted their gaze or were too sympathetic or too full of advice, when neighbors were too kind or too unkind, when strangers stared?

"Role books" abound for normal child-parent interactions. The plethora of books that offer guidance to "you and your child," to parents who are assured that they are, indeed, "people," to parents who want to know whether their child is "developing," "maturing," "adapting" in ways that are approved by their society—all these clarify "normal" expectations and anticipations of what the child is supposed to do and be, and under what circumstances, and what in turn the parent is supposed to put in and may expect to draw out. But until recently, there were no role books for parents of the mentally defective child. Deviance from what is expected always disrupts and skews a person's coping. He must seek to get hold of the nature of this different situation. If it is not defined, he will grope, be confused, be inconsistent in his feelings and behaviors.

In two ways—in his transactions with his problematic child and in his transactions with his small or wide circle of relatives, friends, and acquaintances—the parent of the mentally retarded child suffered from the clouded social definitions of this particular but amorphous role.

Then a dramatic change took place. In a clear-eyed, defiant, but high-hearted way a group of these parents reached out to find one another, to band together about their common problem, to name the problem out loud, to define its dimensions, to make it socially "legitimate"—even more, to place it in the public view as a social and not simply a personal problem. A number of factors combined to give the problem of "mental retardation" prominence and, as a center of concern and endeavor, even prestige. As a result, there is today an open, spoken-out admission that one is the parent of a mentally retarded (or mentally defective, or neurologically damaged) child. With this affirmed (though always hurtful and sorrowful) status, the parents of such children may seek openly to know and to establish the "parts" they are to play, their present and ongoing roles. Whereas formerly they sought advice and guidance in whispered sessions with what were often poorly informed pediatricians or misinformed relatives and friends, or they grasped at straws in popular magazines that printed accounts of glandular cures or miraculous metamorphoses, today they seek, and their demands yield, the opinions of medicine and psychology based upon a growing body of reliable research and renewed clinical interests. For each such parent, of course, there remains the individual anguish and the repeated need to find his personal footing in the repeated stress that his deviant child will experience and bring to him. But today, as he tries to find his precarious balance, every such parent is supported by his knowledge that he carries a socially recognized and legitimized role with increasingly clarified prescriptions for what is expectable and expected in his actions, his understanding, and even in his emotional responses.

So a "whole person" is sustained by social definitions and social affirmation of his status and its dynamic role actions. His sense of orientation, his feelings of uncertainty or security, his effective or inept behavior rest on these (when, one must add, he is able to perceive and accept them). This movement from ambiguity to increasing clarity in the role of parent of a deviate child holds its lesson: in any given situation, a person's choices and decisions and consequent actions will be signally assisted by his clarity and security about his role's demands and rewards and by its being socially recognized as legitimate.

Some role ambiguities, to be sure, defy or elude anyone's capture or definition simply because the roles themselves are in flux, responding to rapid culture changes. In any such single instance when a person does not see or know what he is "supposed to do" or how he can find his footing in shifting grounds, then his helper can, step by step, work out with him and his role partners their own script and agreements. They can be helped to spell out their own rules and expectations, to anticipate and block out their own modes of behavior that will be socially acceptable and mutually satisfying, satisfying at least in the sense of providing some center of orientation and certainty for behavior. As for the helper himself, caught up as he so often is in the myriad details of his client's problems, the framework offered him by considerations of role clarity (or ambiguity) in relation to competent (or inadequate) coping and adaptation gives him one vantage point from which to assess his client's problems.

7

Intake and Some
Role Considerations

Fore-note: One of the ambiguous roles in our social structure, it has seemed to me, is that of applicant to a social agency or to a clinic when help is sought for a problem that is neither tangible nor visible. The need for help with something as amorphous as a relationship to another person or as internal malaise—a problem often difficult even to define or explain to oneself—makes amorphous the perception of the need and of oneself too. One reaches out to a place, the name or reputation of which carries promise of such help; one encounters there a person who is this place "in person." And one is aware, suddenly, of a new area of uncertainty: Who and what is this person? What are his powers? What will he do *for* me or *to* me if I put myself and my problem in his hands? What will he expect of me? What will this cost me (not just in money)? And does he have—or promise—what I want? In short, what an applicant for help with a personal or inter-personal problem encounters as he first faces his potential helper is a host of questions about the rights and obligations and reciprocities involved in the helped-helper roles.

Does this have some bearing on the beginning transactions between a helper and an applicant for help, I wondered? What makes for the transition from being an "applicant"—that is, a petitioner or a candidate—to being a "client"—that is, one who undertakes to employ and to use service? What marks the move from role ambiguity

This essay, with a few editorial changes, was first published in *Social Casework,* April 1960, and was reprinted in Cora Kasius, ed., *Social Casework in the Fifties* (New York: Family Service Association of America, 1962). Its forenote and postscript appear for the first time.

to clarity? What definitions of mutual and reciprocal expectations may need to occur?

It was such questions as these that needled me when I ruminated on that too-frequent phenomenon in clinic and social agency experience—the application for help that is subsequently withdrawn, the applicant who brings in his problem and who then drops out.

In the paper that follows I made an attempt to view a social agency's intake procedures in relation to role considerations. In its brief postscript there is an account of a small effort I made to test my propositions and hunches.

This paper might be given an alternate title, "The Case of the Third Man," for it came about because of my concern with this person. The present title is derived from a proposition I am offering for discussion and testing by caseworkers, as a possible approach to the "third man" problem.

People in trouble in some aspect of their daily living appear at the door of the social agency or clinic and present themselves and their problems. They are recognized as needing the help these agencies are equipped to give. They are given some promise of help or at least of further attention. Two-thirds of them return for a second interview. One-third do not. Of every three persons given the time, attention, and beginning casework help at the agency's intake desk, one drops out before the second interview.

This is a troubling situation. It is troubling from several points of view. Most obvious is the economic waste. The intake process, even if it is one interview, absorbs time, money, and the energies of the casework, supervisory, and clerical staff members. That one-third of such expenditures should be fruitless is a discomfiting fact, and one that we are rightly embarrassed to reveal even to our most loyal supporters.

But there is a more serious loss involved. It is the loss of the chance ˈ to give help not only where it is manifestly needed but at the moment in time when both stress and motivation are high enough to push a person to reach out for help. It is the loss of the moment of white heat, when change and even prevention may be most achievable.

A person who brings himself, or is brought, to a social agency is a person in a critical moment of living. His problem may have arisen suddenly or it may be an old, long-festering one, suddenly come to a head. This person puts on his shoes and goes to open the agency door because he has come to a point where he can no longer tolerate, or others can no longer tolerate, the strain of his problem. Even the unwilling applicant—who has been forced into the agency by the volition of someone else—experiences this first encounter with the social agency as potentially crucial, although his problem is not one that he brings but one with which the agency confronts him.

Every applicant, then, is at a point of mobilization to get (or to avoid) help. In this mobilization of himself in relation to his problem and the agency, lies the dynamic potential for a shift in his adaptive mechanisms. Since high discomfort cannot be sustained without defensive moves to regain stability, and since stability may be gained by poor adaptation as well as constructive adaptation, the effective or ineffective intervention by the caseworkers affects the direction the applicant's balancing efforts will take. Thus, this moment or hour that we call "intake" is a critical one in the life of the person applying for help. Moreover, it is often the case that not only does the applicant "feel" his problem to be a crisis but it actually is one. The forces creating his problem may have come to a point where one or a series of breakdowns and maladaptations may occur in his life situation unless effective intervention takes place. Social workers are increasingly concerned with the idea of prevention. Here, in the intake phase of casework, is a potent opportunity to do preventive work. This is the opportunity to lose or waste when the applicant who needs help fails to take it.

A number of recent studies concerned with the problem of "dropouts" have attempted to analyze possible reasons for them.[1] A recurrent explanation, reported by Dr. Shyne, is this: the applicant's understanding and expectations of the agency were not clear. This explanation, stated in two different ways, appears again in the caseworkers' study reported by Frances Stark. One explanation is that "the misconception that all clients have some knowledge and acceptance of the purposes of social agencies created barriers between caseworker and client." The other is that the caseworker operated in an unproductive way because of "certain misconceptions of the role of the client and caseworker." These explanations seem to have a vital bearing on the problem of dropouts. They point to poor communication between the applicant and the caseworker due to faulty perception or actual misconception of the reciprocal expectations involved in a client's help-taking and a caseworker's help-giving.

It must, of course, be noted that other possible reasons for dropouts are also suggested in these studies. None of them, however, has been less explored than this idea: that the applicant may not have any real understanding of what he is applying *for* or *to*, that his expectations may be quite at odds with the reality he encounters; that, on the other side, the caseworker may be assuming that what he asks, does, and proposes make complete sense to the applicant because they are so manifestly sensible to *him*. One cannot overlook the fact that many subtle factors and also simple ones, known and unknown, operate to make for dropouts after intake. But here, plainly before us, is an explanation that says, in a common-sense way, that an applicant's continuance or discontinuance with an agency beyond the point of intake may be affected by the understanding and agreements between applicant and caseworker as to what in the way of service and behavior is wanted, expected, and realizable. This proposition, it seems to me, deserves to be tested as one possible approach to the problem of the third man.

Elsewhere I have proposed that the aim of the beginning phase in casework (and this phase may be completed in one interview, although it usually requires more) is "to engage this client with his problem and his will to do something about it in a working relationship with this agency, its intentions and special means of helpfulness."[2] The focus implied is somewhat different from the position taken by some other casework writers who consider the initial phase of the casework process to be chiefly a study or exploratory phase.[3] In the latter, emphasis is placed on the caseworker's gaining as much understanding as possible about the nature of the problem and of the person who carries it. In the former, the major emphasis is on the caseworker's active effort to *engage the applicant in wanting to use the help the agency can offer him.*

It goes without saying that the caseworker must first have elicited enough of the nature of the problem to be sure that it falls within the agency's purview. Doing this properly means that the caseworker has not only asked for certain information but has responded to it with warmth and intelligent concern; has not only observed the behavior of the applicant but has drawn some implications for it to guide the "what" and "how" of his reciprocal behavior. But when this much has been done, the essential next step is to bring the applicant into a working agreement or a "compact" with the agency. If an applicant for casework help has been brought to the point where he indicates verbally or in other explicit ways that he sees and partially understands the agency's place in relation to his problem and that he is willing to try its ways of getting at the problem, then the caseworker has a "client." Then he may "study," "explore," "understand," as far and as deeply as necessary. But unless this compact is reached, the applicant may never come again no matter how splendid the exploratory study.

This suggests, then, that my original formulation can be condensed into this idea: *the aim of the beginning phase of casework is to help an "applicant" to undertake the role of "client."*

Immediately, the terms within this condensation—"applicant," "client," and "role"—must be defined. An "applicant" is one who makes a request for something he wants. The person who comes to the social agency or clinic is an "applicant"; he is not yet a "client."

According to Webster, a "client" is "one who employs the services of any profession or business." Mary Richmond first made consistent use of this term in social work.

> Those with whom social case workers are dealing are called by many names. . . . One word will be used for all, usually, in this volume—the word "client." Its history is one of advancement from low estate to higher. First it meant "a suitor, a dependent." Later it meant "one who listens to advice," and later still "one who employs professional service of any kind."[4]

What Miss Richmond indicated is that the concept of client in our profession as in others has undergone an evolution from that of being a recipient of another's largesse and protection, as in the days of the Roman patrons, to that of being one who has undertaken to use a service. It is "undertaking to use a service" which marks the role of client as different from that of applicant. Thus, certain understandings must evolve between caseworker and applicant before the latter becomes a client.

"Role" is a word that carries a considerable freightage of meaning and emotion in social work today. As it is used here it means a person's organized pattern or modes of behaving, fashioned by the status or functions he carries in relation to one or more other persons. Such a behavior pattern is selected, shaped, and colored by several dynamic factors: (1) the person's needs and drives—what he wants, consciously and unconsciously; (2) the person's ideas of the mutual obligations and expectations that have been invested (by custom, tradition, convention) in the particular status and functions he undertakes; (3) the compatibility or conflict between the person's conceptions of obligations and expectations and those held by the other person(s) with whom he is in reciprocation.

One can say, then, that any person who wants something of another person or organization—job, scholarship, counsel, membership, service or grant—assumes the role of an applicant. In the applicant role, one behaves not only in line with his particular personality organization but also in such ways as he feels or believes are called for in a petitioner, and also in relation to his perception and ideas of the circumstances and functions of the person and place to which he applies. The applicant's ideas as to what he wants, what he can get, and his expectations of what the potential grantor will do and require of him (in money, gratitude, promises, behavior) may be vague and half-formed, totally erroneous, or quite correct. A person's behavior as an applicant will be heavily determined by these ideas and expectations.

The role of client, too, is given dimension and color by a person's ideas and expectations of what "undertaking to use the services" of a professional person involves. Becoming a client of a lawyer, an architect, or a broker means not simply that one brings a problem-to-be-solved or a goal-to-be-gained and asks for help with it. Beyond this, it involves a working agreement or compact arrived at between applicant and helper. This agreement or compact includes some exchange of mutual understandings about what the applicant wants and expects of the helper and what the helper can or cannot, will or will not, do about the problem-to-be-worked. It includes agreements as to "who does what" and "where we go from here"—of joint and separate tasks, and of next steps. This process constitutes, in essence, a definition of reciprocal roles and aims arrived at by a professional helper and the applicant who decides to become a client—tentative and limited though this definition must be. It follows that the caseworker does not have a client, whether at intake or later, until he and the applicant have come to some rudimentary agreements about their relationship to one another and to the problem.

If the caseworker assumes from the first that an "applicant" is already a "client," he tends, I believe, to take for granted that the applicant has achieved certain understandings, perceptions, and commitments which the latter may not have come near to reaching. What the worker says and does will be subject to the applicant's misconceptions or partial apprehensions and, therefore, "barriers to communication" will arise. Perhaps this is why we lose the third man.

The proposition I suggest for testing is this: What an applicant will do in the beginning phase of a case is heavily conditioned by his conception of what is expected of him and what he may expect, in return, from the caseworker and agency—in short, *by his conception of his and the caseworker's roles in relation to the problem he brings.* If this is so, the process of intake must have as one primary purpose the clarification of at least preliminary ideas and expectations of reciprocal roles and working relationships. When these are accepted by the applicant and the caseworker, the applicant then becomes a client.

It is rather remarkable how little attention we have paid to this question of who and what the applicant has presumed the caseworker and agency to be. We ourselves have been so immersed in our functions and skills, and so sure about our helping intents and services, that we have quite lost sight of the possibility that the person who faces us across the desk may have very little idea of any of these. On the other hand, he may have many ideas about all of these, and all of them may be seriously mistaken. Sometimes as the applicant presents himself and his story with one part of his mind, considerable mental juggling is going on, unspoken, in another part of his mind, in his effort to determine just who and what this potential helper is or can be to him. The name of the agency to which the applicant brings his problem tells him only in the most general way what the agency is for. What it actually can do for him, how it will do it, where he "comes in" or where he "gets off"—of these he has little comprehension or often much misapprehension. If the setting is one to which the person has applied for one kind of service—for example, medical or psychiatric—and he is then sent to the social service division, his perception may be further confused.

One does not need to examine the perceptions of applicants in order to know how little general understanding there is of the role of the social caseworker. Every caseworker knows persons who have been active in supporting and developing casework agencies not only by money but by hard work and interest, who may even be board members of his agency, but who show by questions or comments that they have only the vaguest idea of what casework services actually entail. These are interested, even devoted, people. Many of them have had considerably more education and greater access to interpretation of casework services than have most applicants. In the light of our chagrin that at times even members of our own families display appalling ignorance of what it is we do, and who we are as caseworkers, is it not interesting that we assume that a person coming to us because of his troubles perceives us accurately, and understands our function and role? We even assume that the applicant, following this supposedly correct perception, has the capacity to adapt, un-aided, to the requirements of the part he must play if he is to be a client.

The recent professional literature is replete with self-exhortations to understand the culture and class membership of our individual clients. Perceptions and role expectations are undoubtedly condi-tioned by these social factors. Yet we have taken small account of them in the intake process and have tended to proceed as if each applicant's perception and ideas of us, and of himself in relation to us, is like every other applicant's. We have paid little attention to the problem of who and what he thinks we are or can be to him.

One of the truest ways by which to know the feelings and neces-sary defenses of another person was taught us in our professional infancy: step into the other's shoes. It is not even necessary to imagine being an applicant to a social agency. Imagine you are making an application for a job. (There is an immediate difference here from an application for help because the person who is looking for a job is offering, at the very least, potential competence; an applicant for social service usually begins from a position of failure with the prob-lem for which he seeks help.) Watch what you are doing and feeling as you apply for the job. You will be telling an interviewer what you want, why you want it, and what you have to offer. Simultaneously you will be trying to assess what this place and person are like; you will wonder if you are telling and asking too much or too little; you will be trying to "size up" what the employer's expectations are. If they are not explicitly stated, you will ask questions to find out what will be expected of you and what you can expect in return—what the reciprocal obligations and rights are. If you are not so bold as to ask them, you will remain uneasy and dissatisfied, plagued by doubts as to whether you want to commit yourself to these vague unknowns. It is in the latter position that the applicant to a social agency so often finds himself. Since he is usually under greater stress than an employment applicant, since he knows less about "the com-pany" to which he is applying, since he offers only "trouble" and not competence, and often feels he is asking for "something for nothing," he is not at all free to ask the questions that we can imagine we would ask.

The more one thinks about this the more surprising it is that most of the applicants to agencies actually do continue past the first interview. Two possible reasons suggest themselves. One is that need for help is so great or is felt so keenly that the applicant clings to the promise of agency concern and on-going attention. As Charlotte Towle has put it, "The needful man is not a free man." The other reason may be that the caseworker's warmth and actual demonstration of helpfulness, by manner, attitudes, and indications of understanding and know-how, provide the necessary security for going on. Yet even here, there remains the question of what the applicant conceives to be his part in relation to that of the caseworker. Perhaps the phenomena of participation, of dependency, and of transference are related to this question.[5]

We are primarily concerned here with those applicants who "discontinue" and with what we can do to help those who need help to undertake the role of client. Regardless of the profession that is offering the service, the client role has these components:

1. Help is sought in some area of difficulty or in moving toward some goal.

2. It is expected that the helper has a willingness to help and the necessary expertness.

3. It is expected that, either at once or within a reasonably short time, some counsel, guidance, tangible means, or promises will be given by which the problem may be solved or the goals achieved.

4. It is expected that some "payment" will be required for the service given; this payment is often money, but when it is, and certainly when it is not, the applicant anticipates (if he is part of our Western give-and-take, take-and-give culture) that there will be certain reciprocal obligations.

5. It is expected that some agreement or understanding will be reached between the applicant and his professional helper as to their on-going roles and direction.

The applicant for casework service is faced with some added complications. He does not choose his helper, the person he meets at intake. Therefore he may be even more involved in trying to make out the nature of his helper than he would be if beforehand he had chosen to go to Dr. Jones or Lawyer Smith or Caseworker Doe. He does not usually pay in money for the service he asks. (Fee-paying clients in social work constitute a small minority.) This circumstance makes him especially uncertain about what he is supposed to put into the venture, or where his obligations begin and his expectations end.

To induct an applicant into the role of client involves our giving thoughtful and imaginative consideration to the conditions and expectations outlined above. To bring a person who needs and wants help to the point where he perceives what help is available for his problem, what possibilities, limits, and conditions are involved, what he may expect and what may be expected of him as a participant, and then to come to mutual agreement as to where and how he and the caseworker can move ahead—this, I believe, is to help a person consciously to undertake to become a client. He may still, of course, choose not to become one, since what has been suggested is no magic formula. It is only a proposition, based on everyday understanding of people in our culture, that offers a possible bridge between the person who wants and needs help and the institutions set up to give it.[6]

The question of *how* roles are to be clarified and operating agreements are to be reached is a subject that cannot be dealt with here. Despite space limits, however, two things must be said. We must still begin where the applicant is. He is involved in a problem and is under stress. Therefore, our first effort must be to help him tell his trouble and what he wants, and simultaneously to elicit and respond to the expressive and defensive emotions which both the problem and the application excite. Only when this matter has been given the caseworker's attentive, compassionate understanding can discussion be held about what the applicant wants or thinks he can get in coming to the agency; what the caseworker and agency realistically are and can do in relation to his particular problem; and what their mutual expectations are. It is in this discussion that misapprehensions, unrealistic expectations, confusions, fears, and immediate mutual goals are clarified. Only then can the applicant say, by his explicit or tacit agreements or his behavior, "I will be your client."

It cannot be overemphasized that this kind of discussion is in no sense the final paragraph of an interview. It is in no sense a tidy summing up of the "rules of play," so to speak. An applicant's conception of his and the caseworker's roles may be charged with emotion; his ideas of what he wants and how he is to get it may also be so charged. Because the caseworker is rarely able to offer a packaged solution to the problem, there are inevitable frustrations involved which the applicant must be helped to face and try to bear. In brief, there are emotional involvements as well as ideas to which the caseworker must relate and with which he must deal in offering casework help.

In sum, I have tried here to state a problem and to present a proposition by which the problem may better be understood and coped with. My argument is simply this: If the caseworker conceives of intake as a "study" or "exploratory process" and the applicant conceives of it as a help-getting experience, the two participants will have a hard time understanding one another. If the caseworker conceives of the applicant as his "client," that is, a person who is ready to use his services, and the applicant conceives of himself and the caseworker in who-knows-what ways, they will have a hard time communicating with one another. If some preliminary and partial agreements and expectations as to reciprocal roles are not clarified at intake, the applicant may still continue with the agency, but he is likely to have confused or even unrealistic expectations which may affect the ensuing course of relationship and treatment. Or he may not return at all.

In recent years, it has been the fashion for a writer to conclude his paper by suggesting that "only further research will tell us" whether or not the proposition he has put forth has value. I shall not place this burden on the overloaded shoulders of social work researchers. It must be placed, I think, on the overloaded shoulders of social caseworkers. Only practice will tell; only actual try-outs, and assessments of those try-outs, will say whether, in fact, this proposition offers a way to solve the troublesome problem of that "intake" which becomes instead a "dropout."

Postscript, Summer 1967: Several years after this article was published I had the chance to try out one of the major propositions in it: that the applicant's return to the agency, to become its client for needed and ostensibly wanted services, might be significantly dependent upon "the clarification of at least preliminary ideas and expectation of reciprocal roles and working relationships." Here I present only a few highlights of what was a small "trial run."[7]

Three experienced caseworkers, two agency staff members and I, agreed to do a series of intake interviews that would differ from the usual ones in that the most specific attention would be given to the applicant's ideas and expectations of the agency, to the clarification and if necessary the correction of those anticipations, and to the ongoing agreements about immediate next steps (actions) to be taken by agency and client. The major difference in intake interview content was that of the focus. Only enough exploration of the presented problem would be done to ascertain that it was appropriately within the agency's function; only enough exploration of the person's involvement in the problem would be done to establish for himself and his listener that he *was* involved, emotionally and as an actor. The main emphasis was to be on drawing out his conceptions and expectations of the help available to him, on clarifying disparities between expectation and reality, on drawing out and relating to his reactions, feelingful or other, to the possibilities and limitations of available help. In brief, the focus was to be upon *aiding him to understand and accept the actuality of beginning role transactions between him and the agency.*

To that end a rough guide for interviewing was set up. Following the applicant's expression of his problem and its effects on him, the caseworker was to draw out his expectations of what the agency could do for him, what he wanted of it, and then, as necessary, to supplement, correct, or affirm those expectations. More, in the recognition that what a person wants has emotional content, the caseworker was to recognize and deal with the feelings that would accompany any disparity between the applicant's expectation and the agency's reality. If resistance was discerned, it was to be recognized openly and dealt with (within the limits of the one interview). With mutual agreement reached between caseworker and applicant as to beginning expectations, the interviewer was to present some necessary next steps on the part of applicant and agency. Here again, if it seemed that such proposals had aroused feeling-reactions or resistance, these were to be recognized and talked over. The major effort was to try out the effect of clarification and responsive discussion of applicant-agency relationships.

So we set to work. Between May and November 1962, we interviewed persons who had called the agency and made an appointment for an interview. In the time we had available we gathered twenty-six persons in twenty-two cases who, the individual interviewer believed, had been moved from being applicants to becoming clients and were therefore expected to return for a second interview.

The first question that leaps to mind of course is, "How many did in fact return?" The answer: twenty out of twenty-six returned; about one-fourth dropped out. But the first leap of pleasure at this lowered dropout rate is quickly dampened by the recognition that ours was a selected, not a random, sample. This sample group was *expected* to return; the obvious nonreturners or the cases we were dubious about were not included in it. So the answer to "how many?" is not useful for comparison with the usual one-third dropout rate. That statistic includes, one assumes, all cases which intake interviewers *invited* to return; our group was *expected* to return.

More pertinent is the question that hews to the central proposition: Was the achievement of mutual and realistic expectations a reliable predictor of an applicant's return? Did his return seem associated with this?

All interviews had been taped. As "investigator" I listened to them with no knowledge of whether the applicant had or had not returned. A schedule was filled out for each interview in which (among other items not relevant here) three major items were assessed in terms of whether the interviewer had handled them "adequately," "partially," or "not at all." Added to these was a global item called "general overall relationship or feeling tone," to be assessed as "good," "adequate," or "poor."

The item that was held to be "most decisive" and thus most likely to predict return or dropout was that which expressed the central proposition: that the applicant's ideas of solutions and his expectations of agency help, if realistic and accepted by the end of the interview, would be highly associated with his return. This proved to be so. It correctly predicted outcomes in twenty out of the twenty-six interviews, or about three times out of four. That is, when the interview was assessed as having achieved clarity of expectation and mutual agreements, the prediction was for return. Three times out of four, returns did indeed occur. When the interview was assessed as not having achieved such understandings, the prediction was for dropout; and this occurred in like ratio.

An almost equally good predictive item was the global "general feeling tone." This will surprise no caseworker. A relationship of warmth between interviewer and applicant or of emotional needfulness in the applicant may be expected to transcend faults in cognition or communication. This global and impressionistic item also predicted twenty out of twenty-six returns. In one way however it was not as good a predictor as the first: it did not catch the dropouts as accurately.

Two other "decisive" items were unfortunately vitiated as predictors because of imprecisions in my schedule. One pertained to resistance: if this was present it would need to be recognized and dealt with if return was to occur. The other dealt with the applicant's understanding and acceptance of the specific next steps: this would have to be achieved if a return was to be expected. But I had not defined the items well enough to judge them reliably. When these four items— clarity of expectations achieved, good relationship, resistance worked (or not present), and agreement as to next steps achieved—were examined (the latter two in their rough state) for their association with returns and dropouts, some interesting connections appeared. It should be noted first that this group of twenty-six "expected returners" was representative of those applicants for whom there are usually high dropout rates in family service agencies and psychiatric clinics. Their economic status, except in two instances, was at a "poverty" or "deprivation" level. Their educational level was predominantly lower than high school completion.

Of the whole group, as has been noted, about seventy-five percent returned. However, for cases where the two decisive items—clarity of expectations and good relationship—were found in combination either with resistance worked (or none present) or with achieved agreement on next steps, *there was a ninety percent return.* And in those cases where only two (or less) of these four items were present, *only fifty percent returned.* (I fully recognize the limited number of cases on which I cite these impressive percentages. Nevertheless, it seems to me that the dropout differences are so wide as to warrant having notice taken of them.)

Further, in regard to the "expectation" item: The problems brought by all the applicants were appropriate to the agency's function since inappropriate requests had been screened out. The requests were for help with interpersonal difficulties, chiefly marital conflicts and parent-child problems. Yet *only six of the twenty-six persons came with realistic conceptions* of what the agency might do with or for them in their troubles. Eighteen of them expressed some general idea—"You'll give us lectures?"—or unrealistic expectations (wishes, really) that the spouse or child being complained of could somehow be brought into line, or that some solution for long-standing problems would be ready for action. (Two remaining interviewees gave insufficient evidence of their expectations.) These need- or wish-propelled expectations confirmed once more what by now several studies have shown: that applicants for help with interpersonal problems are likely to bring vague or need-distorted or uninformed anticipations to the helping-agent.

That such incorrect perceptions or expectations are likely to result in consequent maladaptive behavior seems almost inevitable unless they are recognized and dealt with by the helper. Whether they are dominant or only secondary forces among the many variables that determine whether an applicant moves into the role of service-using client deserves more rigorous testing.

No sooner had I set this down than I came upon a report of such a test done under rigorously controlled conditions. In 1963, operating on essentially the same hypotheses as had guided my loosely organized trial-run, a group of psychiatrists followed their intake interviews with a "role induction interview," the purpose of which was "to arouse or strengthen in the patient certain appropriate anticipations of the psychotherapeutic process, particularly with respect to patient and therapist roles." Carefully matched control and experimental groups of twenty patients each were used; "role induction" was given to one but not the other.

The therapists to whom patients were assigned did not know whether their patients were in the control or experimental group. At the end of a stipulated period in therapy the patients in both groups were assessed, again "blind," with no knowledge on the judges' part of the group to which they belonged. Those who had had the role induction interview were judged as showing "better therapy behavior," having better relationship, better attendance, and showing more favorable responses to treatment.[8]

Identity Problems, Role,
and Casework Treatment

There is epidemic today a common malaise, a sickness of spirit, a disease that has been recognized, named, delineated by both psychoanalysts and social scientists. It has been the theme of a rising tide of literature, played out in the theatre of the absurd and in the novel of the lost soul: the seeking-but-never-finding personality. It has its graphic expression in art works that have neither form nor structure, that express (if art is considered to be a form of communication) "I am not sure what I have to say" or "I am sure only that there is atomization and confusion." It has been called by many names, but its characteristic syndrome is a sense of lost or never-achieved affirmative selfhood. The searching insights of Erikson[1] first identified and illuminated this phenomenon and traced out its roots and foliations. He has named it "identity diffusion" and, at points of its acuteness, "identity crisis." Taking off from him, others have spoken and written of the "quest for identity" as a pervasive problem (or explanation of other problems) in adolescents and young adults.

Its symptoms are these: The person is permeated by a sense of un-ease within his own skin. He experiences confusion, self-doubt, aimlessness, no tensile sense of being someone, going somewhere. He looks out from himself to other persons and surrounding conditions, searching for but failing to find some positive recognition or affirmation that he is valued, good, useful, essential, lovable, competent—at least one, preferably several, of these—or that the others in whose eyes he seeks his reflection hold some such meaning for him. He is characterized by a melancholy sense of futility, hollowness, inability

This article is a revised version of one by the same title published in *Social Service Review*, Vol. 37, No. 3. (September, 1963) and in *Social Work Practice, Selected Papers*, NCSW (New York: Columbia University Press, 1963).

to take hold, or by a restless, directionless pursuit of questions for which he can find no certain answers: "Who am I? What am I? What am I *for*? Where am I going? Why? What is my plan and purpose?"

No thinking man has gone past puberty without having wrestled with these existential questions or at least having vaguely felt their surge in him. In adolescence, as Erikson has made manifest, this search for the secure sense of self is a normal and crucial process; its achievement, tenuous or firm, is the mark of growth and readiness for the tasks and trials of adulthood. Moreover (again Erikson is the author of the idea) the sense of identity is subject to unsettling and dispersion at other critical times in life and may have to be resought, hopefully regained and reintegrated, often with some differences in nature and level. In these passing phases every one of us has come to know experientially the nature and the feel of identity problems. Our concern is with that seemingly increasing mass of persons for whom this problem has become chronically unresolved, one might say characterologically embedded, and also for those individual persons who, caught in identity crises, might be helped to avoid the possibility of taking uncertainty and self-other doubt into the marrow of their personality.

The reasons and explanations for this century's existential malaise are so complex and also so frequently analyzed as to need no repeating here. Sped-up changes in ways of doing things, in ways of conceiving of the world itself, uprooted families shuttling from place to place whether by outer pressure or inner restiveness, social and economic as well as geographic mobility, thinking-machines and skill-machines that edge out the work of human brains and hands, revolutions that pock-mark the face of the earth, phallic capsules that drive into other worlds—all these factors and forces are shaking and even uprooting a society that once stood fairly firm. Although that society has had its inner quakes and upturnings in the past, these were more gradual, often imperceptible. (Of course, the fact that radical changes were not readily perceived and thus not given cognizance as problematic is in itself indicative of how a time and culture determines what each human being perceives and considers to be his suffering. I have often thought, for instance, that when feudalism crumbled and when the industrial revolution turned masses of men out of their work, the rootless cast-off sturdy beggars must have felt, along with hunger and cold, an "identity crisis." Who and what were they, indeed, and where did they belong? But of course they and their society had not advanced to the place where psychic discomfort or despair was given house-room in the minds of men. That it is central in our concerns today is one of those recurring ironic evidences of how many other kinds of security we have achieved, that we can afford the luxury of striving for inner well-being!) The analyses of the sociocultural causes of the apparent growth and spread of identity problems are open to read and are often trenchant. Indeed it might be said, if one were to be flippant, that many sociological and psychological investigators have at least found their occupational identities as interpreters of the reasons why others have not. Unresolved is the problem of what to do about it.

Social work is among the several helping professions that comes face to face with this problem, not (let it be said at once) in its mass manifestations but as it appears in the personal misery and incompetent functioning of individual men and women. In a society pushing to penetrate outer space, social work stubbornly affirms the importance of each man's *inner* space, that which lies within the boundaries of his skin and extends into the wider but still encompassable orbit of his family-work-friendship circles. The concern of social work, especially of its casework practitioners, is with such problems as undermine the human capacity to invest the self in such relationships and tasks that by their yielding to his efforts affirm his worth and competence. The lack or loss of the sense of identity is a frequent aspect of such problems. (One must take care that "identity" should not be applied as a catch-all diagnosis. There is a tendency in all of us to shape what we see by the template of our latest insights.) There is hard and convincing evidence in many situations brought to those who deal with interpersonal and person-to-task problems that identity diffusion or identity dwarfism or some temporary loss of the inner sense of anchorage and aim is associated with such problems as cause or consequence. The problems are not recognized or brought by their sufferers in identity terms; rather they are usually expressed in terms of some role malfunctioning with accompanying emotional distress. But threading through them often is the applicant's anxiousness about himself, about his purpose, place, and meaning in the lives of those that matter to him, about his proper or possible goals. For such individuals, social workers must ponder the question of what to do, how to help this or that individual human being cope with his particular version of identity problems.

Here I come to the potential usefulness of the idea of role in this quest for ways of aiding people to restore or reinforce their sense of identity. It is my thought that when a person is enabled to put himself into some role that seems and feels vital to him, and when he can draw out from his deposit of energy and interest some reward in the form of a sense of mastery (even in small part) and a sense of mattering to others, then his sense of identity is enhanced.

It must be said at once that there is no claim here that any role, paramount though it may be, is a substitute for personal identity in any sense of its being the same kind of thing. It is true, of course, that many people know and feel themselves *only* as they inhabit and act out certain roles. Their roles are their only floor-boards; beneath them lies hollowness. These are persons who, for manifold reasons in their life development, have no inner-core self. This fact has been deplored by commentators on our current social scene, from existential philosophers to professional social critics; but beyond being recognized, it is a fact to be reckoned with. Since "identity" cannot be reinstated or put into the adult personality in the ingenious way that a surgeon, for example, can insert an electric heart pump into the chest cavity, then some reasonable facsimiles for it must be found. Pale and vulnerable as they may be, roles are better than nothing in sustaining the uncertain or empty person's image and sense of himself and his relation to fellowmen. The engagement of the self in some vital role may offer this identity facsimile, and it is not to be taken lightly. Even the most secure of us need our social masks and scripts at times.

Clinicians see identity problems as they are present in middle and late adolescence and in adulthood, when it is largely an end product of the life process to that point. It is an end product that interferes with adequate performance of work and love roles. But paradoxically it is the product of a life history of deficits or difficulties in the carriage of work and love tasks. Where indeed does identity begin? What conditions and occurrences bring it to fullness or hamper its development? If it is that "the accrued confidence that one's ability to maintain inner sameness and continuity . . . is matched by the sameness and continuity of one's meaning for others,"[2] if "the fate of *childhood identifications* . . . depends on the child's satisfactory interaction with a trustworthy and meaningful hierarchy of roles as provided by the generations living together in some form of *family*,"[3] then, obviously, identity begins and grows on the experience of the sensing, feeling, moving, cogitating self in transaction with objects and people from infancy onward. This experience is never formless and random. It is always in some role context and pattern of expectation.

Of course the suckling babe does not know that by his eager intake of mother's milk he is performing his baby role to perfection, nor does he know in any conscious way that when he turns his head away from the nipple and screams with some unaccountable frustration, he is being a disappointing role partner. But knowing or not, he will not be left untouched by his mother's responsiveness of warm enclosure in the one instance or anxious shiftings in the other. Of course the toddler is not aware that social prescriptions govern the time and place of his body eliminations. But by the time he is up on his feet he is learning that if he wants to hold or increase the love of the person most dear to him he must work to "make" or "do" under prescribed conditions. Already by this time his sex identity and its role expectations are in constant view; the toys he has been given and what he is expected to do with them all mark out his destiny. By the time he enters school he is brimming with conscious awareness that he is the child of a mother and a father and he is expected to act (or not act) in certain ways towards them, that he is a brother and that this has its privileges and problems, that he is a school-boy with work-and-play actions and attitudes and relationships—and so onward. His sense of identity, of comfortableness and confidence with himself will grow sturdy and sound only as he acts, does, engages himself with other people and things, and finds, as a result of such engagements, that he feels competent as a doer and that he sees love or admiration or affirmation of his being in the eyes of those who matter to him. It is, in brief, through his experiences of self-and-other in an expanding repertoire of roles that he incorporates and builds his deepest layers of selfhood.

Other factors make their contributions to this accruing sense of identity too. One is the young child's incorporation of parental persons—or parts of them—through his identification and feelings of at-one-ness with them. Another is the emerging consciousness of belonging to a family, of having a life-history backwards in time beyond the self. In other times and places this latter sense of knowing oneself through one's forebears and family connections gave firmer grounding to the sense of identity than it does here and today. "I am of such and such a family," said to the person himself and to his hearer, "I belong. I carry the 'good' blood, the prestige or the character of this socially recognized, firmly rooted group." But in our mobile action-oriented society, a society that is "on-the-make," there is decreasing value placed on forebears. Families are to be detached from, certainly in physical terms; and a man must "make it on his own" even if there is no economic necessity for it. At an unconscious level the family still makes its way into the core of identity. Yet its own loss of stability and rootedness may signally contribute to the rising sense of identity lack in its members. More and more, it seems people need to know themselves by what they experience as doers and by their "take" from these experiences in terms of love, the sense of competence and self-realization, and the reflections and echoes of the recognition and affirmation from others. Role performance and identity, then, are in a continuous cause-effect-cause interplay, the one authenticating the person's sense of selfhood, the other freeing the person to involve himself in love and work tasks with confidence and flexibility.

By the time a social worker or other professional counselor is asked for help with some problem in which identity diffusion is cause or consequence, it is past the time of basic identity formation and development. The core sense of self-trust, self-confidence, self directedness is already there. If it is not, there will not be found just an empty space in the psychic structure, waiting to be filled by attention and affirmation from the helper. That "space" will have been filled—nature abhors a vacuum. There will be found a sense of identity that is more negative than positive: a pervading sense of uneasiness, mistrust, uncertainty, self-doubt, self-and-other denigra tion. Two polar defensive manifestations will be seen (with shade and variations in between being most common, of course) by which the person protects himself from his inner discomforts about lack of self-and-social esteem and sense of status. The one is largely a mask ing operation—acquiescence covers negation, "fitting in," conform ing, taking on the forms if not the substances of roles and carrying them with rigorous inflexibility—these protect against the inner sense of helplessness and dubiousness. The other is an assertive taking on (in?) of a socially frowned upon identity, a repudiation of "good ness" (since this cannot be felt as real). This defense grows strong on the reaction it excites from those who are in opposition; it may be given further support by the person's identifications with others groups or gangs, who align themselves as outsiders or as enemies of the society they perceive as the "ins" or the "haves." This may become an identity of some strength, but its strength is dependent on opposition. When such defenses, used repetitively, become engrained in the total character structure, they will not readily yield to change efforts.

If there were only these polar positions and characterologically entrenched defenses against identity diffusion or deficit, there would be small margin of hope for therapeutic help, whether by social work or more intensive methods. But identity problems differ in degree and chronicity and also in "that to which they are attached"—which is to say, by the particular individual in the particular social situation in which he is found. So there are degrees of help that can be given to strengthen, undergird, feed into, revitalize the uncertain sense of identity, and, of course, degrees of successful achievement of these aims.

Two major kinds of help may build into a person's affirmative sense of identity. One is the love and social recognition consistently conveyed in the relationship proferred by the helper. The other is the support and exercise of the person's capacities to cope with some role which he values and with which he is presently having trouble. This is where the identity-role-identity interweaving comes in. If, in the sustaining and nurturing interchange of relationship, a person can be helped to experience some valued role more gratifyingly and can know himself as having been the instrument by which this change came into being, if he can get even the minimal reward of recognition for trying to handle himself more effectively in interactions with others, there will result for him some heightened sense of self as having both power and purpose.

Obviously such a change will not come about simply because the helper encourages him to "try to behave in school" or "try to be nicer to your wife." To help a person re-shoulder and carry a familiar role in new ways or to learn to try out new patterns of behaving and reacting requires some motivation in the client and a repertoire of skills in the helper. Everything the social caseworker knows, for example, of how to release and receive the client's feelings, of how to promote the client's reflection on them, of how to clarify his understandings, of how to enable him to perceive himself and his "others," himself and his goals, the relation between his actions and feelings, between his actions and their consequences—all these and the further helping modes that cannot be detailed here will need to be used in what sounds like the humdrum business of helping someone to carry a homely daily task with greater satisfaction. Yet it is by these homely daily tasks that we take our own measure and know our own powers

The case example that follows presents a good example of an identity problem and role problem inextricably bound together and poses some of the treatment considerations:

Wade X is a seventeen-year-old Negro boy, brought by his mother to a family agency with the agreement of his probation officer. Wade has been involved in a number of delinquencies. He was with a gang when the police raided the house of a girl who claimed gang-rape; he has stolen a car for a joy ride; he has smoked "reefers"; recently, after mounting defiance in school, which culminated in his striking a teacher, he was expelled. But there is margin for hope. Wade's mother is a responsible woman, worried about her son. Wade seems to have good intelligence. Moreover, he has registered in night school classes in art and psychology because he wants "to show" his teachers. In fact, he thinks he wants to *be* a teacher.

In his first interview with the family caseworker, he is glib and blame-projecting. But he is also puzzled and worried about himself. He says he sometimes wonders if he's crazy. He takes long walks but he finds himself going nowhere; sometimes he finds he is talking to himself. And his mother has told him that he does not have the right feelings about things. He wonders.

Fragments of past history begin to reveal the reasons for the boy's particular diffusion of identity. Wade's father deserted when Wade was three and his brother was five. His mother placed each child with different relatives in different cities. Wade lived with his cousins, an elderly childless couple who lived in a small town several hundred miles from New York. While they did not adopt him he was called by their surname, X. His mother visited occasionally, but Wade does not recall these visits, until one day, about four years ago, she visited him and told him that she had remarried and that he could come to live with her if he chose. Not long afterward, Wade walked out of his foster-parents' home "as if I was going to school" and came to live with his mother, his stepfather and his brother, who had also recently arrived.

Living together at home now are his stepfather and his mother, Mr. and Mrs. Y; his brother, who carries his own father's name

Charles Z; and our boy, Wade X. Mrs. Y, his mother, speaks of her uncertainty about her current roles. She has continued to work, even though married, because it did not seem right to ask her new husband to support her children. Should she quit? She finds herself suddenly a mother, but of sons who are virtually men. Her husband accepts them—but passively—and one of Wade's complaints is that his stepfather does not "come right out" and tell him what to do.

The identity problem is a complicated one here and for obvious reasons. Wade is in adolescence, the period of normal identity crisis, when the common questions of "Who am I?" "Why and what for?" "Where am I to go?" are endemic. For him, as for every young person who struggles with them, these questions are poignant and shaking. But for him they drive even deeper, deep into his babyhood, as far back, perhaps, as when on the threshold of forming some bonds of identification with his father, he lost him, and when, suddenly thereafter, he found himself motherless too, and with strangers. Probably his mother thought or hoped he was too young to be hurt by this change and probably, like so many children torn from their parents in their most vulnerable years, he furthered the impression that he was unaffected by letting no feeling show through. That he did not give himself over to his foster parents is suggested in his having walked out of their lives "as if I was going to school." So he must, from babyhood on, have wondered who he belonged to, and why he was given away, and where his real mother and father were, and what was to become of him. Added to all this is his being black: by this accident of birth he inherited a racial identity problem, the problem of difference, of alienation from the dominant group, some sense of being socially undervalued. Now on top of all this comes his migration back to his mother's home. But it is not the mother or the home he knew or must have fantasied. She is a different mother, not only because she has grown older, and so has he, and their relationship to one another must have some considerably different qualities from what he dreamed of or yearned for, but also because she has another man who is not his father, either in reality or in the image he seeks (someone who will be the authority he wants, either in order to feel safe and little-boy again or to test and defy in a power struggle). Wade has migrated from a small town community and school into a metropolis and into a new school which is itself a small city. The changes he is experiencing not only push up inside himself but wind about him in dizzying widening circles of family life, school life, peer-play life.

Wade has made some blind efforts to steady himself. Their inconsistency bespeaks his conflict and confusion. He wants to be a teacher; he has enough feeling, bad or good, deposited in his teachers that he wants to "show them" that he is worth something; yet he has fought with them—or with them as representative of "the system." He hands a good line to the social worker, presents himself as blameless; yet he worries about himself, thinks he may be crazy, walks and wonders alone. He has joined delinquents—or at least with young people whose sex-theft-drug exploits are under legal prohibition. One does not yet know whether these playmates and their activities were the only ones available to a young man who simply wanted companionship and fun or whether Wade is seeking a negative identity, seeking to find defiant expression for what must be inner feelings, long in the growing, of betrayal, desertion, unconnectedness. If it is the latter it is a matter for quick concern. There seem to be in Wade's consciousness enough ambivalent wish and bent to give hope that therapeutic interventions may tip the balance in a more positive direction. One further diagnostic speculation, and this is on the pessimistic side: the social caseworker reported blandness of affect in the boy, glibness, and a kind of disarming avoidance of blame. Were these persistent behaviors, they, coupled with the mother's complaint that Wade does not have "the right feelings," would suggest serious character defect, perhaps with a schizoid underlay. Yet there is evidence of conscious anxiety and conflict in him.

Whatever the nature of this boy's psychosocial pathology—and that nature and its severity can only be revealed when efforts to engage his motivation for help and change bring out his responsive behavior—this boy has little sense of identity. His restless, impulsive feelingless behavior is quite out of line with his good intelligence, his family's standards, his conscious goals. Neither his past nor his present anchors him.

What does one do about personal problems that have run so long and spread their tentacles so pervasively? Or about an ingrained character disorder? Or about the festering social and behavioral problems that may, to be sure, be "only symptoms," as is sometimes said (and yet today's symptoms are the causes of tomorrow's new problems)? What aspect or part of such proliferating deep-long-lying problems does a helper take hold of?

The first criterion for the choice of an entry point is that it be where the client hurts. Where emotion is, there motivation will be found. But since in a jungle-growth of problems the client himself often cannot say what troubles him most or what is uppermost in his today's concerns (two different designations), a second criterion may need to be used: the entry to helping may be in some area of the situation which is in immediate need of attention lest, by its self-propelled dynamics, it adds to or complicates the already present difficulties. Another consideration supports this second criterion. It is not only that by some first aid intervention there may be actual prevention of an otherwise undermining cause-effect spiral but also that such intervention, when it is focussed upon some here and now and tangible problem, makes sense to the client. He sees its relevance to him. This criterion of relevance to the client is of particular importance when one works with people who are action-oriented rather than self-analysis oriented, who expect that something has to happen in their situation before it can happen in themselves.

Where the applicant for help usually first feels and sees his hurt is in some frustrating or unsatisfying transaction between himself and the objects or people in one (or more) of his roles. In any role that he cares about, that feels important to him, will be found the person himself as a feeling, thinking, operating entity. So he can be engaged in significant part there. More, however: in any role there is involved at least one, usually more, significant others; and those others, by their attitudes and actions, constitute in large part the individual person's "circumstances." As dynamic forces with which the applicant is in interplay they must be involved by the helper (with variations dictated by the particulars of the case) so that their power for hurting or healing may be within the helper's purview and influence.

Wade is a case in point. Where to take hold of this boy whose sense of selfhood, of identity, is like a loose, thready floss, or whose sense of selfhood depends chiefly on being in opposition? What would *he* see as real and useful to him, what would he want from a person purporting to be there to help him (not to control or check on him)? In the eddying circles of his daily relationships what persons and conditions would need to be known and influenced? What behavior and aids on the part of his helper, the social caseworker, would serve to give him a sense of at least temporary anchorage and of direction in which to go forward?

Within every one of his vital relationships, Wade is having trouble or feeling discomfort—with his mother, his stepfather, his peers, his school. School is in the forefront of his present concerns (forefront, not necessarily most basic nor deepest, but simply in the center of his conscious awareness and worry). For him and at this moment, the most troubling, most tangible, most consciously desired, and most readily achieved role is that of student. In this role he sees and feels his troubles plainly; in this role he knows that his actions count, for other people will decide his future unless he undertakes some part in that decision. His success or failure in that role matters to his family, to his community, but more, to this boy's whole unfolding image of himself. Expelled from school, without occupation, without direction, he is a nothing going nowhere and talking to himself. If he could return to school with some determination to meet its requirements responsibly he might experience some restoration of his sense of doing something (that is socially expected and approved), going somewhere (that has regularity and certainty), and being somebody (a student working and learning). This sense of self as being and acting to a purpose may even be enhanced by the fact that his resumption of these responsible tasks is the result of his own decision and choice. And this will have emerged not from his being coaxed and pushed into going back to school but as the result of discussions with his caseworker in which they have scrutinized his wishes and aspirations for himself, his actions and their consequences, and in which they have considered and rehearsed alternative ways of dealing with school personnel, and what rewards or frustrations could be anticipated, and so on. To this the caseworker might have to add direct work with school personnel to first get their version of Wade's problems and potentials and then (if desirable) their agreements and conditions for his return to school. And the possibility of involving Wade's mother or other family members in their support of his constructive behaviors would also need consideration.

The caseworker who understands what a meaningful role involves will know that the feelings, actions, reciprocal expectations, and interactions involved in such a role will become the subject matter of the ongoing work with Wade. Moreover, the concept of focus includes not only the idea of partializing but also that of viewing in depth. Thus, if the caseworker and Wade were to focus upon his problematic role of student, such focus would involve talking over and feeling through this problem in depth and detail. What brought about the breakdown in this role? How does Wade see it, feel it, think about it? What does he want us to help him do about it? What is he willing and able to invest in the solution? To be a student he must act in certain ways; how does he feel about this? Can he, with the caseworker's help, begin to see himself as acting as well as acted upon? As affecting as well as affected? Can he, supported in the relationship, get into the shoes of another—his teacher, for example —and see another's position? What difference does his being in or out of school make to his mother? Does he care? And so on.

There is, of course, always the possibility that the choice of focus —in this instance the boy's school problems—may lead to another area which for the client feels more hazardous or more vital. Then a shift must take place to that other area. What remains constant will be the concentration upon the transactional interchanges between the client and the others in whatever role relationships and tasks are under scrutiny.

The repeated expression and examination of self as actor and interactor, of self as affector as well as affected, of actions as driven by emotions, of emotions and ideas as subjects for understanding and consideration—all this would be the content of the ongoing interviews between Wade and his caseworker. Such interviews would have boundary and depth and vital reality for Wade because they would be about what he is and does and feels *now* in a clearly delineated interaction experience. This is the food for thought, for expressed and reflected upon feeling, for behavior experiments. But the basic nurturance will flow from the relationship proferred and sustained by the caseworker, taken in and responded to (this is being assumed now) by the client.

The meaning of the words we use when we describe the casework relationship—acceptance, warmth, empathy, receptivity—is essentially this: "I look at you as a human being. But more than that, I see and hear you, I take you in, as a particular human being: *you.* You are worth my attentiveness, my interest, my lending myself to your need." By these demonstrated attitudes, the caseworker first affirms the applicant's unique identity.

Relationship deepens as the threads of his emotional involvement in his problems are drawn from client to caseworker. The caseworker's responsive comments, his attentive receptivity, his guidance of the talk together say, in effect: "I accept you, and I can feel with you. You are worth my help, not only because you need it, but also because you have within you the potential for coping with what hurts or frustrates you. That 'wanting' or drive in you, combined with the help I can offer you, is what makes our being together have a purpose." By these spoken or implicit affirmations the caseworker injects into the relationship not only support but stimulation, not only acceptance but expectation. "I take you as you are, in your *being*. But our business together is your *becoming*." This is what the ongoing relationship conveys.

As the client begins to feel himself "received," accepted in his own being, he comes to feel a sense of at-one-ness with his caseworker. In part unconsciously, in part consciously, he incorporates his caseworker's view of him. The danger now is that some loss of self may occur, some blurring of the reality sense of his separate identity, which we know as one aspect of "transference." The caseworker's clarity about the purpose and the focus of their work together—to help the client engage himself more effectively in some present life-role—is one brake upon neurotic transference.

The client's role problem may actually be the symptom of basic personality problems, as Wade's problems are symptoms of his pervasive identity diffusion. But while they may be seen and diagnosed whole, personality problems cannot be dealt with whole. They can best be identified, taken hold of, observed, and worked over as they show themselves in some partial and tangible aspect of today's life-experience.

Some explorations of the beginning and course of Wade's problems may be necessary at some point in the treatment, and surely in dealing with problems of the here and now the relevant past will thread its way through repeatedly. But the exploration of past events and feelings may lead into an endless labyrinth unless it is consistently examined in its meaning and uses for the present. And the present is known and felt and taken on as a time for coping only as it is lived out in person-to-other, person-to-circumstance transactions.

The permeation effect of improvement and gratification in one role upon other parts of a person's life is not hard to imagine. If Wade could find some security in being reinstated in the position of student; if his (probably awkward and tentative) efforts to control his impulses meet with some recognition by his teachers, his mother, his caseworker, perhaps even some of his peers; if he can see the steps by which he can achieve what he wants for the future instead of blindly banking on "breaks"; if his mastery of school subjects gives him some pleasure—if these small changes can be made to happen, they will combine to build into his general sense of himself. One can expect in him a rising feeling of self-respect, a growing self-aware-ness, some greater sense of direction and purpose, and, undergirding all this, the sense of being worth the attention of other people. His motivation to put himself into working on his problem will be sus-tained when the task seems encompassable to him, if he can see and feel some small achievement. Work on a tangible role promises such boundaries and rewards.

Of course it may happen in Wade's case, as with any other client, that as much as he wants to handle himself and his difficulty differ-ently, he cannot. Try as he may, responsive within the casework interview as he may be, he might repeatedly find himself unable to carry through on his perceptions and conscious intentions. When this occurs, we know that there are imperious unconscious forces at work. Then there is need for reconsiderations of diagnosis, treat-ment, and goals, perhaps for psychiatric consultation. Even then, however, the therapeutic question remains: "By what means other than taking the role of "sick one" or "patient" can this person experi-ence himself as having some personal competence and know that he *is* something?"

The conscious sense of being something is most real when a person uses himself—his energies, his emotions, his skills—in carrying some work-tasks or love-tasks that he and others feel are important. His sense of self expands when, as in the casework interview, he is accepted and affirmed and then supported as he learns to perceive and modify his feelings and actions. His sense of worth is bulwarked as the caseworker—a person he has become attached to, representa-tive of society—supports the importance and value of the role he works on, as well as his efforts. His sense of aim and of future is sustained as the caseworker keeps before him his realistic goals. His rewards for trying to see himself more clearly, to share his feelings, to modify his behavior, lie in his sense of mastery when he succeeds, in the caseworker's unflagging encouragement when he fails, and in the responses and recognition he gets from other persons involved with him. This last is of great moment, for the testing ground for self-hood and self-worth is the reflection of self we see in the eyes of the people who are part of our everyday life. The eyes of the caseworker are important mirrors; but even more important are the eyes of the people with whom we live, from whom we want love or recognition, whose eyes affirm both our person and our value.

The sense of self, of identity, grows and develops on the experience of the self as having some small powers and capacities in coping with everyday interpersonal and instrumental problems and on the indication by others that one has meaning and value for them. For many persons these have been experienced over the life span in meager measure. There are no ways yet known to undo the frail substructure caused by these psychic vitamin deficiencies. But there are ways by which to shore it up, to compensate for it, to bulwark whatever confidence and certainty remains. These lie in the tangible, immediate-present opportunities to exercise one's powers and find one's purpose in vital life roles. When a caseworker helps his client to find himself and to feel himself adequate to love and work tasks, he reinforces that person's sense and affirmation of identity.

9

Role and Help to Troubled Adults

We all have troubles and problems at some points and in some roles in our lives. We weather them somehow, skirmishing about, mobilizing the extra powers we can call up in ourselves or our families and friends. But there are times and circumstances when those powers and resources are not to be had. Then we reach out to persons outside our usual and natural help-group. When we seek professional help, we seek expertness for our particular problem-area and, often, the access to provisions or resources that are not within our comand. Not only do we expect expert knowledge and know-how and resources to characterize professional help, but we hope that the profferer may be counted upon to be both objective and compassionate. He should be objective in the sense of being personally unentangled in the dilemma, compassionate in the sense of being concerned and caring about our suffering.

Part of the "expert knowledge" of the helper must be knowledge and understanding of the powers for good and evil that lie in people's daily relationships and activities. Underlying this should be a grasp of the ways in which a system of ideas—such as those embraced in "role"—may facilitate the helper's actions. Whatever his skills, the professional person's theoretical stance or his system of beliefs will influence how he sees a problem and how he interrpets it. It will determine his focus of attention. For example, the concept of role will sensitize him to the social determinants of his client's behavior. It will guide his actions and his aims. More: if his client comes to "believe in him," it will influence his client's own view of his problem, of himself in relation to it, and of his expectations of its outcome. What follows here is a discussion of some of the ways in which role concepts shape and color professional help. It is particularly focussed to social work's helping processes, but it has relevance, I believe, to other forms of helping too.

People are helped by many kinds of helpers and many forms of influence. From psychiatrists to witch doctors, from orthodox psychoanalysis to behaviorist conditioning, from miracle shrines to placebos passing as miracle drugs—many divergent and even theoretically polar forms of help have proved beneficial to people in trouble. Yet there persists in most of us some stubborn belief that there is *one* best way. That "best way" is usually the way in which we have been indoctrinated, or have ourselves been helped, or have found compatible with our own bents, and/or have found workable in its application. (Perhaps this fixing of belief and loyalty to "one way" is necessary to our sense of stability and integrity; most of us need fixed stars by which to gauge and guide ourselves, and orthodoxies offer these. There is the further fact that it is easier to *think* with diversity than to *act* so: action demands of us some choice of course and content.)

What is of equal interest (and of proper concern too) is that those who have been helped, patients or clients, tend to become "true believers" too. They tend to accept and to make their own their helper's interpretations of their problems and their helper's conceptions of how they need to cope with them. Indeed, their "treatability" is marked by their capacity so to attach themselves to their helper, so to "relate," "love," "identify," "feel at one with" that they take in his attitudes, appraisals, judgments, and come to possess or to be possessed by them. What happens, then, is that a system of thought about what is good, mature, desirable, allowable, healthy, to-be-valued for the individual and his person-to-person and person-to-task encounters, moves out from helper to be absorbed as an emotionally freighted conviction by those whom he helps. The client or patient comes to express this as *his* belief, *his* guide to his behavior. One result (among others): his perspectives, his view of himself and of significant others, of himself as actor and as acted upon, his idea of what he has a "right" to expect from life and the "responsibility" to be and give and do, even his sense of "happiness"—all these assessments of self-in-living are colored and cast by the value judgments that inhere in a belief system that was first the therapist's and was taken in by the person whom he has helped.[1] In the swift and pervasive communication among people today, what for a time were guiding beliefs within the closed circuit of professional helper and his client begin to spread out into widening circles of influence to become part of the spirit of the times.

This phenomenon of value transmission from the helper to the helped is another reason for my interest in exploring social role. Perhaps we have not sufficiently tapped and plumbed and utilized the powers for healing, for gratification, for self-awareness and self-fulfillment that lie nascent in the humdrum everyday roles of everyday life. Perhaps more is to be found therein than has been tasted, savored, appreciated, valued. Perhaps by the helper's attention to this continuously being woven fabric of role feeling-actions and action-responses the content of people's lives may take on some greater luster and meaning. And perhaps the obvious and pervasive hunger for social acceptance, belonging, affirmation can be fed by deeper awareness of the social support potentials within people's commonplace but vital role transactions.

For many years the theoretical basis for the social work method called "casework" has been that of dynamic psychiatry. In sketch, the pervading belief has been that the maladjustments and frustrations in people's lives were the result of the personality disturbances or deficits they brought to their life circumstances,[2] and that these were the product of an inexorable chain of earlier hurts and frustrations and errors of response. The treatment focus followed logically from this. It was upon the person's subjective self-expression, his emotions, his self-awareness and knowledge, interpretations of his past and present reality, his understanding of what forces in his life-experience had shaped him, and so on. The treatment assumptions were that as he gained confidence in his helper's support and caring for and belief in him, he would be freed to know himself more truly, more open to examine and realistically to appraise his own feelings and behavior. He would feel less impelled to repeat old behavior patterns; he would find tensional release and surcease in the therapeutic permission; he would be able more correctly to understand his impulses and compulsions and to assess what feelings and behavior were realistically called for at a given time and place and thus with greater ease and success would manage himself accordingly.

Countless persons would attest to having been helped by those who worked from this base of problem-as-lying-within-the-personality. But for countless others it has had many limitations, particularly for persons whose present-day problems are crucial and imperative, and for those whose life styles make introspective reflection and self-examination implausible, and for those who may be viewed (sometimes correctly, sometimes not) as more victim than creator of their social circumstances. Of this, more further.

Recently there has emerged in psychiatry as well as in social work a kind of polar reaction against the "personality cult," against concentration upon the individual personality either as source of problems in social functioning or as treatment locus. This reaction has several thrusts, and one is towards the belief and averment that it is in *society* that sickness lies, not in the individual, that a "sick society" offers the individual only sick means by which to express his normal drives and meet his normal needs. This theory stance results in a considerable shake-up of ideas about what helping troubled people should consist of.

When the sick society is taken as a conceptual conviction, the nature of people's problems and the useful modes of help come to be quite differently perceived, defined, and resolved. This shift of sentiment, thought, and action will affect not only the professional helper but also the problem-carrier. "We're depraved because we're deprived," sing the delinquents in *West Side Story,* and they express what is becoming an increasingly popular view. Like its polar counterpart this view of society as sick and of the individual as its victim sets up a particular frame of beliefs and consequent expectations and treatment strategies. It is now being proposed that mental illness is largely a social definition of behavior distorted by social stress and strictures; that some forms of delinquent behavior may be viewed as a healthy protest against social pathologies. The "poor" are being accredited, *ipso facto*, with being "good" or "right" (whatever happened to "honest"?) since their condition of poverty is the fault of society. The "indigenous worker" is being held to be more competent and compassionate than the professional helper, chiefly because he is a product of social exploitation and thus is assumed to be allied by feeling and understanding with the exploited. Not only in social work but in medicine and psychiatry and organized religion, too, there has occurred a shift in interest from work with individual problems to work with larger units—groups and communities. Community surveys to identify pervasive medical-social-psychiatric problems, projects that aim to prevent social deterioration, projects that aim to provide more accessible opportunities for work, schooling, recreation, housing, job training, child-care, and child-stimulation—

all these burgeon today in the striving to mitigate newly recognized socially-induced ills.

Already a number of psychological effects upon the individual, both the professional helper or his client, may be discerned. In some quarters there is a demand, if not to abandon attempts to work with individuals, at least to push it to the sidelines in some determination that all effort should be poured into changes in social provisions and structures. The rise and proliferation of treatment groups in place of the one-person-to-one-helper formula is in part a reflection of the belief that the individual suffers from (and therefore needs help to deal with) his alienation from society and the smaller social groups that represent it. There appears to be a growing sense that since the individual is not to blame for what society has done to him (a kind of magnified mirror image of the earlier idea that the individual is not to blame for what his *parents* did to him) he cannot be held responsible for self-governance or obligation to others. If he is a puppet moved by the hand of a sick social system, he can scarcely be asked to perceive himself and to act as a self-determining person. In some places, it is true, he is being spurred to act in his own behalf towards bringing about change in those sectors of society he can affect. But it is not surprising that such actions, when they are pushed chiefly by his perception of himself as victim, when they are guided by his conception of external "blame," may often be more retaliative than responsible. It would not be surprising that as the individual is held to be "blameless," his sense of personal responsibility and obligation will diminish and with it his sense of himself as actor, effector, owner of himself, shaper (even in small part) of his fate. On the other hand, it should not be surprising either that even when radical social changes are effected and stabilized, there will remain many individual persons who will still need help to know what is available to them, to know how to reach for it, and then to find how best to manage themselves in the on-going adaptations that even a utopian society will require.[3]

In the broad ground between these polar concepts of society-as-sick and personality-as-sick, some of us have been trying to find some broad-gauge theoretical footing and, at the same time, some precision of focus for our treatment perspectives and actions. Those who work with individuals and small groups (families or groups formed around common problems) are increasingly concerned to find the linkages between each man as personality and that segment of "society" or environment of which he feels himself to be a part. Increasingly there is awareness of the connections between a man's sense of his identity and worth and the recognition given him by those he cares about in his society. Increasingly there is conviction that personality develops on the nurture that social interaction provides and that it is both steadied and powered by those social transactions that yield a sense of gratification and confidence. Increasingly, too, the goal of "cure" of personality problems, whether intra- or inter-personal, is being relinquished just as it is in many problems in physical medicine. Taking its place is the more realistic goal of such increased ability and flexibility in coping, such increased gratifications and rewards in problem-solving as will make it possible for the person to carry his inevitably problematic social tasks with some modicum of competence and some margin of pleasure.

The concept of social roles provides a clear, firm perspective for viewing man in his dual nature—as both creature and creator of his society. It provides a major linkage between his always unique personality and the self-other twosome or the massive society with which he continuously interacts. It links man's needs to their social fulfillment, links his personality to its social expression, his hunger for love and recognition to the nurture from the people and circumstances of his everyday living environment. Thus it is a concept that may serve as a useful kind of framework within which a helper views a person in trouble and which holds direction and focus for what might be the most available and manageable form of help. If the carrying of one's social roles with gratification and competence is affirmed as important by the helper, it will inevitably be caught as "belief" and taken in by the helped. It will influence the client's or patient's expectations of self-and-other, of personal rights and responsibilities, of anticipated outcomes, and his feelingful reactions to all of these.

Social role, then, offers a framework both for professional *viewing* and for *doing*. Like other concepts that govern help-giving help-using processes, it is based on certain beliefs, values, and assumptions. Like other concepts, it sensitizes the observer to particular aspects of persons involved in their problems, illuminating some in bold relief and leaving others in shadow. No claim can be made for it (or any other theoretical perspective) that it is the one and true and only perspective. My claim is simply that it is a useful and useable one.

Its usefulness in social work is supported by studies in recent years that point chiefly not to what people's problems in living "are" (by objective judgments) but to what the problem-sufferers *feel* and *perceive* them to be. (As any helper knows, where the person feels and sees his problem to be is where his motivation is.)

Most people who bring their problems in personal and social functioning to social work rather than to psychiatry see those problems as lying in large part outside themselves.[4] When a person goes to a psychiatrist, he says in effect, "*I* am the problem" or "I carry a problem—like a sickness—*within myself*" or "*I* feel and I act in ways that destroy me." He undertakes the role of a patient. The person who chooses to go to a social agency (or whose choice is made for him) tends to place the difficulty in some transactions *between* himself and other persons or himself and circumstances. "I am having a problem *with*—(some other person—"my husband is impossible," "my child is incorrigible," "my teachers are unfair"). Or he complains of problems in transactions with some person-situational tasks ("school is boring," "I don't have enough money to manage," "I hate my job and my job hates me.") In brief, most people place and define their problems in terms of current transactions between themselves and others *in specific social roles*. Some, less insightful, place them totally in the other, seeing themselves only as "acted upon" victims. The problem, they feel, lies not in themselves but in their "others," not in the forces in themselves but in the forces called into play when two or more personalities act in some role interchange.

Their diagnosis may be correct in some instances, incorrect in others. But even if it is incorrect, the action of the professional helper must be guided by this practice-tested fact: people are motivated to work on their problems only in the terms in which they see, feel, and define them. If they see the problem as their marriage relationship and not as themselves, as their child's inborn badness and not in their projections on him, they will not see the point of, nor stay with, the helper whose conceptual stance is that the problem lies in the personal drives and demands they bring to the relationship. The helper might be right. But his rightness will not hold his client for long. Certainly at the entry phase in any helping process—a phase that may in one instance extend over many weeks and in another be completed in one interview—the helper must ally himself with the view and definition of the situation that is his client's. This is how they come together and, for a time, how they will hold together.

Now a second off-shoot of "role" as a viewing and doing perspective emerges. It is this: since no role can be carried alone, the role's "other" must be taken into diagnostic and treatment consideration. The persons and conditions with whom the client is in problematic transaction must be met by the helpers and appropriately influenced. These others must be taken cognizance of and dealt with both as part of the vicious cycle of interaction and for their potential power in its reversal. These others, the role partners or those involved in the problem network, are seen and felt as the butts, the blights, the scapegoats, the provocateurs, the eroders of the client-person's life. But with help they may become his partners, his reciprocators, his supporters, his nurturers.

If this other side of the role transaction see-saw is ignored, the helper will find that he is dealing with a single force in what is a two-force situation. He will have neither knowledge nor control over what may be either a balance-power or an undermining force. Supported within a therapeutic relationship, the individual client may come to feel better. But his social situation may at the same time deteriorate.

I recall a dramatic example of this. A young married woman, mother of a three year old boy, applied to a family agency for help to "save her marriage" to an "inconsiderate," "undependable" husband. Their child was being shunted weekly from father, who had taken up lodging elsewhere, to mother to grandparents. The young woman was taken on for help with her many personal—and fluently articulated—conflicts, about her marriage, about herself as wife, as former sweetheart, as daughter, as child—the threads moved backwards into her personal labyrinth. After a number of interviews she said she felt immeasurably better—less tense, more poised, freer, free enough, indeed, to begin dating other men. All her efforts to "save the marriage" had ceased. All the problems ordinarily talked out or fought out between husband and wife were spilled out to the social worker. The husband? He remained an unknown. The child? Since his mother had become a girl-on-the-make again, he and his fate lay somewhere outside the periphery of concern. One person was, for the moment, happy in her easily achieved separation from a problematic situation. Two persons, husband and child, were—happy? unhappy? in limbo? Nobody knew.

In this instance neither husband nor child interfered with the wife and mother's separation decision. But—and now an ethical question enters in—should they have been taken account of by an agent of society, a social worker? Should the other side of the role contract involved in marriage and motherhood have been looked at, weighed, and influenced? The pros and cons of this issue cannot be argued here. The point here is simply that one individual's sense of well-being does not necessarily result in the well-being of those others who are tied by bonds of love and social contract to the one, and that unless the helper establishes some working connection with the others involved in the problem under work, he has no basis for either assessing or influencing their powers for good or evil. Perhaps the question of values—whether individual or family welfare is paramount in a given instance—is peculiarly the gadfly of social work. It cannot be ignored by any helper, however. Change in one person in a role network will affect the whole network. The effect will not necessarily be in the desirable direction unless both (or all) reciprocators are at least taken account of within the sphere of professional influence. And the "desirable direction" is a value-judgement that the helper holds, consciously or not. Subtly, insidiously, or (preferably) openly recognized and honestly shared, these values and beliefs of the helper will color and shape those of his client.

Another major focus that role-sights provide is upon the here and now present-day actions and forces that shape people's feelings and behavior. People suffer from their present problems more than from their past memories, said the psychoanalyst Franz Alexander. As we all know, when life today goes well for us our past memories of mistakes and hurts bother us very little. When life goes badly, on the other hand, the sleeping dogs of the past are roused, and often a "cause" in the past is sought and found and mourned. Sometimes this is appropriate, often useful. But too often it may serve as an escape from present-day coping and responsibility. "Cause" becomes excuse. The focus upon what is happening in today's problematic relationships and behavior and by what various means it may be worked at ("worked at," different from "cured"!) does not allow for the relinquishment of this day's responsibilities, this day's necessities. (Always to be excepted, of course, are those persons whose ego disorganization or failure makes their temporary retreat a necessity.)

The anguished—and often releasing—examination of times past, of what I should have done, of what others should have done to and for me, has its particular therapeutic purposes. But it is not enough. Nor is wistful or blind hope in the day ahead, or faith in the "stroke of luck," or "growing out of" some problem. The past flows into the present, and in a moment the future is present. The present is the only point in time and place where we can perceive, know, feel, understand, and interpret our past. ("We see our past," said Santayana, "only through the lenses of the present.") The past can be re-experienced. But it can be reworked, reformed only within the perspectives and transactions of this day, the present. As for the future, the old saw states it; today is tomorrow's yesterday. Today's experience of self-and-other is internalized as tomorrow's scar or boost to the personality. So this moment in time and space and action must be grasped, held, probed, and worked for its life enhancement. Within our emotionally significant roles lie the blights or the blessings of life experience.

For the person whose today's life situations feel crucial, the circumstances and interpersonal relationships that are upsetting today and in the too-near tomorrow simply will not wait or stand still. The person in trouble must cope now, at once, continuously. Freud once said that psychoanalysis was an excellent therapy for those whose ego was strong. He might have added, "and for those whose life situation is in relatively good balance" so that their energies do not have to be poured continuously into trying to find footing in a precarious life situation and so that some gratifications might cushion their discomfort and stress. For when the realistic circumstances of daily life, especially interpersonal relationships, give constant provocation to anger or guilt or anxiousness, then the here-and-now becomes "cause" in itself. As a locus for treatment attention it can scarcely be put aside.

There are, moreover, many people who need help with their day-by-day functioning because they are actually beset by one dilemma or catastrophe after the other. Their problems proliferate. It is sometimes hard to guage diagnostically which came first, the crisis-prone personality or a malevolent fate. One knows that some of their problems are created and some exacerbated by ego deficits or depletions and that these may be the end results of the onslaught of social trauma. But at the point of entry by the helper, at the point of intervention that is calculated to cut into the vicious circle, the "problem of the day" in its heart-felt, spirit-eroding, action-driven aspect becomes the problem to be worked.

Many persons known to social workers have never experienced self-awareness or the introspection that is basic if one is to know oneself as actor. Still others are so characteristically impulse-ridden, so present-oriented that they are able to perceive and comprehend only what is plain and clear in the hum-drum "he did and then I said," "she said and then I thought," "I felt like, and then she said" of today's or last night's interplay. There are, further, those for whom belief in talk, or even in the trustworthiness of the helper, is all but absent. For all of these—and their name is legion—one must seek and find the practical, tangible, action-oriented help-ways that focus on the problems that are sufficient unto the day. Role considerations may provide this perspective.

Client as well as his helper will be affected by viewing himself within the framework of today's roles. The idea that emotionally freighted encounters between persons and between them and their social circumstances may resonate deeply into the personality has a consequence. It is that the person is in continuous process, not just of "having been" and now "being," but of "becoming." He is becoming, pushed, pulled, shaped, turned-over, steadied, bulwarked, or stripped down; he masks and defends or retreats, he detours or drives forward—all in his continuous effort to cope and adapt. Moreover, it suggests that "becoming" is motored not only by drives derived from the past but also by potent forces in the here and now. In this perspective the here and now becomes the location and time staked out for exploration between client and helper, for being mined in depth. (Focus means narrowing of sights, but it thereby allows for detailed and depth insights.) Moreover, the here and now becomes the field of action for experimenting with changed circumstances and behaviors. What the persons involved in role difficulties do, say, feel, believe, want *now;* and what the consequences of their actions are for themselves and for the other(s) with whom they struggle; and what, then, they want different or better for tomorrow; and how this might come into being—all this shuttling of feeling, impulse, action, thought that weaves to and fro and about the several persons tied by role bonds—these become the subjects for the explorations, ruminations, emotional outpourings, and planned actions called "treatment." Treatment is the effort to change the directions and qualities of the powers that inhere in person-to-person, person-to-task transactions. And these are in continuous communication with the inner man.

This savoring of the emotionally significant details of daily living is too generally missing from most of our lives. Most days for most people arrive and vanish unheeded, noted and felt in a vague subliminal way as tiring, pleasant, boring, interesting, irritating, numbing, or nice enough as days go. For most people daily role tasks are dispatched with a kind of automatic efficiency or a grudging make-do. Overall there lies some unspoken wish that something "big" might happen, something that will thrust up the dead-level of daily life into a high peak of excitement, that will lift flat emotion to some pitch of intensity. Catastrophes do this, not just happy events. A great fire or a flood or a storm that paralyzes a city, bringing discomfort or actual tragedy to its victims—these happenings cheer people immensely. They become freshly aware of their luck at having escaped hurt or death, or they are proud to have mastered such danger as they were exposed to. Moreover, they feel bound together, affiliated by a shared calamity. Pervasive in all the shared feeling is the awareness of self alive, pulse going, feelings known, connection to others, and the experience of a break in the grey monotony of daily rounds.

Of course most people do not wish for catastrophes to brighten their lives. Most wish for something to happen that will be "exciting," "unexpected in some wonderful way," something to heighten the level of conscious experience of physical sensation, of joyousness, of social affirmation and affiliation, and of being to some purpose. Perhaps many of the expressive experiences people seek today, different though they are in kind, may have at their core these common needs to feel and experience in the self some greater intensity and actuality. Psychedelic and other drug experiments, group confessionals and conversions (now conducted in psychiatric rather than religious jargons) seem to promise some fresh and heightened awareness of the self. The shift from our traditional ideals of "utility" or "beauty" as primary values to that of "excitement" as the prime value (art, college courses, marriage, jobs, people one meets, must all be "exciting") is a shift in search of the senses and emotions that seem absent in homely every-day living.

The fact is that in most human lives very few "big" things happen. Past the impressionable days of childhood, when all the senses are open and all the feelers out, past the sexually sensitized and emotionally rocketing years of adolescence, there are a few "exciting" things that happen—but only a few: a first job, the first few promotions, falling in love, marrying, becoming a parent, and then for many years the vicarious excitements accompanying milestone events in one's child's life. In between, where can the sense of self as feeling person, as involved, as contented, as person with a purpose, as person loved by and respected by others, as person within his own skin and yet part of the bigger world—where can these tastings and knowledge of the self be savored for their bitter-sweet and occasionally elating pleasures?

In daily life roles, I propose. Not by blotting them out, either through defending ourselves against full consciousness of what we are doing and with whom, or through artificially arranged escape hatches. But only by studied, conscious practice in and attention to savoring (I know no better word to describe the attentive exploration of experiences by the senses) the meanings and essences of the persons and tasks with which we are in emotionally meaningful transaction. Such studied, conscious practice means taking pause, at given moments of experience or in afterthought, to become fully aware of oneself as emotionally involved with the other (person or object), taking in (rather than taking for granted) the sense or "feel" of the other at this time and in this place, asking and answering what he means to me and asks of me and what I mean to him and ask of him, viewing how my actions affect him and his me, what I find that is good and heartening in our interchange, and what might make it better. And so on. It is exercise of our powers of awareness.

In short, if we—any of us—are to find life's small pleasures, they must be found in life's small daily experiences. One of the poignant moments in Thornton Wilder's "Our Town" catches the essence of this need in a small life space. The dead Emily returns to relive one happy day of her life—her fourteenth birthday. In the warm family kitchen her mother bustles about making all the mundane comfortable noises of family life. But Emily, yearning to feel and realize the moment deeply, cries out, "Oh, Mama, just *look* at me one minute, as though you really saw me . . . . Mama, just for a moment we're happy. Let's look at one another." But the clatter of pots and pans and small talk goes on. "Do human beings ever realize life while they live it?" asks Emily.

Why can't people handle their own problems? Why can't they gird up their loins and stand on their own feet and determine that they will cope and prevail?

This is a different question from that which asks, "What *causes* lie at the base of people's problems?" Such causes may be past or recent, deep or shallow, single or multiple; they may lie in the flawed fabric of the personality or in the accident of circumstance. The practitioner's pursuit of "cause" is a quest for an explanation of the presenting problem. "How did it get to be this way?" is the question, and the accompanying assumption is that this "how," if disclosed, may be eradicated or ameliorated so that its off-shoots are no longer potent. That this quest has often led the helper into a veritable mesh-work of cause-effect is well known. That sometimes "the" cause, when it is relatively recent and overt and simplex, may be removed or its effects diluted is also a commonplace. But there remains a "cause" that has not had sufficient attention from professional helpers. It is not "What causes the problem?" Rather it is: "What causes the person's inability to cope with this problem? What is missing in his motivation, in his capacities, in his resources that makes him unable to deal with his problematic situation unaided?"

Let it be said at once that sometimes the problem and the person's inability to cope with it are one and the same. If the problem, say, is caused by disturbances in personality, the incapacity to cope with it is self-explained. Even so, there may be value in asking, "Why can't the person cope?" And the value is this: This question places a spot-light on the person, the problem-sufferer, as he is now, immediately. As he is now, he is a living being, which is to say that he is mentally, emotionally, physically active, at work trying to cope with his intolerable situation. To be sure he may be coping in signally inappropriate and increasingly problematic ways. He may be retreating, denying, projecting, or engaging in all manner of blind, panic-driven actions that only worsen the difficulty. But the important thing is that he is trying, still, to solve his problem or his connection with it. All his life he has been problem-solving. He may have done it badly all his life, and his present dilemma may be the end result. But why has his mode of coping broken down *now*? He may, on the other hand, have been a relatively successful problem-solver. ("Relatively" because which of us is able to master all his problems all the time?) So why, now, must he turn for help?

Very few people come to adulthood without having had all kinds of crises, decisions, hazards, threatening circumstances in their lives. They have dealt with them with whatever personal or outside resources they could muster. Why not now? The purpose of this question, in short, is to prevent the helper from concentrating all his energies on exploring and understanding problem-causes while the person's coping efforts grind to a complete halt. Rather he should

concentrate upon keeping active and alive the person's own responsibility and capacity as actor and doer in his own behalf. Certainly
in many instances the helper will need to change the modes and
directions of the person's problem-solving behavior; certainly he will
need to open new perceptions and perspectives, to correct and even
halt destructive operations; often he will need to provide the lenses
and the tangible material means by which problems may be seen,
felt, and dealt with differently, or even dissolved. But the central idea
is that the helper should connect himself and his service not simply to
a person who has a problem but to a *person who is in pursuit of some
solution.*

Why is a person unable to carry one of his vital roles? Why is he
unable to draw from the role the satisfactions that make it a rewarding one, one that fulfills him? This, I submit, is the initial question
that must be asked and answered when a helper faces his client. It
is the first diagnostic question—though of course it may not be the
last.[5]

Three main kinds of difficulties hamper a person's motivation or
capacity to cope with a vital role. For mnemonic ease they may be
tabbed by the letter D: deficiencies, disturbances or disorders, and
discrepancies. They are not mutually exclusive; all may occur together and each will have differing degrees of potency. They are
sketched roughly in what follows.

First among the deficiencies is that of material means. A person
cannot carry a role adequately if he does not have the things required
for role performance. This is so obvious as to seem silly in the saying,
and it is the most readily understood deficiency. Yet its consequences
to the role carrier are not always recognized. A husband and father
will have some difficulty in maintaining his status as family head
when he is jobless or does not provide money-support. A wife and
mother cannot be a good house-keeper when soap and mops are not
in her purchase power or when dresser drawers or closet space are
missing. A youngster cannot function well as student when there is
literally no table at home where he can set down his books, no corner
where he can study. Sometimes the person himself overlooks these
rudimentary but essential instrumental means to role performance.
All such deficiencies call for provision of tangible material means.

A second deficiency lies in certain personal capacity lacks, temporary or chronic deficits in the person's makeup. They may be of
a physical or mental or emotional sort. Illness, disability, physical

incapacities all will restrict and even thwart role performance. A bed-ridden mother or a chronically sick father cannot carry all the usual role expectations of work or protection or succoring. They may still carry parental authority, still provide affection and guidance, but major changes and shifts will have to occur in their and their children's expectations and in acceptance of their mutual and changed obligations and privileges. The child with limited intellectual capacities cannot carry the role of student with competence; his mentally defective mother may make mountains out of molehill household duties. Personal capacities may, in other instances, be temporarily drained by fatigue or depression or a bombardment of trauma.

Deficiencies of personal capacities call for two major kinds of help to stabilize or enhance role functioning: one, the provision of substitute or rehabilitative means to make up for losses or lacks; two, the helper's recognition of the shift in behavioral and attitude expectations of self and other that might have to be brought about in the role participants themselves.

Deficiency of knowledge or preparation is another blank space in a person's readiness to carry a role. There are times and conditions when people undertake or are thrust into new roles when they simply do not know what is involved in them, what they may realistically expect of themselves or of others. To enter a new and unfamiliar role is to make a kind of "migration." The person who moves from rural south to urban north, from the Puerto Rican sugar plantation to the New York slum, may be frightened, paralyzed, or mobilized into aggression as the case may be, may act "stupid" or "crazy" or withdrawn, chiefly because he does not know what is expected of him and what to anticipate in his new encounters. Not all migrations are from one culture to another. Some are from one role-set to another, and in these migrations some of the same reactions may be observed. The young woman thrust unwittingly and unwillingly into motherhood, the girl and boy who marry without having planned further than the color of the bridesmaid's dresses and the honeymoon, the school dropout who takes a job with considerations only of quick pay, not of his in-put—all these and other new role undertakings may cause a person to founder and fail because of lack of both knowledge and know-how.

Many of these "foreigners" to new roles have lacked adequate role models in parents or peers by which consciously or unconsciously to pattern themselves. Many have not taken or been offered the chance to think over, talk over, rehearse in the mind "what you are supposed to act like, to expect."[6]

Unlike the two first forms of deficiency which are open and evident to the helper (though sometimes not so to the client himself) this deficiency of knowledge and know-how has been less obvious and very little explored. There has been some overriding assumption that one knows what one *wants* to know—that is, if one hasn't caught on to that which he who runs may read, it is because there have been emotional or psychological blinders present and that, therefore, the first diagnostic and helping approach is to lift these scales from the client's eyes. But facts contradict this assumption. It has been found, for example, that pregnant young women, college graduates, who knew all about the "facts of life" and of gestation were grossly ignorant—and therefore in high anxiety—about what their babies and they were supposed to be like and act like in the first days and weeks following child-birth. Intelligent young couples, eager for parenthood, complained in another study that no one had prepared them for the difficulties that follow on bringing the first baby home.[7] Marriage counsellors will attest to the frequent incidence of lack of knowledge or of misinformation among young couples about marriage expectancies—and these young people are both eager and ready to plan a good married life.

The pursuit of the question of why people cannot adequately carry their roles may reveal these knowledge and preparation deficiencies. "What is your idea of what a woman is supposed to do for her husband?" "What do you expect you'll have to act like (dress like, do, etc.) on this job?" "When you say Tim is bad to his little sister, do you think this is different from most three year olds when the mother brings home a new baby?" "What would you advise your mother to do about you if you were in her shoes?" "How do you think I should be able to help you?" (This latter question is based on the expectation that how a client will act and what he will say will heavily depend on his knowledge and valid expectations of his helper.) These are some of the kinds of questions that explore what actual knowledge or realistic grasp the person has of role requirements. Moreover, they open the possibility that he wants and can use information and that he and the helper can anticipate and prepare for more adequate role performance. Incidentally, this may involve some new awareness of the problems being felt by the "other."

"Disturbances" or "disorders" refer to those intrapsychic turmoils, constrictions, or distortions, those emotional-psychological difficulties that make the carrying of relationships and responsibilities in role tasks either impossible or too taxing and ungratifying. Such emotional and intrapersonal disturbances may be acute but transient, or intense but chronic. In either instance one or both role partners may be unable to meet role obligations or gain gratifications from its rewards. Motivations and capacity to carry the role may be temporarily or regularly undermined. But some signal differences between the transient and the chronic disturbance should be noted.

The chronically disturbed person is one who suffers fairly continuous internal conflict, unrealistic anxiety, uncertain control of imperious unconscious drives. The chronically disordered person is one whose impulses run away with him and for which he then finds "reasons" that to him are plausible. The former may be said to be pervaded by neurotic drives, the latter by character defects. (I am acutely aware of the oversimplifications that occur when one tries to put complex phenomena into a nutshell. I am aware, too, of the ambiguities inherent in the psychiatric diagnoses of "neurosis" and "character disorders." These are in-the-rough designations.) In either instance the person behaves less in relation to the actualities of the present situation and more in relation to his inner push or skewed "reading" of the social actuality. Thus he may "know," above the eyebrows, what a given role calls for from him and his partner, but he is unable to carry what he knows into action. Or his very capacity to perceive and comprehend may be clouded by emotions that belong to another time and place but are roused somehow by the new situation.

Personality disturbances or entrenched disorders may indeed be a major cause of inability to cope with sudden stress or a pyramiding of problems. But few persons' capacity or incapacity is *total*, even though we have sometimes acted as if it were. We have tended to write off as totally sick a person diagnosed has having schizophrenia, calling him "a schizophrenic," one who is totally characterized by his mental-emotional disorder. But interestingly, the person diagnosed as having incurable cancer or a long-term deteriorating illness such as multiple sclerosis is not named as whole self by his illness name. Rather, he is said to *have* the sickness, certainly to be *affected* by it in every aspect of his living; *but he is assumed to be more than his sickness*. Some years ago Thomas Mann spoke of this. In an essay on Nietzsche he wrote of the philosopher's last weeks, when he was wracked with paresis, fevered and hallucinating at times, yet at other times lucid enough to speak and write with greatness. "Sickness," said Mann, "is something purely schematic. What is important is *that to which the sickness is joined.*" "That to which the sickness is joined" is the human material with which the nonmedical helper works. "That to which the sickness is joined" calls for attentive testing and assessment. The testing and assessment lies in whether the person's willingness to use help results in some changed capacity and comfort through modifying some necessarily small part of his current life role. As has been suggested before, the clue that personality disturbance is pervasive and overriding is that, despite the person's *wanting* to operate differently and *knowing* how to do so and *having no realistic obstacles* in his way, he cannot take the appropriate action. When this proves to be so, we can know that he is victim of the unconscious powers within him.

When this is the case he needs intensive psychotherapeutic help, whether from psychiatry or from especially skilled therapists in other professions of which social work is one. For many reasons—lack of money and paucity of qualified personnel are among them—such help is often not available. But more than this, many persons who may be judged to need such help are not necessarily able to use it productively. For them, then, the best help may be to enable them—by provision of supports from the helper, from others in their role networks, from palliative drugs, money, and resource aids—to function at least marginally in relation to the requirements of daily life roles.

Each of us has his Achilles heel. Disturbances or disorders of motivation and capacity to deal with daily problems may arise in even the best-balanced of persons in response to overwhelming stress. For any one of us there may be some situational crisis, some shocking blow to our usual but emotionally invested life circumstances that may temporarily paralyze us. "Ego strength," "maturity," "problem-solving capacity"—all these ideal norms against which we judge a person's coping ability cannot be assessed except by viewing a person's behavior in the context of the actual situation in which he is involved. A death in the family, a life- or status-threatening physical disablement, a failure in job or school or marriage, some social "disgrace"—these and other trauma and insults to the personality may cause breakdown in or impairment of usual role relationships and tasks. When such breakdowns feed into an already shaken equilibrium, a vicious cycle may be set in motion. Recently, both in psychiatric and social work practice and writing, considerable attention has been given to these crisis events and their outcomes. A considerable literature currently deals with the "first aid" treatment of personality-shaking crises. The aim is to avoid entrenchment of the maladaptations that may follow on traumatic experience. The method often includes, along with the release and reconsideration of emotional reactions, emotional work-over, the work-over of the knowledge and behaviors that new role relationships and tasks require.[8]

Perhaps the least examined and explored explanation for a person's impaired problem-solving lies in the discrepancies that may be found within vital roles themselves. Such discrepancies, like deficiencies, are of several kinds. They may occur between several roles carried by one person; they may occur between the differing (and emotionally charged) expectations of self and other that role partners hold; they may occur between demands of a role and the equally imperious demands of personal drives and wishes; or they may occur because of ambiguously or contradictorily defined role norms themselves. If one or more such discrepancies exist and are not recognized as such either by the role carrier or the person to whom he looks for help, the problem may be attributed to other causes or the role carrier himself may be aware only of pervasive tension and malaise, of being pulled apart by uncertainties, indecisions, inevitable ambivalences. So each of these discrepancies deserve a brief identification.

Discrepancy between several valued roles: In our present day culture the classic example of this conflict, which at its least produces irritability and at its worst produces chronic anxiousness, is that of working mother. For the woman who works because she must, because her income is necessary to meet actual family need or family desires, there may be tensions and stress, but she is bulwarked by her sense of righteousness, even sacrifice. For the woman who works of her own free will, because she wants to, there ensue all the usual double burdens of home-and-children plus job responsibilities, to which are added the guilts engendered by her society, which reiterates that her place is "in the home." Indeed, the more she enjoys her job the more likely she is to feel guilty, to snatch avidly at such studies that show, for example, that there is no significant association between children's delinquency and mother's working. But there are serious pull-aparts too—when her child's illness weighs heavily upon her, when she doubts her housekeeper's capacity, and so on. Men too face these dual role problems. The pull between driving for job achievement and being a good husband and father is a frequent strain. The opposing pulls of loyalty to wife and loyalty to mother may be another, or of companionship with wife versus comraderie with bachelorhood friends. Another example: in a working situation it is not uncommon for one of a pair of colleagues or work-mates to be promoted above the other. Now both will feel the discrepancies between equality friendship status and unequal hierarchal status, and conflict or distancing or considerable shuffling about for role-footing may occur with resultant relationship strains unless the discrepancy is faced up to and accepted with its inevitable awkwardness.

Discrepancies between the anticipations and expectations of self-and-other in any role may be a major cause of conflict, whether between partners in marriage, between parents and their small children or parents and their adult children, between students and their teachers, between employers and employees.

The practice experience of caseworkers abounds in examples of these misapprehensions or misconceptions on the part of one or both role partners, of gaping and heretofore unexplored hiatuses between what one thinks he or the other "is supposed to be or act like." During a considerable experience of work with marital problems I was repeatedly aware of how few couples had, during courtship or afterwards, considered together what marriage would ask of each and give them. Buoyant and avid with love or infatuation or pulled inexorably forward by all the social approvals and rites that accompany the passage from courtship to marriage, many couples enter marriage all but ignorant of what their partners'—or even their own —conceptions of the roles of spouse involve. Prepared for marriage only by their parental role models, which they unconsciously imitate (or consciously reject, or both at once), oblivious to the shift of their own roles from "sweethearts" or "steadies" to husband-and-wife, they were often surprised or hurt or angered by the differences of expectation and gratification they harbored and had not shared. "He thinks I should stay home all the time." "She thinks she's the boss." "She's always running to her mother for advice, and *I'm* her husband." "He believes I don't have to know what he does with his pay check, but I say it's my business too." And so on.

Parents in trouble with their children often exhibit wide-of-the-norm expectations that may be the result not just of their own needs but also of the discrepancy between their guiding ideas and the realistic expectation. The mother who believes that her child should be toilet-trained and "accident" free by age two (because her neighbor's or her sister's child was) may grow anxious and tense at what she considers her retarded or recalcitrant little one. The father of the adolescent girl who, out of his own adolescent exploits, anticipates that every boy friend has sexual designs on his daughter, is likely to be in wrangling tyrannical conflict with his at first bewildered and then rebellious child. "Children are supposed to take care of parents in their old age," says a dutiful daughter who urges her frail old mother to come to live with her (and sleep on the couch in the sun parlor), while her mother resists with, "I love my children—but God forbid I should have to ask them for help!"

"What do you want? What do you expect? What do you know or understand of what is usual, realistic, possible in this kind of role and its relationship?" These are the beginning inquiries of people in trouble that open discrepant expectations between role partners to plain view and on-going consideration.

It may be argued that differing perceptions and expectations of role performance and relationships rise out of the personality needs each person brings to each role he undertakes. There can be no question but that a strong and unconscious selective process goes on in each one of us all the time, filtering out and taking in what we hear, see, come to believe, to value, to invest in. So what we believe is right or wrong, good or bad, acceptable or intolerable, expectable or unforseen is, of course, that which is compatible with our personality bent and makeup. Nevertheless, we all have had the experience of changes in how we see things and how we interpret them simply by the acquisition of greater knowledge and understanding of them. What we may once have considered a "sin" may, for instance, come to be seen by us as a "sickness" because we have been exposed to knowledge that cast new light upon it. What we may once have branded "wrong" or "intolerable" may come to seem understandable or "acceptable." Differences between ourselves and others have given way to truces or even strong changes of sentiment, largely through examining the often unreasoned sources of those differences.

In brief, many self-other expectations, while emotionally charged, are not necessarily fixed. They are often subject to the cool light of reason and to cognitive input and consideration and then to compromises on both sides. True, the personality brought to any given role determines in considerable part how the role will be perceived, defined, and coped with. But it seems also to be true that enlightening knowledge coupled with experiences of new coping behavior, when it is felt as successful, gives birth to beliefs and sentiments and assumptions about self-and-others or self-and-situation. This is one way that personal change occurs.

One must always add, of course, that the motivation, the willingness to listen to and receive the "other," to learn, and to attempt new behaviors is basic to such changes. It suggests further that the possibly discrepant assumptions of role partners (or those held by one of them) ought to be the stuff of early exploration when people cannot seem to solve their inter-personal problems. The person who needs help with such problems, before he begins to plumb his depths, needs to know first his own conscious wishes and beliefs about his relationship behaviors and to consider their consequences for him and for the partnership in which he is involved. His and his partner's conscious and discrepant expectations and their desired ends are the most readily accessible material for work-over.

As has been said earlier, such work-over will clearly reveal whether, indeed, personality needs and drives are discrepant with role requirements. This is a third sort of discrepancy that explains a person's inability to solve his difficulties in carrying some vital role. The child-wife who becomes a mother may suffer between her infant's demands of her (along with those of her pediatrician, her husband, her mother-in-law, her friends and neighbors) and her need and desire to be something of a baby herself, cared for and catered to. The unwed mother whose decision to keep her baby is based upon her need, often innocently expressed, to "have somebody love me"; the husband who, on becoming a father, finds himself locked in a kind of sibling rivalry with his child; the person seeking for friends and nurturing relationships who repeatedly alienates people by his acid attitudes—all these exemplify the kinds of discrepancy that may occur between what one *is* and what one is expected or even required to do.

For many people their most valued roles are "second nature." That is they "fit" with personality needs; they are syntonic to the personality. For others, one or more of their vital roles, with their requirements and even their rewards, may be "wanted" consciously but may be alien to the personality, dystonic. Such roles do not feel comfortable or true. They are "put on," carried precariously. They consume excess energy, they lack spontaneity, they often feel burdensome beyond tolerence. Then they are fought openly in transactions with the role partners, or rigidified and ritualized so that the personality is defended against them, or relinquished in whole or in significant part. Help to persons whose inability to solve their role problem lies in a discrepancy between characteristic and entrenched personality needs and role needs is neither easily provided nor taken. As has been said earlier, such help is within the province of the experienced and highly skilled therapist when the person is able and willing to undertake facing his inmost self as "cause."

The last of the discrepancies that block people's problem-solving efforts are those that may occur because of the vague and ambiguous definition and expectations of certain roles. Role ambiguity has been given a separate essay of its own.

Past the perspectives on the nature and potentials of everyday lives that role concepts provide for the professional helper, past its provision of a viewing lens for assessing people with problems of relationship or task-involvement, does it have any specific "treatment" usefulness? That is, does it offer or suggest different ways by which a helper might influence his client and/or the configuration of person-with-problem in pursuit of a solution? Granting that when the client comes to share his helper's viewpoint he is already influenced thereby in his perception and definition of his problem and that, therefore, his sense of it will be affected, are there any further active ingredients within the concept of role that shape or change the actions of the helper?

The basic methods (sometimes called "techniques") of influencing human behavior are common to all helping processes. They have grown out of solid, repeated observations of what actions in person-to-person or person-to-group transactions seem to spark and sustain human motivation, to nurture and expand human potentials, either to block people or to release them, and make them either anxious or free. These ways of relating to and influencing people will be variously played out depending upon what an individual case calls for and upon the style and skill and special function of the helper. But except for the actual provision of tangible goods or services which social work frequently offers, these helping techniques are all forms of communication that have their roots in the dynamics of spontaneous or learned change. They consist, in the main, of attitudes and verbal communications that seek to reach into the help-needing person's feelings and thought process. They are generally held to include the helper's demonstrated empathy and caring for his client; his respectfulness; his affirmation of the client's social worth; the inquiries by which he and his client establish the problem; receptivity and attentiveness; clarifications and explanation; reflective or challenging comments for consideration; counsel and advice when called for; confrontation and comments that stimulate self-and-situation exploration and interpretation; planning and rehearsal of actions to be taken—and so forth. These ways of influence by communication will not, as far as I can see, be affected by whether or not one works within a role framework.

But there are other aspects of the helping process and of the content and substance of help-giving that are signally affected by ideas inherent in role.

First among these is the nature of the working relationship itself. As soon as the helper is aware that both "client" and "helper" are roles with certain generally expectable norms of rights and responsibilities and actions and sentiments, so soon he realizes that for many reasons outside the immediate situation the applicant for help may have misconceptions and misapprehensions about what he and his helper are to be together and do together. Then, at once, he must give his attention to clarifications and agreements between himself and the applicant about their separate and joint purposes and operations. He must motivate the applicant for help to want to be his client —that is, to be one who chooses to employ his services.[9] Those mutual agreements about the valid expectations of each and other form a beginning "contract" for a working relationship.

That relationship will have to be taken stock of now and again, because no relationship is "established" in a static once-and-for-all sense. All relationships, if they are alive, require work-over at one time or another. When mutually understood and agreed upon expectations are part of a beginning relationship, however, they not only constitute a kind of working contract, a reference point of stability, but they tend to hold relationship within its valid and realistic bounds. Transference and counter-transference reactions may occur with less frequency and certainly with less provocation when helper-client roles and role tasks are clarified or subject to reclarification. So the concept of role as it applies to applicant, client, and helper (or patient and helper) will shape and color the beginning and on-going relationship whether it is chiefly a socializing or chiefly a therapeutic one.

Another way in which role immediately affects the helping mode becomes obvious in consideration of problems of interpersonal relationships. Family diagnosis, family treatment, "conjoint therapy," family-group interviews—all these newly emerging efforts attempt to treat inter-personal problems within the inter-personal system rather than with isolated units, the individuals in that system. The theories that underlie these practices are as yet an uneasy amalgam and are often given minimal heed. But one fact seems clear: whether "small group theory" or "communication theory" or "systems theory" or "learning theory" is the rationale, place must be found for the concepts embraced by "role" if treatment is of the interpersonal situation and is to simultaneously involve the two or more persons in transaction. If both partners in a marital conflict are to be involved in its solution, whether together or singly, they and their helper must come to some clarity and definitions and reflective examinations of what the role of each is supposed by each to be, what is wanted that is missing, what is done to get it, how that action affects the feelings and responses of each, and so on. If a parent-child problem is viewed as a three-sided (or more complex) interchange, then the constant stuff of reference and examination and talk must be the ideas and counter-ideas, feelings and counter-feelings, expectations and counter-expectations invested in the transactional roles. Without the focal center that role and its dynamic contents provide, neither the helper nor the participants in the tangled role web-work will be clear about rights or obligations or resolutions.

Now yet another way in which role affects the helper's action presents itself. Role offers a clear and understandable and readily grasped *focus*. As any caseworker will attest—particularly he who works with so-called multiproblem and socially- or physically-disorganized families or persons—focus is no small feat. Problems generate problems, and the client and then caseworker may be flooded with their prolificacy, and find themselves now attending to this, next attending to that, all fingers in the dike, so to speak, and new leaks springing up all about. The mental mechanism of focus, of selective and concentrated attention, is an essential part of good ego functioning. Those whose inner or outer experience has continuously pulled them apart and has kept them running to stay where they are have not developed this capacity. They leap from one brink of anxiety to another, touch ground and go. But even he who is a competent problem-solver may be swamped with too many stimuli and dimensions at one time. This is why the idea of deliberate focus, a kind of partialization of the whole, has value.

Role provides focus at the same time that it includes the person's feeling, thinking, acting, and interchange behaviors. The focus provided by role is upon some here and now problem the person is experiencing in some transaction between himself and one or more others or between himself and essential activities. It says, "Here, within some vital relationship, is the feeling, knowing, acting, *you* in combat or in futile feinting with an 'other' (or hostile circumstances). And it is here that, with help, you may want to regain stability (or achieve a better level of functioning) and earn some greater satisfactions from your efforts." It says, further, by implication, "Perhaps what you learn here—about how your expectations affect your feelings and your feelings your actions and your actions your thoughts and feelings, and about how you must stop to 'read' the other person or to figure out what the situation calls for before you leap, and so on—these learnings, when they are reinforced by some small successes, can be carried over to other roles and aspects in your life." In brief: focus upon one problematic area of a person's social functioning not only partializes the task so that the ego does not need to run from it or defend against it, but it also provides a repeated exercise of selective attention which is basic to competent coping.

There is nothing in the idea of focus that prevents a helper from shifting his locus of attention from one to another role problem if this seems called for. Nor is there anything but the helper's rigidity that would rule out considerations of the past as it bears on today's problems. And certainly considerations of the near future are the very essence of stretching forward.

When "treatment" is aimed at coping with some role problems more effectively and satisfyingly, then the goals to be achieved tend, on the part of both client and helper, to become more realistic and more readily arrived at. The illusion of "cure" or of some fixed state of adjustment tends to dissolve because nothing affirms the reality that life is a necessarily continuous problem-solving process more than attention to the daily interchanges between people and their circumstances. The treatment goal, then, will be to restore or reinforce or reform the client's role-carrying capacities and motivations. The extent to which such modifications will successfully occur will depend upon the personalities of the clients, the nature of their problems, the reasons for their inability to cope unaided, the resources open to them, and so forth. Goal, then, becomes a contracting or expanding idea, subject to the on-going assessments that can be made only as client and helper work together. Goal achievement is held within modest and realistic bounds for client and helper, both, when it is viewed as *relative* to all the particular factors in the particular case, and when it is gauged by the client's demonstrated increase of competence and of felt gratification in his daily coping with his erstwhile problematic-others or problematic-tasks.

The client as person is always affected by this role-work. When his role behavior changes, it is because he has been motivated and enabled to act differently. When it is rewarded, it is he, as personality, that experiences the sense of competence or pleasure. True, all his *needs* will not have been met. Needs are life-long. But his problems in meeting his needs in one life area will have been modified or lessened. From this flows new energy to grapple further and new hope for what lies ahead.

A role, as has been said, is "where the action is." Each day, under the searchlight of their helpers' inquiries or comments, the role participants can see and hear and feel and know themselves as actors. They are doing well or badly; they are being victimized by their interactions or are themselves the injurers. They are in a living situation which is now, perhaps for the first time, under attention and scrutiny. It is, provided they are so moved, subject to try-outs of new strategies —some different response to a familiar stimulus, some often fumbling but earnest efforts to do and say something calculated to break their usual and ungratifying cycle of give-take. When these try-outs bring some wanted results, they are in themselves rewards. Even when they fall flat, when they are brought back to the helper as report or accusation, the *effort* is rewarded by the helper's affirmation of the client's investment. What is most important is that both client and helper are talking about what is real, here and now, and subject to further conscious and calculated change efforts.

Action and its resonant effects upon feelings and attitudes has already been touched upon. One further comment here in the context of helping people to change themselves and/or their circumstances: We have clung to the notion that feeling changes must *precede* behavioral change. There is growing evidence that a reverse movement may also occur, that consciously undertaken behavioral changes, when they bring satisfying and consistent responses from others (people or objects), may yield a changed sense of self and of affect. When motivation is present, control and management of behavior becomes possible. The underlying personality dynamics may remain untouched, to be sure, but rewarded behavior will yield change in feelings, sentiments, and anticipations.[10] Feelings about oneself and other are not only the cause but also the product and consequence of action and behavior that is seen, heard, felt and reinforced within living present roles.

In the frequent use today of joint interviewing, involving both (or more) role partners, the helper is present at a live play-out of characteristic relationships and transactions. It scarcely needs to be said that this is far more "real" than *ex post facto* accounts by either role partner. It is first-hand action. (This is also what makes it difficult —the helper is at the scene of the action, no longer the receptive viewer of a motion picture or listener to a tape recorder!) Again, its treatment value lies in the possibility that it can be intervened with on the spot, in the play-out, as it were. Intervention by the helper may be to call attention to what is occurring in the transaction, to raise again (and again) the question of whether this mode of relating yields the participants what they want, to suggest thinking together about alternate behaviors, and so on. "I and thou," or more commonly "me and you," come to know themselves most vividly as they come to observe themselves in their present behavior and the response it calls forth in others.

The question of whether problems in role interplay are always best dealt with in groups of two or more persons, or whether intensive interviews with one member at a time may often be indicated, can and has been argued several ways. What is important is that when self as role partner is the central consideration, the self as actor cannot be lost sight of. What I do, what I say, how I react, how I feel—these are subjects not just to be nursed and fondled. They require that the doer, sayer, reactor, feeler be helped to perceive himself as an actor, as one who by his behavior calls forth responsive behaviors or reactions in other people and things. He must come to feel himself *not simply as pawn but as power.* What he does has consequences. And this is never better examined or seen than in his current role transactions.

The realness of present-moment or present-day interchanges is of particular use for those adults who have had little experience with introspection. Many people's lives have not afforded them the luxury of combing over their feelings and thoughts as a prelude to action. Typically their action is driven by unrecognized impulse. Words carry small symbolic freightage for them, and they seem to know themselves, their feelings, their thoughts and reactions more as epilogue than as prologue to their acts. For them the concentration on some limited area of active transaction between themselves and others is clamorous, open, tangibly real. Those helpers whose special concern today is with the people called "culturally deprived" (deprived of the cultivation and integration of their thought and feeling processes) would do well to recognize the place of action in the lives of these people.

One further way in which role contributes to the substance of treatment: it maintains and enhances the necessary links and interdependencies between the client and his natural sources of love, of recognition, and gratification. No helper—social worker, psychoanalyst, clergyman, teacher—can undertake to be an on-going part of a help-needer's life for long. His role imposes limits of time and relationship. Yet sometimes this is what the person being helped yearns for: that this person, who understands and forgives him beyond all others, who gives much and asks little, should remain his "alter," his life-staff. And sometimes, too, pulled in by the natural gratification of being needed and responded to, the helper himself may lose his view of the fact that the client cannot live off the bread of a prolonged therapeutic relationship but must be prepared for chewing and digesting the tougher crusts of ordinary relationships. That helper-persons should be present and available to vulnerable or stress-ridden people at any and recurrent points of crisis or needfulness goes without saying. But some conception and criterion of termination should thread through any artificially created helping situation.

All of us must find among the people who make up our work-friendship-family life the major sources of our nurture by love and of our undergirding by social affirmation. A helper can lead a person to use himself more effectively with such people so as to get more out of his relationships to them. More, a helper can lead him to expand the too-narrow boundaries of the small society he knows or to break out of its fetters, if need be, towards new or more rewarding relationships. But the helper can substitute for these natural sources of nurturance only in order to prepare him for those others.

When difficulty in role functioning is taken as the problem-to-be-worked, the therapeutic problems of excessive dependency upon the helper, of unreadiness to end the helping relationship, of the transfer of gratification-seeking from natural sources to the person of the helper are minimized. They are minimized simply because role problems always include at least one "other," and that other must be a partner in the problem-solving, though he need not always be an "equal partner." Always in the center of work is the client in relation to his employer or his workmates or his wife or his children. It is for his "interpersonal competence" that he labors.

An interesting by-product occurs when a person works on himself-in-relation-to-others. Under the helper's guidance he will not only be encouraged to speak of himself and his own feelings and actions but also to imagine, if he can, how he feels to the "other," how the other might see and interpret what he does, and so forth. He will, in brief, be encouraged now and again to step into the shoes of his role reciprocator, to imagine how the situation feels or is perceived by the other. There is a very telling diagnostic clue that this reveals, the clue to whether the person has any capacity for what Freud called "einfuhlung," literally "in-feeling," to another. Empathy is the name we give it. Empathy bespeaks, among other things, some flexibility of personality, some capacity to leave one's own skin and role and to momentarily enter the skin and take on the role of another. The person who cannot imagine what the other feels, or who stonily attributes to him only his own projections, is one for whom the change prognosis is poor. He who, on the other hand, has the ability (combined with the willingness) to take a look at himself from the other fellow's stance, or to try to see how the other might feel or think, or to play with ideas of what he would do were he in the other's place—that person is a good prospect for behavior modification. In working on his role relationships, his capacity for empathy, the basic quality for understanding and relating to other people, will have been exercised and perhaps even expanded.

Nowhere within the thought-action perspectives that social role provides is there prescription for imposing the helper's norms upon the helped, nor for imprisoning the helped person in the mores and standards, middle-class or other, of the helper. Nothing in the role concept bespeaks rigidity or authoritarianism. Rather, the basic diagnostic and treatment perspectives take into account the fact that every human being, certainly by adulthood, has been socialized by his particular society. From those persons who have had feelingful and powerful meaning for him he has absorbed beliefs, concepts, patterned behaviors that shape and guide his adaptational behavior and the feelings that accompany it. Everybody has assumptions about what he is supposed to do and be in certain roles and what he can expect to get from them. Everybody has positive or negative feelings and sentiments that infuse these beliefs, often both, ambivalently. Everybody may find himself at one time or another involved in some role for which he has no adequate preparation, no necessary resources of material means or competence, or to which he and his role partner bring discrepant expectations. Recognizing these phenomena, the helper moves not to say: "But this is the way you *should* act." "This is what a wife *ought* to be." "Let me fit you into my little role-box." Not at all. Rather, he says: "Tell me what *your* ideas are of what *you* (and he) should be doing and saying, of what *you* want out of this relationship, of what *you* feel and expect to get. Why, as *you* see it, are you not getting the satisfactions you want? What can you (each and both) do differently to get what you're after? Is what you want actually achievable? Is it possible within what the community around you permits or provides for? If it is not permitted, what will it get you and cost you; what are the consequences likely to be for you if you continue to flaunt law or established custom?" (Each man is still free, in the final analysis, to choose to "take a chance" with the outcomes of his behavior or to choose self-destruction, when he must; but he cannot be said to be "free" or "self-determining" unless his actions follow on conscious consideration of the alternatives open to him, both action alternatives and their foreseeable outcomes.) "If what you want is socially acceptable but not available to you, how can you act to get it?" And so forth.

The helper will operate continuously to draw out the client's own conceptions of what he wants in his role(s) and what he will be obliged to put in to gain what he desires, to examine the incongruities between his and his role partner's expectations, the inconsistencies between his verbalized aims and his actions, and so on. The client will be led to look at what is realistically possible and what can be made possible, what he values and what compromises he may have to make, what different actions he may have to take to come close to his own goals. The *client's* role affects and ideas are brought to the forefront, not the helper's; the demands and requirements lie in his reality, in his transactions with people and tasks, not in some prestructured imposition by his helper. The helper holds up a mirror to his client's examination, now reflecting the client, his wishes and actions, now reflecting the realistic social scene with its demands and its rewards.

Most people want the same kinds of rewards. Their differences do not lie in conceptions of what they would like themselves and their children to have or to be. They lie more in the hope and opportunity and the capacities available to win those common human "goods." Class differences, ethnic differences, personality differences will determine the specific forms these human strivings will take. But on the whole we are, as Harry Stack Sullivan once said, "all much more human than otherwise"; and the good things we all want are fundamentally the same: love, a small place in the social sun, physical and economic security, and the open opportunity to reach beyond ourselves. When he understands this, the helper sets about, together with his client, to search out whether any one or all of these are present or possible in any part of his daily life roles.

What makes a person willing and able to make such changes in his behavior? What makes him open to "changes of heart" and beliefs and thence of action? When one looks at the helping process closely one sees that in its most meaningful forms it contains the same dynamics, in varying degree, as have been postulated as the moving powers in adulthood.

To be cared about and to be cared *for*, to be believed in, received with compassion, attended to with concern—these are akin to being loved. Some persons, it is true, no longer have the capacity to receive love; they cannot trust another. But for those who once knew love and who can retrieve their trust, the warmth and caring of a helpful relationship is taken in avidly. It offers sustenance and an expanded sense of the self, as all love does; and some part of the helper is drawn into the self in that phenomenon called "identification" which yields both support and spur.

To be recognized as a valued, or potentially valuable member of society, if only because one is struggling to make a go of it, and to have one's efforts affirmed by a person who represents social sanctions—this undergirds a person's sense of self as a socially connected being. When he experiences his helper as a benign arm of his society, when he is given needed aids or provided with additional resources, then what has seemed to be a hostile society begins to seem hospitable to him. When his use of such social opportunities brings him the reward of lessened tension or, further, some increased affirmation of his efforts from his intimates and some increased sense of himself as a doer, he feels some growing sense of having place and part in at least the microcosm of his personal life.

Because professional helpers are usually called upon at times of needfulness when people's own problem-solving efforts have proved inadequate, they often encounter people at points of crisis. Crucial states are turning points. A turning point may be a learning point, when one reaches out for new and better ways by which to cope with one's self and one's problem. Accompanying the warmth and nurture of the helper's relationship and his undergirding support is the work of feeling and thinking through and experimenting with such actions within the problem area as are expected to be more effective and gratifying to the persons involved. If they prove to be so, then they become "learned," taken in by the "actor" as part of himself.

Hope is the fourth ingredient in motivation for change. Hope is implicit in the presence and expected resources of a helper. But it can be felt by him who needs help only if he has experienced some real-feeling basis for believing that something different or better is available to him—for the working if not for the asking. That basis for confidence and hope is most firm when the floor-boards of physical, economic, social, and affectional security are to be counted on.

To realize living while we live it—this is the necessity for each of us. Within our vital roles, working and loving and striving, we need to keep alert to every potential for affectionate giving and getting, for gaining self-esteem and giving affirmation to others, for the exercise and management of self and circumstance that will develop into the necessary sense of being responsibly competent. Such opportunities often lie unheeded and unplumbed in our daily transactions.

This is no plea of a latter-day Candide that we obliterate from our consciousness (and consciences) the hurts and ravages and bitterness that are present in every human life—and excessively present in some. I know that this is not the best of all possible worlds. But it is all we have. And so rather than turning from it in despair into "absurdity," rather than searching for "meaning" and "authenticity" and "realness" in experiences that substitute sensation for self-knowledge, that substitute body-closeness for communion, that substitute head-talk for heart-feeling, rather than assuming that only *past* roles had the power to shape our lives, I plead for stopping to look and to listen deeply for the self-and-other enhancements, self-and-other gratifying powers that might be drawn from and put into this day's love and work roles. This is the primary value, I believe, in the professional helper's exploration and study and working within the content of vital roles in people's everyday lives. Whatever reforms or revolutions may or must be brought about—in civil rights, in economic provision, in the sciences and the arts, in all the expandable opportunities that exist for man to recreate and realize himself—the fact remains that for most human beings life will hold its deepest meaning and relevance in man's age-long use of himself as worker, lover, friend, generator and shaper of new human beings. Let us help him—and ourselves—to savor and to know these work and love tasks for their deepest meaning and their fullest promise.

Notes

1. ADULTHOOD AND PERSONAL CHANGE

[1] There are a few notable exceptions to this generalization. Among them: Robert White's *Lives in Progress*, 2d. ed., (New York: Holt, Rinehart & Winston, 1966) in which three young adults are studied in detail over two time periods. Another is the on-going program of research on middle age, in progress since 1952 in the Committee on Human Development, University of Chicago. See Bernice Neugarten and Associates, *Personality in Middle and Late Life*, (New York: Atherton Press, 1964).

[2] One of the leaders of psychoanalysis, Franz Alexander, M.D., made some of these same observations in his essay "Development of the Fundamental Concepts of Psychoanalysis," in *Dynamic Psychiatry* (University of Chicago Press, 1952). He wrote: "It is only recently that students of personality have become impressed by the fact that personality development does not stop at a certain age, that significant changes take place in all phases of the life-curve, and particularly that the formative experience of early years do not necessarily leave irreversible effects. Many of the adverse influences of early childhood can be corrected by later experiences in life. Indeed, psychoanalytic therapy is based on this view. . . . All psychoanalysts conform implicitly to this view, in that they practice a therapy by which they endeavor to bring changes into personality structure. Yet many psychoanalysts are strangely inconsistent, in that they underestimate the influence of later experiences in life, to which they ascribe only a precipitating significance. While this often may be the case, profound experiences in later life, such as migration from one culture to another, continued contact with certain persons, as well as many vicissitudes of life, may produce deep changes in personality. If this were not the case, psychoanalytic therapy of adults, in itself a form of later experience, could not alter a patient's personality."

[3] From among a growing number of studies that bear upon this assumption I select the following: A. Thomas, S. Chess, H. Birch, M. Hertzig, S. Korn, *Behavioral Individuality in Early Childhood* (New York: New York University Press, 1963). In this careful longitudinal study of eighty babies from birth through two years of age it was found that innate and "identifiable characteristics of reactivity are persistent. . . ."

Jerome Kagan, "Change and Continuity in Development," *Relations of Development and Aging*, ed. James Birren (Springfield, Ill.: Charles C. Thomas, 1964). In his study of seventy-one adults (ages 20–30) who had been studied in childhood, Kagan found that several kinds of behavior noted between ages 6–10 were good predictors of like behavior in adulthood. "Passive withdrawal from stress," "ease of anger arousal," "involvement in intellectual mastery" were among them. (An interesting finding in this study bears upon sex role: the degree of stability of response depended on its congruence with traditional sex-role expectations. Passive-dependency maintained itself in females from childhood to adulthood, but not in males. Childhood rage reactions predicted aggressive behavior in males, but not in females. In short, *overt* behavior was molded to social expectations.)

Benjamin S. Bloom, *Stability and Change in Human Characteristics* (New York: John Wiley & Sons, 1964). In his search to "identify 'stable' characteristics, to describe the extent to which [they] are stabilized at various ages . . . ," Bloom has examined and assessed major sets of longitudinal studies, chiefly those of physical, academic, intelligence and "interest, attitudes, personality" development. In summary, a basic finding is "that less and less change is likely . . . as the curve of development of a characteristic reaches a virtual plateau" and that a characteristic "can be more drastically affected by the environment in its most rapid period of growth. . . ." From these studies it is apparent that the most stable characteristics in human beings are acquired in the earliest years of life, as psychoanalytic theory postulates. Yet, as Neugarten (and others) point out, there are inconsistencies in the findings of investigators attemping to predict, say, adult achievement based upon that of adolescence—enough disparities to warrant continuing examination of exactly what personality characteristics are being examined, by what tests, under what conditions, and with what sampling. For a quick resumé of such studies see Bernice Neugarten, "Personality Changes During the Adult Years," in *Psychological Backgrounds of Adult Education*, ed. Raymond G. Kuhlen, Center for the Study of Liberal Education for Adults (Chicago, 1963).

[4] The by now well-known experiments of Harry F. Harlow with rhesus monkeys show this in dramatic form. See especially "Maternal Behavior in Socially Deprived Rhesus Monkeys," *Journal of Abnormal and Social Psychology*, vol. 69, no. 4 (1964), pp. 345–54; and "Primary Affectional Patterns in Primates," *American Journal of Orthopsychiatry*, vol. 30, no. 4 (October, 1960); and Harry F. and Margaret K. Harlow, "Social Deprivation in Monkeys," *Scientific American* (November, 1962). See also J. P. Scott, "Animal and Human Children," *Children* (September–October, 1957).

[5] Benjamin Bloom, *Stability and Change*, in discussing the possible effectors of change in stable characteristics.

[6] This is one of the propositions put forward by Leonard S. Cottrell, Jr., in his too little used article, "The Adjustment of the Individual to His Age and Sex Roles," *American Sociological Review*, vol. 7, no. 5 (October, 1942).

[7] ". . . early adulthood is the fullest of teachable moments" writes Robert Havighurst in *Developmental Tasks and Education*, 2d ed., (New York: Longmans, Green, 1952).

8 Benjamin Bloom, *Stability and Change*, p. 196.

9 See Allen Wheelis, "The Place of Action in Personality Change," *Psychiatry*, 13 (1950): 135–48.

10 Piaget, speaking at the 1967 annual meeting of the American Ortho-psychiatric Association is quoted in the *Saturday Review* (May 20, 1967) on how knowledge is acquired. "To know an object, to know an event, is not simply to look at it and make a mental copy or image of it. To know an object *is to act on it*. To know is to modify, to transform the object. . . . *An operation* is thus the essence of knowledge; it is an *interiorized action* which modifies the object of knowledge." (Italics mine.)

See also Lois Barclay Murphy, *The Widening World of Childhood* (New York: Basic Books, 1962), in which she, in her sensitive observations of young children, repeatedly records the connection between "doing" and the sense of "knowing" both self and object.

2. SOCIAL ROLE AND THE ADULT PERSONALITY

1 Robert Havighurst, *Developmental Tasks and Education*, 2d ed. (New York: Longmans, Green, 1952).

2 For proof of this see Lionel Neiman and James Hughes, "The Problem of the Concept of Role—A Re-survey of the Literature," *Social Forces*, (December, 1951), pp. 141–149, reprinted in *Social Perspectives on Behavior*, ed. Herman D. Stein and Richard A. Cloward (Glencoe, Ill.: Free Press, 1958).

For the reader who wants to pursue the problems that inhere in role definition and description and to clarify (as well as complicate) his thinking, the book *Role Theory: Concepts & Research*, Bruce Biddle and Edwin J. Thomas, eds. (New York: John Wiley & Sons, 1966), offers a compendium. See especially Chapter 1, "The Nature and History of Role Theory."

3 Roy S. Grinker, Sr., Helen MacGregor, Kate Selan, Annette Klein, and Janet Kohrman, *Psychiatric Social Work: A Transactional Case Book* (New York: Basic Books, 1961).

4 The thesis of Jessie Bernard's book, *Social Problems at Midcentury* (New York: Holt Rinehart & Winston, 1961) is that in the economy of abundance the "pervasive motif of social problems has changed from concern with mere survival . . . to concern with the malfunctions of role and status."

5 For a fully developed presentation of essentially these same ideas see the essay by Talcott Parsons, "Social Structure and the Development of Personality: Freud's Contribution to the Integration of Psychology and Sociology," in his *Social Sructure and Personality* (New York: Free Press of Glencoe, 1964); also in *Psychiatry*, 21 (1958): 321–40. In this essay Parsons traces Freud's concepts of object-choice and object cathexsis, identification, and internalization through the role transactions beween child and mother and child and larger family collectivity from birth through latency.

6 Ralph Linton, "Concepts of Role and Status," *The Cultural Background of Personality* (New York: Appleton-Century, 1945).

7 Erik Erikson, "Reality and Actuality," *Journal of the American Psychoanalytic Association*, 10 (1962): 451–74.

8 My beginning efforts to explore the dynamic content of roles in action, from which much of the material herein has been developed, are as follows: "Social Components of Casework Practice," *Social Welfare Forum National Conference of Social Work* (New York: Columbia University Press, 1953); "Psychotherapy and Counseling: Some Distinctions in Social Casework," *Annals of the New York Academy of Sciences*, 63 (November, 1955). See especially, "The Role Concept and Social Casework: Some Explorations, I: The 'Social' in Social Casework," *Social Service Review*, vol. 35, no. 4 (December, 1961), and "The Role Concept and Social Casework: Some Explorations, II: What is Social Diagnosis?" *Social Service Review*, vol. 36, no. 1 (March, 1962). In these latter two articles will be found references to other readings that bear on role in its particular import for social work.

9 Seymour Lieberman, "The Effects of Changes in Role on the Attitudes of Role Occupants," *Human Relations*, 9 (1950), reprinted in Neil J. Smelser and Wm. T. Smelser, eds., *Personality and Social Systems* (New York: John Wiley & Sons, 1963), pp. 264–79.

10 ". . . intelligence as at present measured does reach a virtual plateau in the period ages 10 to 17," writes Benjamin Bloom in his *Stability and Change in Human Characteristics* (New York: John Wiley & Sons, 1964), p. 81. He goes on: ". . . further development is likely only if powerful forces in the environment encourage further growth and development."

11 Nancy Bayley has been the major purveyor of this heartening information, based upon several studies. See Nancy Bayley and M. H. Oden, "The Maintenance of Intellectual Ability in Gifted Adults," *Journal of Gerontology*, 10 (1955); Bloom, *Stability and Change*, pp. 80–91, where Bayley's other studies on adult intelligence are listed and commented upon by Bloom.

12 "As individuals leave one environment and enter another they seem to be especially susceptible to the effects of the new environment in the initial period in the new environment," writes Bloom (*Stability and Change*, p. 196). The studies he cites are chiefly of youngsters making school changes. Migrants from one country to another and from one area to another (rural to urban, for example) show this same shake-up and reorganization of themselves with greater or lesser success at adaptation. A new role, insofar as it embraces a new position in a social network and calls for new modes of transaction with other persons, may be viewed as a kind of "migration."

3. WORK

1 *Civilization and Its Discontents* (London: Hogarth Press, 1930). One cannot help but wonder how Freud matched this pessimistic view of

work with his own driving avidity for it. His so-called autobiography is an account of his *work*, not of himself as person.

² Erikson writes: "Cases of severe identity diffusion also suffer from an acute upset in the sense of workmanship . . ." ("Identity and the Life Cycle," *Psychological Issues*, vol. 1, no. 1, monograph 1 [New York: International Universities Press, 1959], p. 127).

³ Harlan W. Gilmore, *The Beggar* (Chapel Hill: University of North Carolina Press, 1940).

⁴ Robert Dubin, "Industrial Workers' Worlds: A Study of the 'Central Life Interests' of Industrial Workers," *Social Problems*, vol. 3, no. 3 (January, 1956); reprinted in E. O. Smigel, ed., *Work and Leisure* (New Haven: College & University Press, 1963).

⁵ Nancy Morse and Robert Weiss, "The Function and Meaning of Work and the Job." *American Sociological Review*, vol. 20, no. 2 (April, 1955).

⁶ Robert H. Grant, "Work Careers and Aspirations of Automobile Workers," *American Sociological Review*, vol. 19, no. 2 (April, 1954); reprinted in Herman D. Stein and Richard Cloward, eds., *Social Perspectives on Behavior* (Glencoe: The Free Press, 1958).

⁷ A good review of such studies is Ruth S. Cavan's "Unemployment— Crisis of the Common Man," *Marriage and Family Living*, 21 (May, 1959).

⁸ Robert Dubin, "Industrial Workers' Worlds."

⁹ Herman J. Loether studied, in 1963, a random sample of 101 retired county employees. Among the blue-collar employees the "most missed" aspects of work was companionship with other workers—although these men had been more eager to retire than had the white-collar workers! ("Meaning of Work and Adjustment to Retirement," reprinted in Arthur Shostak and William Gomberg, eds., *Blue Collar World* [New Jersey: Prentice Hall, 1964]).

¹⁰ Erik Erikson, *Insight and Responsibility* (New York: W. W. Norton, 1964), p. 23.

¹¹ Numerous work studies and rearrangements of work systems have been done over a number of years in the effort to increase production and to engage the interest and involvement of the worker. For condensed accounts of these, as well as for a knowledgeable and concerned overview of today's work and its problems, see Georges Friedmann, *The Anatomy of Work*, First Free Press Paperback Edition (New York: Crowell, Collier, 1964).

¹² On the "necessary forerunner of any individual's acquisition of the capacity to work," see Anna Freud, *Normality and Pathology in Childhood* (New York: International Universities Press, 1965), pp. 79–82; and Erik Erikson, "Identity and the Life Cycle," *Psychological Issues*, vol. 1, no. 1 (New York: International Universities Press, 1959), pp. 86–88.

¹³ On "effectance" and for a trenchant and readable summary of recent trends in ego psychology, see Robert W. White, "Ego and Reality in Psy-

choanalytic Theory," *Psychological Issues*, vol. 3, no. 3 (1963). See also his "Motivation Reconsidered: the Concept of Competence," *Psychological Review*, vol. 66 (September, 1959). Also available as reprint no. P-364, Bobbs-Merrill Co., Indianapolis, Ind.

14 Alexander Solzhenitsyn, *One Day in the Life of Ivan Denisovich*, (New York: Frederick A. Praeger, 1963).

15 Robert Blauner in *Alienation and Freedom* (Chicago: University of Chicago Press, 1964), found that printers rated work interests high. They gave variety, creativity, challenge, educational stimulus as major reasons for liking their work. Auto workers, while they are the highest paid among blue-collar workers, find their jobs routine and gave the possibility of buying a better outside-of-work-life as their chief satisfaction.

16 Appropos of this, Louis Orzack, taking off from Dubin's study ("Industrial Workers' World") of work as a central interest in the lives of industrial workers, investigated work and work-place as central life interests in the lives of 150 professional nurses. (See Louis H. Orzack, "Work as a Central Life Interest of Professionals," *Social Problems*, vol. 7, no. 2 [Fall, 1959]; reprinted in Erwin O. Smigel, ed., *Work and Leisure* [New Haven: College and University Press, 1963].) In contrast with industrial workers, nurses reported in four out of five instances that work and work-place *were* their central life interest. There are, of course, important factors which may explain this, such as the fact that the industrial workers were men and the nurses women. But the nurses placed "personal satisfaction," informal group experiences, and formal organization attachments high among the gratifications of their work. All of these "personal satisfactions" surely must include, too, the sense of competence that derives from performing nursing tasks.

17 Two cheerfully audacious researchers have recently published their initial studies on "happiness." For some nine hundred men interviewed, ". . . work is of crucial importance" to their happiness. Thirty-three percent of unemployed men report themselves "not too happy" as compared with twelve percent of men employed. See Norman M. Bradburn and David Caplovitz, *Reports on Happiness*, National Opinion Research Center, Monographs in Social Research (Chicago: Aldine Publishing Co., 1965), pp. 14–15.

4. MARRIAGE

1 In his article, "The Cult of Personality and Sexual Relations," *Psychiatry*, 4 (1941) Arnold Green sets forth the different expectations generally held in middle-class relations between the sexes and from those of a lower-class Polish group. So generalizations about marriage must be set within specific group "culture."

2 Those of us who have worked professionally or as confidantes with marital problems have had repeated indication that it is possible to have sexual pleasure despite many nagging and turbulent problems in marriage and, vice versa, that it is possible to have only minimally satisfying sex

and yet to find considerable satisfactions and mutualities in other areas of marriage. Mirra Komarovsky in her *Blue Collar Marriage* (New York: Random House, 1962), pp. 82–111, finds that sexual and marital adjustment are not invariably associated. She hypothesizes however that educational level will affect the degree of association, that "among the educated women in our culture, sexual gratification in the face of marital unhappiness carries a greater likelihood of deviant sex needs than among the less-educated." This seems highly plausible since some greater hostility between the sexes seems more taken for granted by lower-class couples. One wonders, however, whether a turnabout is possible also for the educated woman: that sexual disparities may be accommodated to because other aspects of marriage are highly valued. And one also wonders whether age may be a factor in the valuation of sex versus other marriage relationships?

[3] *A Writer's Diary* (New York: Harcourt, Brace & World, 1954), pp. 96–97. This quotation is used with permission of the publisher.

[4] A number of studies consistently report that unmarried men are more "unhappy" and live in a greater "state of anomie" than unmarried women. After this fact has been ascertained, there remains the unanswered question still of whether a man's unmarried state is the effect more than the cause of his unhappiness—that is, whether his failure to court and choose a wife is symptomatic of incapacity to form close personal ties. Here my bias shows—that men in our society are still more free to pursue and decide on marriage than are women. For findings and further references, see Norman Bradburn and David Caplovitz, *Reports on Happiness*, National Opinion Research Center (Chicago: Aldine Publishing Company, 1965).

[5] The driving persistence of the feeling that marriage, any marriage, is a woman's proper destiny was brought home to me many years ago when I was a young and unmarried caseworker. A woman client was embroiled in a marriage that probably was being held together only by the fact that no alternatives were open either to the wife or husband, both were devoted to their four children, neither had resources that could support separate living arrangements. At the end of one interview, during which she had harangued, wept, shouted, denigrated not only her husband but all men as sex-driven pigs, selfish, oafish, lazy "no-goods," she sighed. Then she looked at me afresh, with a kind of maternal tenderness, and said gently, "And so, dolly, when are *you* going to find a husband?"

[6] The emergence and swift spread of a joke about some situation or circumstance usually attests to its being of some common concern, a concern which is managed in part by being laughed off. A current story is of the man who proudly shows his friend the elaborate home of his recently married daughter. "My!" says the impressed friend, "your son-in-law must be doing very well!" " He *is*," says the proud father-in-law, "he got all A's last term!"

[7] See especially Mirra Komarovsky, *Blue Collar Marriage*, (New York: Random House, 1962) for a study that rigorously examines contrasts

between its findings and those researches that have studied the life-modes and expectations of college-educated men and women or upward-mobile young couples. It has an excellent bibliography too. See also, Lee Rainwater, Richard Coleman, and Gerald Handel, *Working Man's Wife*, (New York: Oceana Publications, 1959) for class culture differences of marriage expectations.

[8] I am reminded of an example in contrasts that struck me forcibly some years ago. A client, the wife of a semiskilled garment worker who had had a heart attack, said to me tenderly, "He is such a wonderful husband. Went to work, came home, sat down, ate his supper, read the paper, gave me his pay—quiet, nice, went to bed. He didn't smoke, he didn't swear—nothing was bad." Not long thereafter a college acquaintance of mine was explaining her inability to tolerate her husband any further. It went like this: "He comes home, eats his dinner, says not a word, reads the paper, goes to bed—that's all he wants out of life. He's just a stupid bore and I've had it!"

5. PARENTHOOD

[1] At this writing (summer 1966) I have learned of a longitudinal study being planned by Bernice Neugarten and John Schlien, Committee on Human Development, University of Chicago, "focused upon changes in parent personality" and on the "effects of parenthood upon adult personality." Until this and further systematic research is done, the exposition that follows must be based upon clinical data, everyday observations, and attributed implications.

[2] See Therese Benedek, M.D., "Parenthood as a Developmental Phase," *Journal of American Psychoanalytic Association*, 7 (1959): 389–417.

[3] Aline Auerbach reports that young mothers, regardless of educational background, reveal ignorances and emotional disturbances over what to expect and how to handle their first-born babies. See "Meeting the Needs of New Mothers," *Children* (November–December, 1964).

[4] "Motherhood . . . sets in motion a reorganization in the mother's personality." ". . . motherliness, in its sublimated manifestations, widens the span of the personality." This is the testimony of a clinical observer whose psychoanalytic work with women has been underpinned and enriched by studies of woman's physiology. Therese Benedek, "Personality Development," in *Dynamic Psychiatry*, ed. Franz Alexander and Helen Ross (Chicago: University of Chicago Press, 1952), pp. 74–75.

[5] Supporting this observation (and at some difference from the expectations that used to hold in child guidance clinic anamneses that an unwanted pregnancy inevitably resulted in a rejected child) is the study reported by Sears, Maccoby, and Levin revealing that the attitude towards pregnancy "forecasts slightly—but only slightly—the warmth [a mother] will show her child after he is born. The forecast is even poorer for her warmth five years later." Robert R. Sears, Eleanor E. Maccoby, Harry Levin, *Patterns of Child Rearing* (New York: Row, Peterson, 1957), p. 56.

⁶ Therese Benedek, "Parenthood as a Developmental Phase," p. 393.

⁷ See E.E. Le Masters, "Parenthood as a Crisis," and Everett D. Dyer, "Parenthood as a Crisis: a Re-study," both in *Crisis Intervention: Selected Readings*, ed. Howard Parad (New York: Family Service Association of America, 1965).

⁸ Greta Bibring, M.D., names as one sign of the young mother's maturing the capacity to feel that her own identity and her role in the larger family are interdependent. See Greta L. Bibring, Thomas Dwyer, Dorothy S. Huntington, and Arthur Valenstien, "A Study of the Psychological Processes in Pregnancy and of the Earliest Mother-Child Relation," *The Psychoanalytic Study of the Child*, 16 (New York: International Universities Press, 1961).

⁹ Not only do ethnic and class differences determine maternal levels of discomfort and forms of behavior, but fads and phases of child-rearing beliefs are potent, too. For a swift survey of changing child-rearing norms, see Uri Bronfenbrenner, "Socialization and Social Class Through Time and Space," in Eleanor Maccoby, Theodore Newcomb and Eugene Hartley, eds., *Readings in Social Psychology*, 3d ed. (New York: Holt, Rinehart & Winston, 1958).

¹⁰ Therese Benedek, "Parenthood as a Developmental Phase," p. 415.

¹¹ Moreover, he becomes aware that his margin of useable power to enforce his dicta grows narrower daily. The threat of excommunication from parental favor no longer looms as real or big for the adolescent—there are all those "peers" and play-fellows on the outside to take him in, sympathize, admire, support him. The parent's sheer physical dominance is no more. "There I was," said a mother to me not long ago, "shaking my finger and hollering at what I suddenly realized was this big hulk of a man who, if he wanted to, could have lifted a hand like a ham and pushed me over." When this sudden perspective swept over her, she went on to say, she abruptly shifted her tactics. She lowered her voice and said gently that she realized he was too big and too grown to have her talk to him like this. He looked at her gravely for a moment and then remarked that she ought to do something about controlling her terrible temper. Which, she said, she set about doing, forthwith!

¹² Miriam Elson, "The Reactive Impact of Adolescent and Family Upon Each Other in Separation," *Journal of the American Academy of Child Psychiatry*, vol. 3, no. 4 (October, 1964). Writing of a group of cases seen in a college mental health clinic, Miriam Elson says, "At the time of separation some parents begin to re-examine and re-open their own commitments to marriage, to vocation or profession, and to their children," and she points out that the adolescent's departure for college may in such cases have had "a disturbing if not shattering impact on the family unit."

¹³ "What *is* it," a flippant interior decorator once asked me, "about menopause and new furniture?" But it is probably not simply menopause and the refurbishing of at least the exterior life but also the realistic as well as symbolic shifts in living arrangements.

6. ROLE AMBIGUITY—SOME COMMON PROBLEMS

[1] Some of the examples of role ambiguity discussed herein have been touched on in my earlier publications. For unwed mothers, see "Unmarried Mothers," in Nathan Cohen, ed., *Social Work and Social Problems* (New York: National Association of Social Workers, 1964). On parents of the mentally retarded, see "Social Diagnosis Leading to Social Treatment," in *Social Work in Child Health Projects for Mentally Retarded Children,* (Washington, D.C.: Department of Public Health, 1963).

[2] For an analysis of "patient" as a role, see Talcott Parsons, "Illness and the Role of the Physician: A Sociological Perspective," *American Journal of Orthopsychiatry,* 21 (1951).

[3] Two incidents which illustrate the patient's own awareness of this special role: One patient, a schizophrenic, persisted in walking backwards in hospital corridors and rooms. One day his social worker met him in the nearby town where the patient was out on a pass, greeted him, and commented with pleasure that he was walking forward, like everybody else. The patient withered him with a look of disdain. "You know darn well you can't walk backwards out here!" he said. A second man, discharged from the hospital, was asked to return for tests that were part of a research project. When he was asked to stay overnight to complete the tests, he agreed. But instantly he resumed the disordered appearance he had maintained during his hospitalization—tie off, collar askew, trousers tucked into his shoes. His wry explanation: "If you're going to make me a patient, I'll *be* one." (Robert Brown, then clinical caseworker at Downey Veterans' Administration Hospital, told me of these incidents.)

[4] In support of these observations is the study, "Instrumental Role Expectations and Posthospital Performance of Female Mental Patients," in which, among others, was the finding that "the greater the agreement in expectations between patient and significant other, the greater the tendency for better posthospital performance." (Simon Denitz, Shirley Angrist, Mark Lefton, and Benjamin Pasamanick, in *Social Forces,* 40 (1962): 248–54.

7. INTAKE AND SOME ROLE CONSIDERATIONS

[1] Leonard S. Kogan, "The Short-Term Case in a Family Agency," Part 3, *Social Casework,* vol. 38, no. 7 (1957), pp. 366–74. This study reveals that, of the people applying to the Community Serivce Society who are accepted for service following an intake interview, about one-third do not return.

Lilian Ripple, "Motivation, Capacity, and Opportunity as Related to the Use of Casework Service: Theoretical Base and Plan of Study," *Social Service Review,* vol. 29, no. 2 (1955), pp. 172–93. Sampling for this study in two Chicago family agencies, the Family Service Bureau of the United Charities and the Jewish Family and Community Service, agencies selected in part because of their high standards of practice, reveals a dropout rate of approximately one-third of the clients who were expected to return for a second interview.

Ann W. Shyne, "What Research Tells Us About Short-Terms Cases in Family Agencies," *Social Casework*, vol. 38, no. 5 (1957), pp. 223–31. This article summarizes a number of studies done on cases that continue and those that discontinue, in an effort to understand the causes of dropouts. The one-third dropout rate was characteristic in 64 member agencies of the Family Service Association of America.

Frances B. Stark, "Barriers to Client-Worker Communication at Intake," *Social Casework*, vol. 40, no. 4 (1959), pp. 177–83. This article is of particular interest because it is a self-study by caseworkers of their own experience with cases at intake. Of twenty clients judged to be motivated to seek help only seven were "successfully engaged in contact." The article deals with possible reasons for the loss of almost two-thirds of the applicants.

[2] Helen Harris Perlman, *Social Casework: A Problem-solving Process* (Chicago: University of Chicago Press, 1957), p. 113.

[3] See, for example, the statement on "The Study Phase," in *Method and Process in Social Casework—Report of a Staff Committee, Community Service Society of New York* (New York: Family Service Association of America, 1958); and Frances H. Scherz "Intake: Concept and Process," *Social Casework*, vol. 33, no. 6 (1952), pp. 233–40.

[4] Mary E. Richmond, *Social Diagnosis* (New York: Russell Sage Foundation, 1917), p. 38.

[5] See John P. Spiegel, M.D., "Aspects of Transference and Countertransference," *Science and Psychoanalysis*, vol. 2, *Individual and Familial Dynamics*, Jules H. Masserman, M.D., ed. (New York: Grune and Stratton, 1959), pp. 160–82.

[6] It is of interest that some psychiatrists are giving attention to this same problem: role clarity between patient and doctor. In Karl Menninger's recent book, *Theory of Psychoanalytic Technique* (New York: Basic Books, 1958) developed from his teaching sessions with young psychiatrists, he presents at some length the idea that the psychiatrist and his potential patient must, at the beginning of their relationship, come to a "contract" of agreement about their mutual roles and obligations.

[7] The agency hospitable to this tryout was the Family Service Bureau of the United Charities of Chicago. Jeanette Hanford is its director, and Wilda Dailey the district secretary of its Midway District where the work was done. The two caseworkers who worked with me as intake interviewers were Mrs. Margaret Landram and Mr. Samuel Miller. My colleague, Lilian Ripple, gave me help in the technical details of accounting for findings. I am grateful to each and all of these coworkers.

[8] S. R. Hoehn, J. B. Frank, S. D. Imber, E. H. Nash, A. R. Stone, C. C. Battle, "Systematic Preparation of Patients for Psychotherapy," *Journal of Psychiatric Research*, 2 (1964): 267–81.

See also Betty Overall and H. Aronson, "Expectations of Psychotherapy in Patients of Lower Socio-Economic Class," *American Journal of Orthopsychiatry,* vol. 33, no. 3 (April, 1963).

8. IDENTITY PROBLEMS, ROLE, AND CASEWORK TREATMENT

[1] The author and explorer of the concept "identity" as a central phenomenon in the development of the personality is Erik Erikson. His major writings reveal his unfolding conception of identity and its significances. In his *Childhood and Society* (New York: W. W. Norton, 1950), he writes of the normative crisis of adolescence as "identity and role confusion"; ego identity, he proposes, is made up of integrated identifications, aptitudes developed, and the "opportunities offered in social roles." *Identity and the Life Cycle* (New York: International Universities Press, 1959) is devoted to expanded and deepened scrutiny of the subject. The crisis of adolescence is renamed "identity versus identity diffusion." "Work mastery," says Erikson here, "is in any culture the backbone of identity formation" (p. 163). "Identity and Uprootedness in our Time," an essay written in 1959, published in *Insight and Responsibility* (New York: W. W. Norton, 1964), plays still more light across the person's sense of identity and binds it again (along with other conditions) to "roles and tasks" in which the human being "can recognize himself and feel recognized" (p. 90).

[2] Erik Erikson, "Growth and Crisis of the Health Personality," in *Identity and the Life Cycle,* (New York: International Universities Press, 1959), vol. 1, no. 1, p. 89.

[3] Erik Erikson, "The Problem of Ego Identity," *ibid.*, p. 13.

9. ROLE AND HELP TO TROUBLED ADULTS

[1] For an engaging discussion of the relationship dynamics in psychotherapy (as well as a pointed guide to research in psychotherapeutic theories, processes, and outcomes) see Jerome D. Frank, M.D., *Persuasion and Healing,* (Baltimore, Md.: Johns Hopkins Press, 1961). Among other therapeutic influences is the effect of the therapist's verbal or attitudinal responses to the material brought out by the patient. See also the studies of this phenomenon cited in Dr. Frank's book, Kurt Salzinger and Stephanie Pisoni, "Reinforcement of Verbal Affect Responses of Normal Subjects During the Interview," *Journal of Abnormal and Social Psychology,* vol. 60, no. 1 (1960).

[2] I omit here what social casework does *not* omit: the recognition that there are circumstances that impinge upon people from the outside that are in no sense attributable to personality faults and that are the result of social and economic lacks and deficits.

[3] For a plaintive protestation to this effect see Helen Harris Perlman, "Casework is Dead," *Social Casework,* vol. 48, no. 1 (January, 1967).

⁴ This repeated social work experience of how applicants view and present the problems they bring to social agencies is corroborated by a recent nation-wide survey on people's views of the life problems for which they needed outside help. Of twenty-four hundred "representative Americans" over twenty-one years of age, 83% reported that they sought help for problems which they defined as difficulties *between themselves and other persons or circumstances* (italics mine). Forty-two % asked for help with marriage problems, 12% with a child's problem, 4% with unspecified relationship problems, 6% with job or school problems, and so on. See Gerald Gurin, Joseph Veroff, Sheila Feld, *Americans View Their Mental Health: a Nationwide Interview Study* (New York: Basic Books, 1960), p. 305.

⁵ This same idea was first put forward in my *Social Casework: A Problem-Solving Process* (Chicago: University of Chicago Press, 1957), p. 54–57, as follows: "In order to understand what the casework process must include in its problem-solving help, it is necessary to take stock first of the kinds of blockings which occur in people's normal problem-solving efforts." Development of this idea in the context of role was essayed in my "The Role Concept and Social Casework: Some Explorations II: What is Social Diagnosis?" *Social Service Review*, vol. 36, no. 1 (March, 1962). What is presented here is a revision of that effort.

Several other efforts have been made to develop a classification of the nature and degree of problem-solving difficulties within the purview of role transactions. See notably, John Spiegel, M.D., "Resolution of Role Conflict Within the Family," *Psychiatry*, 20 (February, 1957), in which he delineates "five causes for failure of complementarity . . ."; and Werner Boehm, *The Social Casework Method in Social Work Education* (New York: Council on Social Work Education, 1959), esp. pp. 118–23, in which he proposes "a taxonomy of problems on the basis of the concepts of role and stress."

⁶ Relevant to this, see Leonard S. Cottrell, Jr., "The Adjustment of the Individual to His Age and Sex Roles," *American Sociological Review*, vol. 7, no. 5 (October, 1942).

⁷ See Aline Auerbach, "Meeting the Needs of New Mothers," *Children*, (November–December, 1964); and E. E. Masters, "Parenthood as Crisis," *Marriage and Family Living*, vol. 19, no. 4 (1957).

⁸ A compilation of articles and bibliographical references dealing with the concept of crisis and its treatment is Howard J. Parad, ed., *Crisis Intervention: Selected Readings* (New York: Family Service Association of America, 1965). See also Lola Selby, "Social Work and Crisis Theory," in *Social Work Papers*, 10 (Los Angeles: University of Southern California, 1963).

⁹ For a full development of this point, see the essay "Intake and Some Role Considerations," p. 162.

¹⁰ "There is increasing evidence that enacting a role can also lead to

measurable physiological changes," report Leonard Krasner and Leonard Ullman in *Research in Behavior Modification* (New York: Holt, Rinehart & Winston, 1965,) p. 343. A number of other studies show how cognition and information may be antecedents of emotional states. For a presentation of these see Richard S. Lazarus, *Psychological Stress and the Coping Process* (New York: McGraw-Hill, 1966), esp. pp. 250–57. Bruno Bettelheim, speaking of the effect upon a person of his own behavior, has suggested that "as a man acts so he may become."

Index